# U.S. Occupation of Okinawa

## JAPANESE SOCIETY SERIES
## General Editor: Yoshio Sugimoto

Lives of Young Koreans in Japan
*Yasunori Fukuoka*

Globalization and Social Change in Contemporary Japan
*J.S. Eades, Tom Gill and Harumi Befu*

Coming Out in Japan: The Story of Satoru and Ryuta
*Satoru Ito and Ryuta Yanase*

Japan and Its Others:
Globalization, Difference and the Critique of Modernity
*John Clammer*

Hegemony of Homogeneity: An Anthropological Analysis of Nihonjinron
*Harumi Befu*

Foreign Migrants in Contemporary Japan
*Hiroshi Komai*

A Social History of Science and Technology in Contemporary Japan, Volume 1
*Shigeru Nakayama*

Farewell to Nippon: Japanese Lifestyle Migrants in Australia
*Machiko Sato*

The Peripheral Centre:
Essays on Japanese History and Civilization
*Johann P. Arnason*

A Genealogy of 'Japanese' Self-images
*Eiji Oguma*

Class Structure in Contemporary Japan
*Kenji Hashimoto*

An Ecological View of History
*Tadao Umesao*

Nationalism and Gender
*Chizuko Ueno*

Native Anthropology: The Japanese Challenge to Western Academic Hegemony
*Takami Kuwayama*

Youth Deviance in Japan: Class Reproduction of Non-Conformity
*Robert Stuart Yoder*

Japanese Companies: Theories and Realities
*Masami Nomura and Yoshihiko Kamii*

From Salvation to Spirituality: Popular Religious Movements in Modern Japan
*Susumu Shimazono*

The 'Big Bang' in Japanese Higher Education:
The 2004 Reforms and the Dynamics of Change
*J.S. Eades, Roger Goodman and Yumiko Hada*

Japanese Politics: An Introduction
*Takashi Inoguchi*

A Social History of Science and Technology in Contemporary Japan, Volume 2
*Shigeru Nakayama*

Gender and Japanese Management
*Kimiko Kimoto*

Philosophy of Agricultural Science: A Japanese Perspective
*Osamu Soda*

A Social History of Science and Technology in Contemporary Japan, Volume 3
*Shigeru Nakayama and Kunio Goto*

Japan's Underclass: Day Laborers and the Homeless
*Hideo Aoki*

A Social History of Science and Technology in Contemporary Japan, Volume 4
*Shigeru Nakayama and Hitoshi Yoshioka*

Scams and Sweeteners: A Sociology of Fraud
*Masahiro Ogino*

Toyota's Assembly Line: A View from the Factory Floor
*Ryoji Ihara*

Village Life in Modern Japan: An Environmental Perspective
*Akira Furukawa*

Social Welfare in Japan: Principles and Applications
*Kojun Furukawa*

Escape from Work: Freelancing Youth and the Challenge to Corporate Japan
*Reiko Kosugi*

Japan's Whaling: The Politics of Culture in Historical Perspective
*Hiroyuki Watanabe*

Gender Gymnastics: Performing and Consuming Japan's Takarazuka Revue
*Leonie R. Stickland*

Poverty and Social Welfare in Japan
*Masami Iwata and Akihiko Nishizawa*

The Modern Japanese Family: Its Rise and Fall
*Chizuko Ueno*

Widows of Japan: An Anthropological Perspective
*Deborah McDowell Aoki*

In Pursuit of the Seikatsusha:
A Genealogy of the Autonomous Citizen in Japan
*Masako Amano*

Demographic Change and Inequality in Japan
*Sawako Shirahase*

The Origins of Japanese Credentialism
*Ikuo Amano*

Pop Culture and the Everyday in Japan: Sociological Perspectives
*Katsuya Minamida and Izumi Tsuji*

Japanese Perceptions of Foreigners
*Shunsuke Tanabe*

Migrant Workers in Contemporary Japan:
An Institutional Perspective on Transnational Employment
*Kiyoto Tanno*

The Boundaries of 'the Japanese', Volume 1:
Okinawa 1868–1972 – Inclusion and Exclusion
*Eiji Oguma*

International Migrants in Japan: Contributions in an Era of Population Decline
*Yoshitaka Ishikawa*

Globalizing Japan: Striving to Engage the World
*Ross Mouer*

Beyond Fukushima: Toward a Post-Nuclear Society
*Koichi Hasegawa*

Japan's Ultra Right
*Naoto Higuchi*

The Boundaries of 'the Japanese', volume 2:
Korea, Taiwan and the Ainu 1868–1945
*Eiji Oguma*

Creating Subaltern Counterpublics: Korean Women
In Japan and Their Struggles for Night School
*Akwi Seo*

Aftermath: Fukushima and 3.11 Earthquake
*Yutaka Tsujinaka and Hiroaki Inatsugu*

Learning English in Japan
*Takunori Terasawa*

Others in Japanese Agriculture
*Kenichi Yasuoka*

## Social Stratification and Inequality Series

Inequality amid Affluence: Social Stratification in Japan
*Junsuke Hara and Kazuo Seiyama*

Intentional Social Change: A Rational Choice Theory
*Yoshimichi Sato*

Constructing Civil Society in Japan: Voices of Environmental Movements
*Koichi Hasegawa*

Deciphering Stratification and Inequality: Japan and beyond
*Yoshimichi Sato*

Social Justice in Japan: Concepts, Theories and Paradigms
*Ken-ichi Ohbuchi*

Gender and Career in Japan
*Atsuko Suzuki*

Status and Stratification: Cultural Forms in East and Southeast Asia
*Mutsuhiko Shima*

Globalization, Minorities and Civil Society:
Perspectives from Asian and Western Cities
*Koichi Hasegawa and Naoki Yoshihara*

Fluidity of Place: Globalization and the Transformation of Urban Space
*Naoki Yoshihara*

Japan's New Inequality:
Intersection of Employment Reforms and Welfare Arrangements
*Yoshimichi Sato and Jun Imai*

Minorities and Diversity
*Kunihiro Kimura*

Inequality, Discrimination and Conflict in Japan:
Ways to Social Justice and Cooperation
*Ken-ichi Ohbuchi and Junko Asai*

Social Exclusion: Perspectives from France and Japan
*Marc Humbert and Yoshimichi Sato*

Global Migration and Ethnic Communities:
Studies of Asia and South America
*Naoki Yoshihara*

Stratification in Cultural Contexts: Cases from East and Southeast Asia
*Toshiaki Kimura*

## Advanced Social Research Series

A Sociology of Happiness
*Kenji Kosaka*

Frontiers of Social Research: Japan and Beyond
*Akira Furukawa*

A Quest for Alternative Sociology
*Kenji Kosaka and Masahiro Ogino*

## Modernity and Identity in Asia Series

Globalization, Culture and Inequality in Asia
*Timothy S. Scrase, Todd Miles, Joseph Holden and Scott Baum*

Looking for Money:
Capitalism and Modernity in an Orang Asli Village
*Alberto Gomes*

Governance and Democracy in Asia
*Takashi Inoguchi and Matthew Carlson*

Liberalism: Its Achievements and Failures
*Kazuo Seiyama*

Health Inequalities in Japan: An Empirical Study of Older People
*Katsunori Kondo*

**Uruma Shimpo Newspaper House, 1946**
The Japanese language newspaper published in a civilian camp in Ishikawa, on the eastern part of Okinawa Island, started as a U.S. supported two-page mimeograph of news sources obtained from the U.S. wire services. (Naha City Museum of History, Code # 02001038)

**The Voice of the Ryukyus and its broadcasting staff**
The first civilian Japanese-language radio station in postwar Okinawa. It was established with contribution of CIE Okinawa. (Naha City Museum of History, Code # 10004299)

**American films released at Okinawa Gekijo Theater, 1950**
The only movie theater with a roof at the time that screened American movies. When a new film was released there, a ceremony was held, to which the local notables from the military and civilians were invited.
(Naha City Museum of History, Code # 02000565)

**High Commissioner Watson's Press Conference, 1964**
In accordance with Executive Order 10713, a High Commissioner succeeded the Governor as the highest-ranking officer of the United States within Okinawa. (Okinawa Prefectural Archives, Code # 0000029994, 38-62-3 (9W3))

# U.S. Occupation of Okinawa
## A Soft Power Theory Approach

By

Hideko Yoshimoto

Kyoto University Press

First published in Japanese by Shumpu Publishing, Japan.

This English edition published in 2019 by:

Trans Pacific Press
PO Box 164, Balwyn North
Victoria 3104, Australia
Telephone: +61-(0)3-9859-1112
Fax: +61-(0)3-8611-7989
Email: tpp.mail@gmail.com
Web: http://www.transpacificpress.com

© Hideko Yoshimoto 2019.

Edited by Karl Smith.

Designed and set by Sarah Tuke, Melbourne, Australia.

Printed by Asia Printing Office Corporation, Nagoya, Japan..

**Distributors**

**Australia and New Zealand**
James Bennett Pty Ltd
Locked Bag 537
Frenchs Forest NSW 2086
Australia
Telephone: +61-(0)2-8988-5000
Fax: +61-(0)2-8988-5031
Email: info@bennett.com.au
Web: www.bennett.com.au

**USA and Canada**
Independent Publishers Group (IPG)
814 N. Franklin Street
Chicago, IL 60610
USA
Telephone inquiries: +1-312-337-0747
Order placement: 800-888-4741
   (domestic only)
Fax: +1-312-337-5985
Email: frontdesk@ipgbook.com
Web: http://www.ipgbook.com

**Asia and the Pacific (except Japan)**
Kinokuniya Company Ltd.
*Head office*:
3-7-10 Shimomeguro
Meguro-ku
Tokyo 153-8504
Japan
Telephone: +81-(0)3-6910-0531
Fax: +81-(0)3-6420-1362
Email: bkimp@kinokuniya.co.jp
Web: www.kinokuniya.co.jp
*Asia-Pacific office*:
Kinokuniya Book Stores of Singapore Pte., Ltd.
391B Orchard Road #13-06/07/08
Ngee Ann City Tower B
Singapore 238874
Telephone: +65-6276-5558
Fax: +65-6276-5570
Email: SSO@kinokuniya.co.jp

The publication of this book was supported by a Grant-in-Aid for Publication of Scientific Research Results (Grant Number 18HP5259), provided by the Japan Society for the Promotion of Science, to which we express our sincere appreciation.

All rights reserved. No reproduction of any part of this book may take place without the written permission of Trans Pacific Press.

ISSN    1443–9670 (Japanese Society Series)
ISBN    978–1–925608–88–5

*Cover illustration*: Okinawa Gekijo Theater where American films were released, 1950 (see page vii for details). Courtesy of Naha City Museum of History, Code # 02000565.

# Contents

| | |
|---|---|
| List of Abbreviations | xii |
| Introduction | 1 |

Part I: Congressional Oversight in Foreign Lands

| | |
|---|---|
| 1 Congressional Oversight | 19 |
| 2 Civil Affairs: From Military Government to Public Affairs | 30 |
| 3 U.S. Occupation Policy Defined in JCS 1231 | 40 |
| 4 United States Civil Administration of the Ryukyu Islands, Wartime Directive Revived | 49 |
| 5 Quest for Legitimacy: Army-Congressional Relations | 58 |

Part II: U.S. Foreign Information Policy for Okinawa

| | |
|---|---|
| 6 U.S. Foreign Information Policy | 81 |
| 7 Civil Information and Education Programs 1945–1957 | 97 |
| 8 Public Affairs Department, USCAR: 1957–1972 | 113 |
| 9 U.S.–Japan's Operation Friendship | 131 |
| Conclusion | 147 |
| Appendix | 159 |
| Notes | 165 |
| Bibliography | 185 |
| Name Index | 191 |
| Policy Index | 194 |
| Subject Index | 195 |

# List of Abbreviations

| | |
|---|---|
| CAMG | Civil Affairs and Military Government (Division, Army) |
| CCS | Combined Chiefs of Staff |
| CIA | Central Intelligence Agency |
| CIC | Counter Intelligence Corp. |
| CIE | Civil Information and Education |
| ECA | Economic Cooperation Administration |
| EL | Dwight D. Eisenhower Presidential Library |
| EOP | Executive Office of the President |
| FEC | Far East Command |
| GARIOA | Government Aid and Relief in Occupied Areas |
| GHQ | General Headquarters, SCAP |
| JCS | Joint Chiefs of Staff |
| NA | National Archives |
| NSC | National Security Council |
| OCB | Operations Coordinating Board |
| OSS | Office of Strategic Services |
| OWI | Office of War Information |
| PAO | Public Affairs Officer |
| PSB | Psychological Strategy Board |
| SCAP | Supreme Commander for the Allied Powers |
| TL | Harry S. Truman Presidential Library |
| USCAR | United States Civil Administration of the Ryukyu Islands |
| USIA | United States Information Agency |
| USIS | United States Information Service |

# Introduction
## Reconsidering the U.S. Occupation of Okinawa: A Soft Power Theory Approach

### Democracy and War

The United States maintains military bases around the globe, while advocating democratic ideals, including freedom of the press. Freedom of the press is an essential factor of American democracy. It has thus been a dilemma for the U.S. government and its public affairs activities that the domestic press criticizes U.S. military actions overseas more harshly than the foreign press. Military actions often inflict violence, and even death. Accordingly, the U.S. government has had to coordinate its public affairs activities[1] to avoid criticism from the U.S. press.

As the U.S. case shows, democracy and war are essentially incompatible. Once war starts, democratic states are forced to control their domestic press and public opinion, explicitly rationalizing their military actions. Harold D. Lasswell described the inherent contradiction between democracy and war as "the dilemma of modern states."[2]

Emerging as a major power after World War II, the U.S. government realized the necessity of managing public affairs and commenced transforming and expanding federal departments and agencies, launching a massive public diplomacy campaign to camouflage the dilemma of the democratic state and garner support for the American military and foreign policy from international publics. The nation euphemistically redefined military policy as "national security policy" and declared "military necessity" to protect American democracy. More specifically, it disseminated information promoting the "national security policy" in public relations campaigns both domestically and internationally. A principal objective of these campaigns was to rationalize and justify their overseas military bases. In this rhetoric, killing is heroic and war is a "necessary evil." U.S. military deployment since the beginning of the Cold War has been intertwined with foreign information policy, or so-called public diplomacy.

The U.S. government allocated immense resources to public relations aimed toward both domestic public opinion and public relations in foreign countries. This was public diplomacy as an intricate part of a set of foreign policy channels.[3] Public diplomacy made up an important portion of the U.S. foreign policy throughout the Cold War. Although the State Department was principally responsible for U.S. public diplomacy, other departments and agencies, including Defense and Central Intelligence, provided significant support. Many civilians of U.S. nationality residing in foreign countries were mobilized to support the mission.

Okinawa provides an excellent case study of how the U.S. deployed public diplomacy in support of its military and national security objectives. Okinawa was regarded as an important military installation in East Asia. The U.S. directly engaged in public affairs activities aimed at the local people and the vernacular press in Okinawa throughout twenty-seven years of military occupation from 1945 to 1972. U.S. public affairs activities aimed to persuade the local Okinawan public that the U.S. administration of Okinawa should be maintained. High Commissioners who administered Okinawa as U.S. representatives repeatedly proclaimed that it was a "military necessity" for the U.S. to maintain administrative authority over the islands they called "the keystone of the Pacific." U.S. public affairs personnel disseminated U.S. national policy through press releases and conferences, seeking to be a major influence on the Okinawan press and people.

The U.S. presented itself as pursuing a "friendlier relationship" and cultural exchange with the Okinawan people, while developing public relations campaigns against communism, which it presented as an enemy common to the U.S. and Okinawan people. These campaigns were conducted through the press, but pitched directly to the general public, utilizing all available channels for reaching Okinawan people including official proclamations, managing civilian camps, economic control and press control. The Okinawan press had been destroyed during the Battle of Okinawa, so in the early years of occupation the U.S. engaged in controlling public affairs through direct supervision and education of the local people. Once the local press resumed publication, however, the U.S. administration shifted its focus to control and censorship of the media.

The U.S. public affairs agencies regarded the local mass media as a means to communicate with the local public and supervised their output while actively promoting U.S. national policy and democratic ideals.

During the U.S. occupation of Okinawa from 1945 to 1950, the United States military government referred to its duties to "control" and "supervise" the local population as "civil affairs activities." In 1950, the United States Civil Administration of the Ryukyu Islands, or USCAR, assumed responsibility for the civil affairs activities of the military government and, until 1972, supervised Okinawan politics, media and local organizations through the "area administration unit" of the Army.[4] Although this unit was nominally engaged in managing civil affairs activities concerning the military activities of the U.S. forces in Okinawa, in effect its scope extended to all aspects of "occupation diplomacy"[5] similar to the U.S. occupation of Germany and Japan. The U.S. Congress regarded these activities as "non-traditional" military activities, and the USCAR budget was separated from "traditional" military expenditures.

The U.S. administration of Okinawa can be categorized as "occupation diplomacy" because the National Security Council (NSC), established in 1947, explicitly identified U.S. policy towards Okinawa as part of its foreign policy towards Japan, which had also been governed by U.S. occupation forces since the end of World War II. Although this new inter-departmental coordinating committee was a part of the Executive Office of the President (EOP), the NSC regarded the U.S. administration of Okinawa as a part of U.S. peacetime diplomacy regarding Japan. JCS 1231, a wartime directive of the Joint Chiefs of Staff issued prior to the U.S. landing on Okinawa Island, had provided the guiding principles determining administration policy in Okinawa from the beginning of the occupation. The pre-assault directive remained substantially active into the late 1960s, long after Japan recovered her independence in 1952, following the Japan Peace Treaty.

This book will analyze JCS 1231 and its revisions in Chapters 3 and 4. The wartime directive maximized the authority of the Joint Chiefs of Staff, extending it to the political and economic spheres of Okinawa. Put differently, continuing to administer Okinawa under the wartime directive provided the Joint Chiefs with a tactical advantage and enhanced power in their dealings with other sections of the U.S. federal government, such as the NSC and State Department.

As a result, wartime occupation and peacetime diplomacy were mixed in the U.S. administrative policy for Okinawa. The U.S. administration of Okinawa might be understood as the process of transformation from wartime occupation to peacetime diplomacy. It began in 1945 when the U.S. forces landed on Okinawa, beginning the wartime occupation, and ended in 1972 when the U.S. returned the administration of Okinawa to Japan. Stated earlier, the Executive Office of the President in Washington D.C. regarded it as part of U.S. foreign policy toward Japan. However, the top officials representing the U.S. in Okinawa had been Army officers throughout the occupation. As political advisers, diplomats dispatched from the State Department had been subordinate to Army officers until 1972. This mode of operation, in which diplomats are subordinate to military officers, is typically seen in wartime situations such as in U.S. occupied North Africa during World War II. The Joint Chiefs of Staff did not accept civilian administrators at the top, insisting that the U.S. theater commanders should be the leading officials in the garrison islands. In this sense, the U.S. administration of Okinawa was appropriately called an "overextended occupation."

However, the U.S. administrators intentionally avoided the use of the term "*senryou*" or occupation. They used the term "*touchi*" or administration instead. The official U.S. position is that the U.S. occupation of Okinawa formally ended when the United States Civil Administration of the Ryukyu Islands (USCAR) succeeded the military government in 1950. It rebutted international criticism, insisting that USCAR was not a military but a civilian organization.[6] To this end, USCAR was translated as "*beiminseifu*" or U.S. civilian "government." The Japanese term "*seifu*" means the government and reminds the Okinawan public of governmental authority.[7] The U.S. then established the Government of the Ryukyus, or Ryukyu *Seifu*, consisting of local Okinawan civil servants under the authority of USCAR. Although the U.S. public documents officially stated that USCAR would merely "assist" the Government of the Ryukyus, the latter was in fact a puppet-like government with no rights of self-determination. The Chief Executive, the top official representing the local Okinawan people, was appointed by USCAR until 1968. However, because the U.S. could not govern the Okinawan people without the support of Okinawan civil servants, the Government of the Ryukyus was not a mere puppet but a substantial government.

USCAR did not permit a popular vote for the Okinawan leadership, concerned that it would endanger the U.S. administration. Polls had clearly indicated that the Okinawan people wanted to return to Japanese sovereignty. A unicameral legislature was established, but USCAR reserved veto rights over local legislation and regularly exercised this veto. Thus, the local government was subordinate to the USCAR authority. However, the U.S. kept insisting that it was a "tandem" administration between the U.S. and the Ryukyus, rejecting the term "puppet." In addition, USCAR deployed public relations campaigns to positively spin the U.S. authority over Okinawa, while promoting a favorable image of the U.S. military presence. The U.S. had initially aimed to advocate democratic ideals in its administrative policy, including freedom of the press, but later realized that permitting freedom of the local press would negatively impact the military occupation. The dilemma of the democratic state had become a central problem in the U.S. administration of Okinawa. In response, the U.S. carefully planned public relations programs and psychological operations controlling freedom of speech for the vernacular press and residents.

U.S. public documentation carefully avoided calling the Okinawan public "citizens," using terms such as "inhabitants" or "people" instead. U.S. theater commanders, the highest officials representing U.S. authority, were given non-military titles such as "Governor" and "High Commissioner." The term Okinawa was carefully avoided because it implied the Japanese prefectural name. The U.S. administrators instead referred to "the Ryukyus" – the name for the region, to stimulate the local and historical identity while stressing cultural differences between Okinawa and mainland Japan. These rhetorical techniques were employed to cover up the U.S. military interests and replace negative images with positive ones. However, the domestic U.S. public did not know the Ryukyus, so Okinawa was used in Congress. This book uses Okinawa and Ryukyu interchangeably.

This book focuses on U.S. information and public relations policies toward Okinawa. Politicians typically seek to mobilize the electorate for their own purposes. In democratic states, politicians primarily address the domestic audience. International politics and foreign soils are out of the loop of politicians' domestic electoral campaigns targeting voters. Therefore, they frequently scapegoat foreign countries or people in different cultures as they speak to their political supporters. For instance, President Trump has blamed Mexico, Japan and China for taking jobs away from American citizens. This is a strategic attempt to garner the support of his supporters – American voters. Okinawa is certainly not unique in this regard, but the U.S. administrators of Okinawa had to exercise their public relations duties in a culture in which the majority wanted to return to

Japanese governance. In this sense, the public relations staff of USCAR was clearly burdened by the dilemma of the garrison state from the beginning.

## Purpose of this research

The purpose of this study is to reconsider the U.S. occupation of Okinawa from 1945 to 1972 in the theoretical framework of recent soft power studies. After the reversion to Japan in 1972, more than 70% of U.S. military bases stationed in Japan are concentrated in the small, southernmost islands. The Japanese media called this situation the "Okinawa problem," which previous studies have discussed as a matter of hard power. However, following Joseph S. Nye's soft power theory proposal have begun focusing their attention on U.S. foreign information policy.

"Everyone is familiar with hard power. We know that military and economic might often get others to change their position." However, Nye says, "hard power can rest on inducements ("carrots") or threats ("sticks")" and referred to "the indirect way to get what you want without tangible threats or payoffs" as soft power. Although, he admits, a weakness of soft power is that the outcome rests on the audience and the government cannot control the result, his perspective is basically optimistic, agreeing with George Kennan's assessment that soft power "would help to transform the Soviet Bloc."[8] It can certainly be seen as having been successful in many respects in fostering cooperation in nations such as Okinawa and Japan. But Nye did not discuss the negative aspects of the soft power, such as its impact on freedom of speech in foreign countries. This case study of Okinawa examines some of the negative aspects of soft power.

The U.S. foreign information policy for the southernmost islands of Japan originated in World War II. The United States Military Government of the Ryukyus was established in March 1945 – prior to the Japanese surrender in August 1945 – and was succeeded by the United States Civil Administration of the Ryukyu Islands (hereafter, USCAR) in 1950. USCAR's administration of the local population effectively extended the occupation until 1972. The right of the people to self-determination was subordinated to U.S. military objectives. As an occupying power, USCAR forcibly acquired land to expand its military bases and carefully suppressed the Okinawan press to camouflage the reality of the military regime.

The U.S. administration of Okinawa can be seen as a sort of prototype of the new "nation-building" role of the military. As can be observed more recently in Afghanistan and Iraq, military forces are not only engaged in traditional warfare, but also act as provisional governments to maintain regional security and rebuild governance systems. During and after these wars, the United States deployed troops for postwar reconstruction and peace building operations. Nontraditional military activities included local intelligence gathering and public affairs work involving the local population in different cultures.

U.S. policymakers reportedly understood that the postwar reconstruction of Japan was successful,[9] but the occupation of Okinawa had many problems. The U.S. extended military supremacy into political affairs, exposing the negative aspects of militarism. It is important to examine the problems caused by the military administration. Unfortunately, the U.S. Army has not published an official history of the administration and some archival documents remain classified. Accordingly, the scope of this study is limited, but it nevertheless aims to clarify U.S. policy and the Okinawan administration based on the available archival evidence.

This study aims to answer the following research questions:
1. What was the U.S. policymaking process regarding the administration of Okinawa?
2. How did Congress oversee the U.S. administration of Okinawa?
3. What were the public affairs and mass media policies under the U.S. administration?
4. What is the historical legacy of U.S. soft power policies?

In answering these questions, this study aims to determine how U.S. foreign information policy was carried out in Okinawa.

## Public Affairs Officer as Gatekeeper: Theoretical Framework

As Nye argues, information policy is a crucial factor in foreign relations. The United States engaged in soft power diplomacy throughout the Cold War. In 1948, the Economic Cooperation Administration (hereafter, ECA) began advertising to promote U.S. economic aid in Europe. Once the United States Information Agency (hereafter, USIA) was established in 1953, public diplomacy policy played an important role in U.S. foreign relations. After the Vietnam War, political scientists and communications scholars analyzed policymaking processes focusing on the relationship between the government and mass media. After the Gulf War of 1991, scholars criticized the U.S. government's manipulation of the mass media during the war. Nye's soft power theory contributed to highlighting the information factor in traditional international relations theory. However, U.S. information policy regarding Okinawa has not been researched. This report is a pilot study on that topic.

The study used a historical method and researched the U.S. national archives. At the same time, it addressed Okinawa's case within the theoretical framework of political science. Previous studies in international relations have primarily focused on governmental organizations as the principle actors in policymaking. In addition to the traditional actors, this study approached the political communications process from the perspective of other actors: the U.S. Congress and mass media, both of which have been largely overlooked in previous research. Congressional oversight and the watchdog function of mass media are important factors in the political communications process in a democratic society.

Roger Hilsman divided political communications processes into three layers: 1) the President and Executive Office, 2) departments and agencies, 3) Congress, mass media and civic organizations.[10] Previous studies of the U.S. administration of Okinawa have primarily focused on the first and second layers. In the 1980s, Seigen Miyazato analyzed the U.S. decision-making process based on Hilsman's theory and argued that the third layer analysis is difficult because of an absence of suitable theories. After Nye's soft power theory was proposed, however, U.S. public diplomacy and propaganda during the Cold War has been well researched. This has, in turn, consolidated the theoretical framework for further investigations. We now have the resources for this study to analyze how third layer actors, the Congress and mass media, influenced policymaking in the administration of Okinawa.

The U.S. Congress and the mass media are expected to oversee government performance at the point at which public policy becomes public information. Although military operations contain many secrets, budgetary bills can give American citizens a summary of its military deployments overseas.[11] Representing American taxpayers, Congress authorizes both defense and welfare budgets. Congressional oversight and the watchdog function of mass media are touchstones of democracy.[12] However, these oversight devices do not always function as intended. This study examines whether the oversight functions worked properly during the U.S. administration of Okinawa.

The focal point is the role of public affairs officers (PAOs) as gatekeepers in the political communications process.[13] They control outgoing information from governmental organizations. They are not necessarily high-ranking officers, but work as gatekeepers who decide which information should be released to public audiences. As the title indicates, public affairs officers deal with a range of affairs relating to the public, not merely press relations. The role of public relations officers is to maintain a favorable relationship between their administrative agencies and the public and to maintain a cordial relationship with Congress. In fact, Congressional relations accounted for the most important part of the PAO's role. The U.S. was unable to deploy military forces overseas without Congressional appropriation. In Okinawa, the PAO's role was to garner local support for the U.S. military bases and promote a favorable image of the United States. The PAO's routine work included activities such as writing press releases, managing press conferences, and speech writing for senior officers. This study examines the U.S. administration of Okinawa from the PAO's perspective.

After World War II, the U.S. strengthened its foreign information strategy because policymakers had been convinced that international public opinion would be a crucial factor in policymaking.[14] Throughout the Cold War, the U.S. conducted an information war against communism to influence foreign audiences. The U.S. campaign against communism was underpinned by the hard power of military strength but mobilized through the soft power of public relations. The United States spent a significant proportion of the federal budget on economic aid to Europe and Asia aiming to expand the free economy. Meanwhile, the U.S. extensively promoted its economic contributions as goodwill gifts to the free world. The federal government launched a series of public relations campaigns to promote the American way of life and values, utilizing mass media such as newspapers, magazines, books, movies and radio broadcasting. But in Okinawa, while propagating democratic ideals, the U.S. administration controlled the press, suppressing news and commentaries critical of U.S. Forces.

## Literature Review

Although previous studies established that the Joint Chiefs of Staff had intended to retain Okinawa as early as 1945, the separation of Okinawa from Japan was formally announced at the international conference at

San Francisco Opera House in September 1951 by provisions of the Treaty of Peace with Japan, which defined Japanese independence after the occupation. Article 3 of the Treaty stipulated that:

> Japan will concur in any proposal of the United States to the United Nations to place under its trusteeship system, with the United States as the sole administering authority, Nansei Shoto south of 29° north latitude (including the Ryukyu Islands and the Daito Islands), Nanpo Shoto south of Sofu Gan (including the Bonin Islands, Rosario Island and the Volcano Islands) and Parece Vela and Marcus Islands. Pending the making of such a proposal and affirmative action thereon, the United States will have the right to exercise all and any powers of administration, legislation and jurisdiction over the territory and inhabitants of these islands, including their territorial waters.[15]

Although the language is not clear regarding how long the U.S. would excise the administrative authority over the territory, John Foster Dulles, President Truman's Special Representative for the peace conference, explained that Japan would retain "residual sovereignty" of the Ryukyu Islands while the United States would have the administrative authority for the time being. Since the United States did not proposed a U.N. trusteeship for the Ryukyu Islands, the status of the Ryukyus remained ambiguous, belonging neither to Japan nor the United States. As a result, Okinawans – called Ryukyuans at the time – were required to have a special permit called the "Ryukyuan passport" when they travelled to Japan or other countries, but did not have an independent nation's status. The language of the peace treaty left Okinawans with a neither-fish-nor-fowl status.

However, the status of Okinawa was addressed in the international treaty, so the U.S. administration of Okinawa must have been discussed as a matter of U.S.-Japan relations. Seigen Miyazato argues that the language of the Treaty did not properly authorize the U.S. administration of Okinawa.[16] Nevertheless, the National Security Council had secretly decided on the Okinawa separation in 1948 and the U.S. and Japanese governments agreed to continue the policy.[17] Analyzing the political decision making process, Robert D. Eldridge points out that the Defense Department insisted on maintaining U.S. administrative authority over the islands, but there was resistance from the State Department. Eldridge concludes that the central Okinawa problem is rooted in this inter-departmental confrontation.[18] State Department deliberations on Okinawa's reversion to Japan started as early as 1953, perceiving that the Okinawa situation could be a major obstacle to U.S.-Japan relations. However, the Defense Department continued to insist that the U.S. should maintain administrative authority over the islands to secure the military bases.

U.S.-Japan diplomatic negotiations concerning the Okinawa reversion have been well researched. The Japanese government had petitioned the U.S. for the return of Okinawa, but deliberations proceeded slowly as the U.S. was not prepared to surrender its vested interests in the islands. Finally, in 1969, the U.S agreed to return Okinawa to Japan.[19] Previous studies have primarily focused on the bilateral decision-making process based on the historical documents of the State Department. However, the policy making process regarding the administration of Okinawa remained unclear, since the executive agency was the Department of the Army under the Department of Defense. Who in Washington directed the U.S. administration of Okinawa? Masaaki Gabe observes that a directive of the Joint Chiefs of Staff in January 1945 determined the basic policy of the U. S. postwar administration.[20] The present study further clarifies that the wartime directive remained in effect at least until the 1960s. In the process, we found that the Civil Affairs Division of the Department of the Army had coordinated the administration of Okinawa with the State Department and the final decisions were submitted to the Executive Office of the President.

Public affairs officers at the Civil Affairs Division did not engage in national policy planning, but were responsible for proposing public relations policy in accordance with national policy. For the PAOs, the U.S. administration of Okinawa was a problem from the beginning because it did not have a legal basis for Congressional appropriations. The U.S. administration was legitimate only by the wartime directive of the Joint Chiefs of Staff, which no longer carried the same authority in the postwar era. Therefore, the Army PAOs responsible for Congressional relations had to establish a legal basis for the administration of Okinawa. This study examines the ways in which the Army PAOs sought legitimacy and the Congress's views of the U.S. administration of Okinawa.

The Smith-Mundt Act of 1948 established the principles of U.S. public diplomacy. As discussed in Chapter 6, the United States Information Agency (USIA) was established on these principles in 1953 and became a major institution of the Cold War. Nicholas J. Cull analyzed USIA documents and identified five constructs of U.S. public diplomacy: 1) listening, 2) advocacy, 3) exchange diplomacy, 4) cultural diplomacy, and

5) international broadcasting.[21] All five of the constructs were found during the U.S. administration of Okinawa. As Chapter 7 and 8 discuss, though, USIA did not establish a branch in Okinawa, where the Army PAOs played that role.

Since Nye published his soft power theory in 2004, Japanese scholars have researched U.S.-Japan relations within the theoretical framework of U.S. information policy and its effects on Japan. Yuka Tsuchiya examined U.S. information and education policies for Japan during the postwar occupation, specifically focusing on the role of American movies released from the Civil Information and Education (CIE) section of the General Headquarters of Supreme Commander for the Allied Powers (GHQ/SCAP) under General MacArthur.[22] Tsuchiya and other scholars also analyzed the role of radio and art exhibitions during the occupation.[23] Yasushi Watanabe examined the role of American Centers, U.S. public relations posts, and the United States Information Service (USIS).[24] These studies have addressed U.S. foreign information policy for Japan but not for Okinawa. This study is based on public affairs documents of the Department of the Army, Joint Chiefs of Staff, National Security Council and Central Intelligence Agency and aims to clarify the public affairs perspective of the Okinawa administration.

The U.S. administration severely restricted the rights of people to self-determination, as numerous studies have shown.[25] USCAR appointed the Chief Executive, a political leader representing the local people, and controlled political and economic affairs through him and the Government of the Ryukyus, which were subordinate to USCAR.[26] It was the public affairs professionals' role to hide the true levers of power as much as possible from the Okinawan people. The latter half of this study discusses the role of public affairs officers in Okinawa.

## Chapter Description

The first part of this book explores the Congressional perspective on the U.S. administration of Okinawa. The early chapters clarify that wartime directives remained effective for a long time after World War II had ended. Meanwhile, the Congress never admitted the wartime directive as a legal basis for federal appropriations for the administration of Okinawa. As a result, the Department of the Army had difficulty persuading the Congress to allocate administrative budgets for Okinawa.

Chapter 1 establishes that U.S. Congressional appropriations for the administration of Okinawa were granted for the budget item "Civil Function, Army" throughout the period. The Congress consistently authorized the budgets for the Department of the Army as GARIOA (Government Aid and Relief in Occupied Areas) from fiscal year 1947 to 1957 and ARIA (Administration Ryukyu Islands, Army) from 1958 to 1972. These appropriations consisted of three components: 1) economic aid, 2) information and education programs, 3) administrative costs. Economic aid was by far the largest amount but reduced significantly after its peak in 1950. The information and education programs appropriations were not as large as the economic aid but remained consistent throughout the U.S. administrative period. This suggests that information and education were priorities.

Chapter 2 defines the "Civil Function, Army" based on Army documentation. According to field manuals, the term referred to civil affairs activities of the Army and was understood in broad terms to include public affairs, local information gathering, censorship, and speech control. For the Army Staff, public affairs was regarded as a part of civil affairs and essential for supporting U.S. Forces.

Chapter 3 discusses the pre-assault JCS directive 1231, issued to Admiral Chester W. Nimitz, the Naval theater commander, prior to the Battle of Okinawa in January 1945. This directive, as we will see, provided the overriding policy for the U.S. administration of Okinawa until the reversion. The chapter points out that although the JCS directive had been repeatedly revised, it had also been forgotten for some period.

Chapter 4 describes how the dated wartime directive was revived in 1950, after the Korean War broke out, and revised once again to establish the Civil Administration of the Ryukyu Islands (USCAR) in December 1950. The chapter also verifies that it was the Joint Chiefs of Staff who insisted on maintaining administrative control of Okinawa for strategic military objectives.

Chapter 5 describes the dilemma for the Army in the Congressional hearings regarding the budgets for Okinawa. While the Joint Chiefs of Staff insisted on maintaining U.S. administrative authority over Okinawa, the Congress took a different view, and was not prepared to bear the cost for governing the country out of American taxpayers' pockets. The chapter describes the process by which administrative costs for Okinawa came to be seen as a burden for the United States. As Japan's economy blossomed in 1960, Japanese aid to Okinawa surpassed U.S. appropriations. As a result, the United States' administration of Okinawa gradually lost both substance and rationale. It was a significant step toward the Okinawa reversion, when the U.S. returned administrative rights to Japan while maintaining its military facilities in Okinawa.

Until then, USCAR, an "area administration unit"[27] of the U.S. Army, supervised politics, the mass media, and non-profit organizations. The area administration unit had been established to support U.S. military activities and control the local population. The U.S. administration of Okinawa can be understood as an instance of "occupation diplomacy," which, after WWII, GHQ/SCAP conducted in mainland Japan, other Asian countries and Europe.[28] The administrative cost was appropriated within the framework of postwar civil affairs activities, a separate budget item to traditional military appropriations.

The National Security Council saw U.S. policy towards Okinawa as part of its Japan policy. Meanwhile, the wartime JCS directives continued to be revised for the administration of Okinawa. The wartime directives defined JCS supremacy over Okinawa. Thus, a strange mixture of wartime and peacetime characterized the U.S. administration of Okinawa. The twenty-seven years can be understood as a long transformation from wartime occupation to peacetime diplomacy. The Executive Office regarded the administration of Okinawa as peacetime diplomacy but at the same time accepted tha the military theater commanders of the Ryukyu Command remained at the top of the administration. The diplomats dispatched from the State Department worked as political advisers under the military commanders. The same style was observed under the U.S. occupation of North Africa during World War II. In this sense, the U.S. administration of Okinawa can be understood as military occupation.

The latter part of this book describes the public relations policy executed in Okinawa to camouflage the military occupation.

Chapter 6 summarizes the U.S. foreign information policy from World War II through the Cold War, and aims to provide a theoretical framework for the remaining chapters. U.S. foreign information policy was determined by the National Security Council. Basically, the Defense Department was responsible for wartime information policy, while the State Department took responsibility for peacetime policy. However, as a special exception, the Department of Defense was responsible for information policy in Okinawa.

Chapter 7 describes the Army's public affairs activities in Okinawa during the first half of the administrative period from 1945 to 1957. Prior to landing on Okinawa, U.S. air raids attacked newspaper and radio facilities. As a result, Okinawan society was deprived of media outlets. At the beginning of the occupation, the U.S. military government established a small newspaper printing facility to disseminate information to local people. Under the military government, U.S. public affairs programs began promoting American values using American movies, radios, books and exhibitions.

Chapter 8 reviews the role of the USCAR Public Affairs Department from 1957 to 1972. The purpose of public relations remained basically the same, but gradually softened. The public affairs professionals endeavored to promote American national policies for East Asia, disseminating a series of press releases and frequently holding press conferences. While they promoted friendship and cultural exchange between the United States and Okinawa, they engaged in anti-communist campaigns.

Chapter 9 analyzes Japanese Prime Minister Sato's visit to Okinawa in 1965 and examines the U.S. public relations campaign "Operation Friendship." In the end, the chapter concludes that the United States gradually started to accept the reversion of Okinawa to Japan, but was determined to maintain its military presence. Although the State Department originally insisted that the U.S. administration of Okinawa would be costly as well as cause many problems between United States and Japan, Defense finally agreed to return the administrative authority to Japan because it gradually recognized it as a financial burden. The United States' "nationl security" only required the free use of military bases in Okinawa.

Throughout Part II, the chapters discuss U.S. foreign information policy for Okinawa and local public affairs activities. In conclusion, the public affairs activities functioned to camouflage the weakness of U.S. legitimacy in the administration of Okinawa.

Throughout the Cold War, the United States not only employed public relations domestically, but also strengthened public diplomacy – direct and mass media communication to a foreign populace – as an alternative channel to traditional diplomatic relations between nations. The State Department was responsible for U.S. public diplomacy, but other agencies such as the Defense Department, CIA, American corporations, nonprofit organizations and civilians had supported the national endeavor. Okinawa was one of the targets for this form of public diplomacy.

# Part I
# Congressional Oversight in Foreign Lands

What role did the US Congress play in America's administration of Okinawa? The legitimacy of the U.S. administration was based on a wartime directive issued by the Joint Chiefs of Staff in the final stages of World War II. However, Congress did not regard the wartime directive as a legal base for funding the postwar administration of Okinawa. The Army Staff at the Defense Department struggled to establish a legal language to persuade Congress of its legitimacy.

A long occupation would be subject to international critique. Nevertheless, the U.S. decided to place Okinawa under the Defense Department to maintain the wartime chain of command. This decision derived from the perspective of uniformed staff who were determined to maintain U.S. administrative authority over Okinawa. To a significant extent, the State Department agreed with Defense's policy, and U.S. administration policy in Okinawa swung between democratic ideals and military control.

# 1 Congressional Oversight

How did Congress view the U.S. occupation of Okinawa? Congress, the only body empowered by the U.S. Constitution to make federal laws, is expected to oversee the actions of the United States government and its agencies. Previous studies of the U.S. occupation of Okinawa have discussed the role of presidents and the executive branch but have not examined congressional oversight of U.S. Forces. However, Congress approved a series of appropriations for the administration of Okinawa throughout a twenty-seven-year period, which makes it responsible for U.S. activities in Okinawa and its treatment of the Okinawan people.

It is difficult to determine the exact size of the U.S. Defense budget allocated to Okinawa. Congressional records do not specify the amount allotted to each military base. CIA budgets for Okinawa are also classified. However, it is possible to determine the national budget appropriated for administrative organizations such as the U.S. Civil Administration of the Ryukyu Islands. According to the Budgets of the United States Government, Congress consistently approved the administrative cost for Okinawa as "Civil Function, Army" from July, 1946 to May 1972.[1] This suggests that Congress had a budgetary policy for the U.S. administration of Okinawa except for the first year from March 1945 to June 1946, the period immediately after Battle of Okinawa.[2]

This chapter summarizes how the civil function of the Army was described in Congressional records and analyzes items included in the appropriations.

## House Appropriations Committee

On May 10, 1946, a bill for the next fiscal year was proposed in the House Subcommittee on Appropriations. As described later in this chapter, the Military Establishment Bill for fiscal year 1947 (July 1, 1946 to June 30, 1947) had included items such as Government Aid and Relief in Occupied

Areas (GARIOA), indicating a major shift in the U.S. defense policy after World War II.

Until 1976, the U.S. fiscal year started on July 1 and ended June 30 of the following year. Accordingly, many American federal employees came to Okinawa in July and returned to their homeland in June. The House of Representatives has traditionally deliberated budgetary bills prior to the Senate because the House is regarded as being closer to the American public than the Senate. The House Committee on Appropriations has a special position among the committees since it is responsible for the taxpayers' money. Budgetary planners visited Capitol Hill from early spring to early summer and provided testimony to justify the budgets they proposed. High Commissioners, the highest-ranking U.S. officers in Okinawa, also visited Congress during this season. Although typically domineering in Okinawa, many of them were quite humble when answering questions from Representatives in Congress.

Military budgets are difficult to handle in Congress because they do not obviously benefit taxpayers' directly. "Does the defense budget really benefit us?" the Congressperson often asks representatives of the Defense Department. Secretaries of Defense must present reasonable answers to persuade the Congress. Facing tough questions, Defense representatives often respond: "It is a military necessity!" Army officers from Okinawa repeated this phrase especially often. In fact, what is a "military necessity" is always questionable, but even the sharpest Congresspersons seem to be silenced by that phrase.

## Military Establishment Act of 1947

The Military Establishment Bill for 1947 included important items indicating a turning point in U.S. national security policy from wartime to peacetime. The GARIOA budget for U.S. occupation of Japan and other items indicated that the U.S. would transform into a nontraditional military nation.

Before World War II, the United States was not the garrison state that it is today.[3] Military costs skyrocketed during the war, however, and by 1945, 80% of the federal budget was allocated to military and related activities. The Military Establishment Act of 1947 sought to rein-in the tremendously swollen military budget. One of its provisions was to utilize military personnel for postwar occupations. When the U.S. launched the Marshall

Plan in 1948, a program for the economic rehabilitation of Europe, many of its provisions to divert military assets into peacetime operations had already been included in the Military Establishment Act of 1947.

Funding for the U.S. occupation of Okinawa for fiscal year 1947 was partially allocated from the GARIOA appropriations for the occupation of Japan included in the Military Establishment Act. The GARIOA appropriations bill of fiscal year 1949 (July 1, 1948 to June 30, 1949) was the first to set a special budget allocation exclusively for the "Ryukyu Islands."

At a hearing for the 1949 appropriations, a Congressman asked, "Why do you set a special budget for the Ryukyus?" The answer is marked as "Off the Record." The 1949 bill was submitted to Congress by the State Department, but the following year the bill was submitted by the Office of the President as a supplementary budget for the Ryukyus. GARIOA appropriations continued to be the budgetary source for the U.S. administration of Okinawa until fiscal year 1957 (July 1, 1956 to June 30, 1957).

Besides GARIOA, the 1947 military appropriations bill included items such as civilian staff employment for occupied areas and their training. The bill also proposed expansion of the information sections of the War Department dealing with intelligence, research, communications, and technology. The Secretary of War, Robert Patterson, explained the purposes of the appropriations bill as follows:

> 1) The occupation of Europe, Japan, and Korea, 2) the training of new men to replace long-serving men overseas, 3) the maintenance of lines of communication and support for the installations in the United States for occupied areas, 4) the provision of forces available for the United Nations Organization, 5) the maintenance of key points such as the Panama Canal, Alaska and airfields, 6) the maintenance of adequate programs of intelligence, research and development, 7) the overriding requirement to preserve the peace of this country in the world.[4]

Although somewhat vague about details, these seven points indicate that the United States intended to maintain its overseas bases and communications infrastructure for peacetime national security purposes. The phrase "to preserve the peace of this country" perhaps refers to the conversion of atomic power for peacetime purposes. Patterson proudly stated that atomic energy would eventually be developed for peacetime benefits of all mankind. The Manhattan Project, created for the development of nuclear weapons, would be turned over to a civilian agency of the government. In the meantime, however, while "this item is not a military item," Secretary Patterson demanded that Congress approve the atomic energy research budget for the Army.

The Military Establishment Act of 1947 included other nontraditional line items as well, such as educational and advertising budgets. Re-education programs were funded for military personnel in respect for their contribution to the war. The bill proposed a new education program for military veterans through which they could study in universities and graduate schools, reportedly because the nation would have a continuous need for their human resources in peacetime.

A large advertising budget was also included in the bill in recognition of the idea that continuous advertising would be necessary even in peacetime. The bill instructed that nation-wide advertising campaigns using all forms of mass media materials including newspapers, magazines, and movies be mobilized, from agricultural media to foreign language media. This part of the bill included a budget allocation for a radio network entitled "The Voice of the Army (VOA)," which would be outsourced to civilian contractors. It is not clear from the Congressional hearings what the Voice of the Army was: whether it referred to the Armed Forces Radio Network (AFN) or other radio broadcasting. The U.S Army had produced advertising materials during WWII and intended to continue to utilize its existing human resources such as information specialists for peacetime operations.

It is important to note that the Congress readily approved the War Department's proposed advertising budget. In the same year, the State Department had intended to continue the Voice of America (VOA) broadcasting, established in 1942, for the postwar period, but both Congress and domestic media companies opposed it. The State Department's proposed budget for foreign information programs including Voice of America was significantly reduced as the American Society of Newspaper Editors (ASNE) contended that the government should not directly disseminate information to Americans because it would essentially be state propaganda. Although accepting these arguments against state propaganda directed at the domestic audience, Congress nevertheless approved the advertising budget provisions in the military appropriations bill. The bill also included other nontraditional military appropriations, such as postwar occupation, peacetime atomic energy, and the Army's advertising and broadcasting. The appropriations bill was approved as the Military Establishment Act of 1947.

## Government Aid and Relief in Occupied Areas

The Government Aid and Relief in Occupied Areas (GARIOA) appropriation introduced in the previous section was another item of the military budget. Although both the Navy and Army had been tentatively stationed in Okinawa from March 1945 to June 1946, the Department of the Army was formally designated as the executive agency of "administration" for "occupied" areas as in the Congressional appropriations of July 1, 1946.[5]

U.S. Defense budgets were divided into two categories, military and civilian. The latter increased throughout the Cold War. The civilian category included various nontraditional items such as communication, technology, school and hospital administration, educational support, research and development. Since the postwar occupation of Europe and Japan relied upon the communications and logistics capabilities of the Army, the Department of the Army proposed another budgetary framework for these nontraditional activities. The GARIOA item was approved as an appropriation for Civil Function, Army. The Army had planned a global network infrastructure of communications connecting the United States, the occupied areas, and other areas. This aspect of the budget was approved as traditional military activities. The postwar occupation had been strategically planned to fortify and further develop the communications infrastructure and logistics capabilities of the Department of the Army.

The GARIOA budget included payments for the civilian employees needed for the occupation as well as for purchasing food and medical supplies for the people in war-devastated areas. The appropriations were declared to be "for necessary cost for the United States being obligated and being responsible" and determined to be used for the following purposes:

> 1) temporary employment of persons and organizations by contracts and otherwise; 2) travel expenses and transportation; civilian employees and travel allowances, 3) law books, books of reference, newspapers, periodicals, educational films, translation rights, photographic work, educational

exhibits, and dissemination of information; 4) expenses incidental to the operation of schools for American children; 5) printing and binding; 6) contract stenographic reporting services, 7) purchase, maintenance, repairs and operation of passenger automobiles and aircraft; 8) repair and maintenance of buildings, utilities, facilities and appurtenances.[6]

Furthermore, GARIOA appropriations included a humanitarian aim identified as "such minimum supplies for civilian populations thereof as may be essential to prevent starvation, disease, or unrest." The phrase often quoted in postwar Japan and the humanitarian aspect of GARIOA funds probably contributed to establishing a favorable image of Americans who are "so bountiful and friendly that they demanded no reparations from the former enemy nations." This sentiment, of course, is grossly exaggerated: the Congressional hearings determined that the GARIOA appropriations should be primarily allocated to the management costs of the occupied areas and that supplies for civilian populations should be kept minimal. Arguably, the humanitarian aspects of this funding were mere window-dressing, intended to demonstrate compliance with international laws.

The GARIOA food and supplies distributed to civilian populations in war-devastated areas were not free. According to the Congressional records, the GARIOA supplies were distributed by contractors for a price. When selling the supplies in local currencies, the contractors could deduct certain margins from the sale price. The cash balance was required to be deposited as "counterpart funds" in the bank account of a tentative government in the occupied areas. The cost of the occupation was offset by the counterpart fund.[7] The U.S. military government in Okinawa started to charge GARIOA for food and supplies in 1947 and reserved the counterpart fund in its own local bank account.

In the hearings, a Congressman asked the War Department: "Why would Americans have to feed enemy aliens, using our taxpayer's money?" and "Feeding those people should not be our job but the mission of the United Nations." Secretary of War Patterson replied: "We are turning over food problem in Austria to UNRRA, (but... ) I do not think UNRRA is prepared to undertake the work in (Germany and Japan). That has been discussed. I think they are stretched to their limit in the way of personnel to handle the job." He continued that Army were providing "food supplies to civilian populations under the disease and unrest formula"[8] and insisted that it is the U.S. responsibility to feed these people in order to establish stability in occupied areas. The Secretary demanded a Government Aid and Relief in Occupied Areas (GARIOA) budget, as a distinct appropriation alongside the military budget for the same department.

Other Congressmen queried the employment of "enemy aliens" in occupied areas. As GARIOA appropriations originally could not be used to employ non-U.S. citizens, a separate provision was attached for hiring local workers where necessary.[9] Since the U.S. occupation of Japan required translators and interpreters fluent in Japanese language, another allocation was made for U.S. Intelligence Service personnel to study abroad in Japanese universities.[10]

Another important provision of the GARIOA funding was a currency conversion device through which the U.S. government acquired foreign currency, a necessity in occupied areas.

## "ECA in the Far East"

Congress passed the Economic Cooperation Act of 1948, a principle law for European economic recovery aid, which allocated 43 billion U.S. dollars to several European nations. The counterpart funds method adopted in GARIOA appropriations were applied to distribute supplies in European economic recovery programs. The Economic Cooperation Administration established in Europe managed the counterpart funds, receiving relief supplies from the New York Office of the State Department. The purpose of the U.S. foreign aid was to fortify the free economy against the Soviet Union. It was called the Marshall Plan, named after the man who proposed it, Secretary of State George Marshall.

As for East Asia, Congress approved a series of China Aid Acts to expand a free world economy against the Chinese Communist Party, which was supposedly expanding its power in the Far East. As ECA related aid ballooned, GARIOA, originally an item of military appropriations, transformed into a foreign aid item in Foreign Aid Appropriation Act, Public Law 80-793. Thus, Economic Rehabilitation in Occupied Areas or EROA replaced the GARIOA appropriation in 1950. Yet, while the ECA assumed responsibility for U.S. economic assistance in Europe, the Department of the Army retained executive power for U.S. foreign aid in Asia, the so- called "ECA in the Far East."

At the Committee on Appropriations for fiscal year 1950, Robert R. West, Deputy Assistant Secretary for Far Eastern Affairs, proposed aid of $4.095 billion for Japan and $26 million for the Ryukyu Islands. He introduced General Eichelberger, commanding officer of the Eighth Army, which had just been assigned a role in the occupation of Japan. West described the role of the Army as the "ECA in the Far East," and declared that General Eichelberger would have plenty of information regarding the political and economic situation in Japan. The 1950 foreign aid appropriations for the Ryukyus included numerous industrial supplies, such as fertilizer, petroleum, oil, lubricant, and automobiles.[11]

Foreign aid to Japan was increased at the time in response to fears that the U.S. might lose Japan if the Chinese Communist Party were to prevail in China and extend its influence to Japan. At the same time, a special appropriation exclusively for the Ryukyus was secretly proposed in Congress, although the separation of Okinawa from mainland Japan had not yet been officially announced.

GARIOA appropriations were used to purchase relief supplies in the United States. These supplies, transported to Okinawa, were sold for local currency, which was deposited in a local bank for the U.S. military government. This so-called counterpart fund was later transferred to USCAR. Called the High Commissioner's General Fund, this special account was utilized for constructing social infrastructure and student exchange programs. The Comptroller Department of USCAR had oversight of the alternative wallet as well as the annual Congressional appropriation.

During the twenty years between 1945 and 1964, the U.S. Congress approved over a trillion dollars for foreign aid. The aid was divided into military assistance and non-military assistance. GARIOA and European Economic Relief Funds are usually counted as non-military aid.[12] Even the non-military aid, though, was viewed as an inexpensive investment in U.S. national security, as was the case in Okinawa.

## Okinawa Special Account

Congress had overseen the special account of USCAR. The Congressional hearings on Supplemental Appropriation Act of 1953 clarified that the United States had had a large amount of foreign currency reserves, using the counterpart fund system. Although the fund originated from Congressional appropriations, they were used overseas without reporting to Congress. Responding to this situation, Congress determined that no federal organizations should use funds without Congressional approval after June 30, 1953.

When the deadline approached, on April 24, 1953, the Secretary of the Army sent a letter of inquiry on behalf of USCAR to the Comptroller General of the United States of America, asking whether the Army should follow the Congressional decision or not. On August 17, the Acting Comptroller reluctantly answered the inquiry that USCAR did not have to follow Section 1415 because the funds were not "foreign currencies" but a special account directly under the U.S. Department of Finance. On this basis, USCAR's special counterpart fund was formally accepted for the U.S. administration of Okinawa.[13] Like a commercial developer, USCAR invested the special funds into public corporations such as electricity plants, water companies, and warehouses.

As the United States had invested large sums in foreign aid during the two decades after World War II, it held millions of dollars' worth of foreign currencies in seventy-one foreign countries in 1957. The U.S. counterpart-based fund of $25 million had been stored in Japan as of March 31, 1956. The House approved the bilateral agreement between the United States and Japan under which the fund would be used for educational and cultural exchange programs between the two countries. United States Information Service (USIS) in Tokyo subsequently used the fund as a supplemental budget for educational exchange programs.[14]

In Okinawa, GARIOA funds were used not only for educational and cultural exchange programs, but to establish public corporations as well. The latter use of the GARIOA funds made USCAR a problem as a U.S. federal agency that owned overseas public corporations which were originally purchased from Congressional appropriations. Congress raised questions regarding the USCAR management of the GARIOA counterpart fund account in Okinawa.

Congress occasionally asked questions about the special fund reserve. For example, while the Army Corps of Engineers were building a power plant in Machinato, Okinawa, a Congressman asked why the U.S. federal government was engaged in a power plant business overseas. Nevertheless, Congress eventually legalized the special fund through its approval of the Price Act of 1959.

## Army Civil Function

Congress allocated federal budgets for the U.S. administration of Okinawa from July 1, 1946 to May 15, 1972, under the line item "Civil Function, Army." The first ten years, 1947–1957, were in the form of GARIOA (Government Aid and Relief in Occupied Areas) and afterward, 1958–1972, as ARIA (Administration, Ryukyu Islands, Army).[15] As we have seen, GARIOA was originally approved as a budgetary item in the Military Appropriations Act for the U.S. occupation of Japan.

Congressional appropriations entail accounting and reporting obligations. As will be discussed in more detail later in this chapter, the budget for the early period of the Military Government in Okinawa was allocated to the Far East Command in Tokyo. After USCAR was established in December 1950, a newly established Comptroller Department of USCAR became responsible for the U.S. administration's budget management.

According to Comptroller Department records, USCAR budgets were comprised of three components: 1) economic aid, 2) information and education programs, and 3) administrative costs. The first item, economic aid, included public construction costs as well as food and medical supplies. The second item, education and information programs, was for public relations to promote pro-American sentiment among Okinawans. The third item, administrative costs, was allocated for the salaries of staff and others.[16]

Economic aid was the largest proportion, but drastically reduced after peaking in fiscal year 1950. Although the amount was far less than the economic aid package, the perceived importance of the information and education program can be seen in arguments that it should be directly funded by U.S. Congressional appropriation rather than the counterpart funds. However, these involved many controversies. For example, the U.S. Congress approved funding for the provision of English textbooks but was reluctant to allocate fees for Japanese language textbooks, even though they had been the Okinawan standard. At the same time, USCAR would not permit the Japanese government to pay for Japanese textbooks for Okinawan schools. Japanese textbooks were therefore donated to Okinawan schools through Nampo Doho Engokai (Southern Islands Friends' Association), a nonprofit organization directly supported by the Japanese government,[17] but that did not really resolve the problem.

The third item was the administrative costs, including the salaries of USCAR employees. At the beginning, mainly American citizens worked for USCAR, but the numbers of local Okinawan employees gradually increased. Salaries for Okinawans were much lower than for their American counterparts. Hence, USCAR gradually increased the proportion of Okinawan employees for budgetary purposes. It also covered the salaries of Japanese staff at USCAR's Tokyo Office "immigration bureau," which controlled incoming Japanese travelers and outgoing Okinawans. USCAR insisted to Congress that all these expenditures were necessary for the administration of Okinawa, under the category Civil Function, Army.

## Chapter Summary

The Congress was largely ambivalent about the U.S. administration of Okinawa. From year to year, Congress consistently approved the "Civil Function, Army" budget for the administration of Okinawa in addition to the traditional military budget. Congress attempted to oversee the civil function of the U.S. military activities overseas by separating the obligations for specific appropriations, but at the same time they endorsed the military administration of the foreign people.

The U.S. budget for the administration of Okinawa consisted of three components: 1) economic aid, 2) information and education programs, and 3) general administrative costs. Economic aid and information programs were similar to the Marshall Plan, but administered by the Department of the Army.

Congressmen raised questions such as: Why should the Congress allocate American taxpayers' money for Okinawan people? That question led to another: Why should the United States of America retain administrative authority over Okinawa? The democratic machinery would not function without the open principle of budgetary appropriations processes. However, Congress approved the military administration of Okinawa by appropriating the budget after all.

# 2 Civil Affairs: From Military Government to Public Affairs

As we have seen, the U.S. Congress approved the budget for the administration of Okinawa from 1947 until 1972 as a civil function of the Army. The U.S. Army Civil Affairs Division was established during World War II to prepare for the postwar occupation of Japan and Germany. Its successors supervised the U.S. administration of Okinawa.

This chapter aims to determine the history and organizational changes of the Civil Affairs Division. The basic principles had been defined in the "Field Manual for Military Government and Civil Affairs (FM27-5)" published in 1943 and revised as the "Civil Operations Manual (FM41-10)" in 1957. *Civil Affairs: Soldiers become Governors* is an official history of the Army dealing with the U.S. occupation of French North Africa during WWII. Arnold G. Fisch wrote *Military Government of the Ryukyu Islands, 1945–1950* as an official history of the early military occupation of Okinawa. After USCAR took over the role of the military government, "Civil Affairs Activities of the Ryukyu Islands" was published as a biannual report of the U.S. administration of Okinawa. This chapter examines these manuals and publications to explore how the Civil Affairs Division and its successors viewed the U.S. administration of Okinawa.

## International Law and War

Compliance with international laws was regarded as a basic obligation for the United States. The U.S. started to prepare its postwar occupation planning on March 1, 1943, establishing the Civil Affairs Division. The occupation plan included administration of the territories which Japan, Germany, and Italy had governed prior to the end of World War II.[1] The Army called such area management activities "civil affairs."

The Army's official history *Civil Affairs: Soldiers Become Governors*, by Coles and Weinberg, describes the process through which soldiers suddenly became governors and the confusion that accompanied this change in roles. Article Four, annexed to the Hague Convention of 1907, obliged modern troops to protect civilian populations in battlefield areas. That obligation demanded that the U.S. Army prepare for civilian administration immediately after the cease-fire. The Joint Chiefs of Staff ordered the theater commander in the Pacific to comply with international law and established a military government in Okinawa to manage the civilian population. As we have seen, GARIOA appropriations were justified by "the disease and social unrest formula" for managing post-conflict populations.

It is, of course, quite difficult to deal with former enemy populations immediately after a ceasefire. *Soldiers Become Governors* describes the dilemma between the practical realities of warfare and the idealistic framework of international laws. General Dwight D. Eisenhower initially argued that the State Department should take responsibility for the postwar occupation of Europe. However, the task eventually fell to the Army because of the difficulties diplomats might encounter dealing with subject populations in politically unstable territories without military assistance. Hence, the U.S. Army assumed executive responsibility for the occupation for security reasons, and this became the U.S. standard. Coles and Weinberg also referred to a variety of postwar peacekeeping operations, including the administration of Okinawa, as "civil affairs."[2]

Since the U.S. experience in French North Africa during WWII, civil affairs activities have taken a pivotal role in U.S. military experiences from the occupation of Japan and Germany to the more recent wars in Afghanistan and Iraq. Postwar intervention in war-devastated foreign countries have been called peace-building operations and have become the standard operating procedure of U.S. military deployment. In this sense, the U.S. administration of Okinawa can be understood as a prototype for U.S. civil affairs activities. In fact, USCAR's biannual reports, "Civil Affairs Activities in the Ryukyu Islands," were sent to the National Defense University in Washington D.C. and used as reference materials to educate civilian officers. The university had pioneered the studies of civil affairs activities as well as national security studies. Civil affairs activities are quite complicated tasks because civil affairs officers and their staff face sensitive cultural and linguistic differences in politically unstable areas.[3] The term peace-building is seemingly positive, but its implementation has been rather uneven because the original plans for civil affairs activities have often been obstructed by unexpected difficulties in different cultures.

## Civil Affairs Field Manual

On July 30, 1940, the U.S. Army published "Military Government" (FM27-5), the first field manual to prepare for the Army's postwar civil affairs activities. It refers to the civil affairs staff as "military government staff" because the definition of civil affairs was not yet agreed upon.[4] On December 22, 1943, the Army and Navy jointly revised the first edition and published the new field manual, "United States Army and Navy Manual of Military Government and Civil Affairs" (FM27-5, OPNAV50E-3). This updated version used the term civil affairs in the title and specified the differences between military government and civil affairs. Accordingly, while military government is an authority executing the role of government in occupied areas based on military power or agreements, civil affairs is defined as activities of a military government dealing with civilian populations and supervising civilian life. Although the two concepts overlapped and were often misunderstood, it could be understood that the Military Government in Okinawa was a provisional authority that suspended the previous local government while the mission of its successor, the United States Civil Administration of the Ryukyu Islands, was civil affairs control over local residents.

The field manual obliged the military government to protect unarmed civilians in compliance with international laws. However, it also stipulated that military objectives should override all others, including civil affairs. Based on military supremacy policy, it determined that theater commanders should concurrently assume the position of military governor. Under the military commander, military officers worked as civil affairs officers dealing with civilians.[5] The manual specified that the mission of civil affairs officers was to control the civilian population for the purposes of minimizing belligerence while obtaining their cooperation with military activities. It was regarded as a military advantage to acquire civilian support in occupied areas. Terms frequently used in Okinawa, such as proclamation, civil administration, and chief executive had all been introduced in the field manual as essential devices for civil affairs activities.

Censorship was an essential function of civil affairs. The field manual describes the two-fold purpose of censorship as helping to maintain security for military and civilian personnel and to acquire local intelligence. The manual directed the civil affairs officers to re-establish civilian communications such as radio, telephone, telegram and postal offices, where these had been destroyed. Once the communications were restored, dissemination of information was defined as the primary mission of civil affairs officers, releasing press materials to engender acceptance of the occupation force.[6] Military police, coastguard, and immigration registration could also be used by civil affairs officers, but the manual recommended utilizing local police if they were reliable.[7] In sum, civil affairs activities covered a broad range of roles and activities from military police to public relations.

The manual continued. The first military government should be established as soon as the occupation force acquired the resultant authority after the assault. Proclamations should be issued immediately with the commencement of the occupation to inform residents of the fact. Ordinances, orders, and instructions should be issued when necessary.[8] All of these directives were carried out during the occupation and administration of Okinawa.

The field manual of 1943 had been proposed by two influential figures, George C. Marshall, Army Chief of Staff, and Earnest J. King, Chief of Naval Operations. As Secretary of State after the war, Marshall would later propose the famous European economic recovery program, the so-called Marshall Plan, which, as suggested above, was already foreshadowed by U.S. economic aid to Japan and Okinawa. Earnest J. King drafted the JCS directives which, as we have seen, effectively governed Okinawa from the end of World War II until the late 1960s.

## Military Government in Okinawa

On January 27, 1945, preparations for the military government in Okinawa were included in the joint Army-Navy Operation Iceberg, the Okinawa landing operation. The plan was for two stages: 1) assault, and 2) garrison. The military government in the assault phase was expected to transport military supplies. When the battle was over, the military government was tasked with constructing airfields in Okinawa in preparation for an attack on mainland Japan. In the garrison phase, the Navy provided medical services to civilians, constructed hospitals and engaged in disease prevention programs. The Army transported food, clothes and other supplies. The transportation of necessary civilian supplies was planned from Hawaii and the west coast of the United States based on an estimate of the Okinawan population. The construction of civilian camps, supply storage and military bases by Army Engineers had been planned prior to the landing on Okinawa.[9]

Operation Iceberg primarily aimed to establish military airfields necessary to attack mainland Japan, but also aimed to cut communications between Japan, China, Taiwan, and other Japanese occupied territories in Southeast Asia.[10] The Civil Affairs Section had been established in Hawaii even earlier, on August 15, 1944. The civil affairs officers were trained at the Civil Affairs Staging Area, Fort Ord, California, and landed on the west coast of Okinawa Island. Soon after the landing, the military government took 22,000 surrendered Okinawans into civilian camps for security purposes. One-hundred Japanese-American translators came to Okinawa, but more translators were needed because most Okinawans did not understand English.[11]

The U.S. Commander-in-Chief in the Battle of Okinawa was Admiral Chester W. Nimitz of the Navy. Lieutenant General Simon B. Buckner of the Army was appointed the Military Governor. Under Buckner's command, Brigadier General William E. Crist was acting military governor. Civil affairs officers disseminated Nimitz's Proclamations, which suspended the authority of the local Japanese government while declaring that the U.S. occupation had commenced.[12] The initial civil affairs activities under the military government were counterintelligence activities. In the southern Pacific Islands and the Philippines, Counter Intelligence Corps (CIC) had been interrogating Japanese prisoners of war to extract information necessary for the forthcoming war against Japan. During the Battle of Okinawa, Psychological Warfare Teams persuaded Okinawans to surrender to U.S. forces, using propaganda leaflets. The Counter Intelligence Corps then interrogated them.[13]

According to a Joint Intelligence Center report, the psychological warfare operation was originally prepared in Pearl Harbor, Hawaii, as a joint project of the 10th Army and G-2 in December 1944. The team produced 23 propaganda leaflets. Of these, 12 were prepared exclusively for Okinawa while the rest were produced as a collaboration of the psychological warfare group and Office of War Information in Honolulu. Japanese language leaflets must have been translated back into English and submitted to the commander for approval prior to printing. The voice recordings of a Japanese intelligence officer who had become a prisoner of war were used to call for surrender. Japanese music and disconcerting sounds were also prepared for the psychological warfare operation.[14] According to records of the Department of the Army, five million propaganda leaflets had been dropped from airplanes over Okinawa during the period between March 25 and April 17, 1945. During the first two weeks after landing, the same report says, 85,000 civilians surrendered, and 9,108 Japanese soldiers died, while 391 were captured as prisoners of war.[15]

## Civil Affairs Handbook

Prior to the Okinawa landing, the Army's Military Intelligence Service had photographed major beaches and drafted a detailed map locating radio stations, communication cables, seaports, airports, hospitals and stockyards.[16] Successful operations rely on an excellent network of intelligence.[17] Local intelligence gathering was believed to be essential to the military operations planning process. The War Department, Office of Naval Intelligence, Office of War Information, and Foreign Broadcasting Information Service had engaged in intelligence gathering in the occupation planning process. The Research and Analysis Division, Office of Strategic Services (OSS) collected intelligence to prepare for the occupation of Japan.[18] Based on research of Japanese language sources, for instance, the Division wrote a detailed analysis concerning the Japanese regard for Emperor Hirohito.[19]

American academics were also mobilized into the war. Edwin O. Reischauer, a Harvard University professor, moved to Washington D.C., where he worked for the State and War Departments, and engaged in censorship of Japanese language newspapers published in the United States. Probably, Reischauer did not read all the contents. Japanese or Japanese Americans were engaged in reading those newspapers and Reischauer was presumably asked his opinion about anything that was ambiguous or uncertain. The Army later invited him to the Presidio in San Francisco, where Reischauer taught Japanese culture and history to prospective civil affairs officers.

The Library of Congress gathered all available resources regarding Japan, including Japanese books, periodicals, newspapers and other materials. Harold D. Lasswell engaged in propaganda analysis at the Library of Congress. Americans who had been in Japan, Japanese Americans, and Japanese in America were all regarded as information sources and summoned to government activities such as translation. Japanese language materials were systematically translated into English and compiled into the "Civil Affairs Handbook, Japan."[20]

Local information was presented in the Okinawan chapter, a three-hundred-page booklet, of the Civil Affairs Handbook, published by the Department of the Navy in November 1944. The Office of Naval Intelligence and the Army Military Intelligence Service had a contract with Columbia University to educate military government staff, and ordered anthropologist George Murdock to research Japan mandated islands, including Okinawa. The Civil Affairs Handbook on the Ryukyu Islands was based on the translation of Japanese language resources including government documents and statistics.[21]

While the field manuals described in the previous section provided guidelines for civil affairs officers and staff, civil affairs handbooks were geographical information guidebooks. Since the civil affairs handbook used pre-war information and statistics of Japanese government, the military government rescinded the dated handbook soon after the landing on Okinawa as they immediately embarked on a new round of information gathering.[22]

## Civil Affairs Division History

The Civil Affairs Division established under the Army Special Staff in 1943 was reorganized as the Army Staff and Office for Occupied Areas in 1945. The former took over the operations planning tasks of the Civil Affairs Division and the latter took logistics such as the transportation of relief supplies and information materials.

The Office of Occupied Areas administered the procurement and transportation of relief supplies based on the GARIOA appropriations. Early GARIOA supplies to Okinawa were appropriated as part of the Japanese aid, which also included Korea. The GARIOA supplies to Korea were regarded as the most important, as the United States estimated that Korea was at serious risk of succumbing to communism. The U.S. intended to empower the free economy of Korea by GARIOA supplies.

As the U.S. occupation of Germany and Japan ended, the Office of Occupied Areas was abolished and reorganized into the Office of the Chiefs of Civil Affairs and Military Government (CAMG) under the Army Staff on April 14, 1952. The Army Staff included the Deputy Chiefs of Planning Staff and Operation and five other divisions such as Budget, Economy, Public Affairs, Research and Analysis, and Military Operation Directorates.[23] Through the reorganization, CAMG began supervising the Ryukyu Islands as well as the Trieste Free Zone in Europe. When Trieste declared independence in 1954, CAMG became exclusively focused on administering the Ryukyus. The CAMG was further reorganized into the Office of the Chief of Civil Affairs in 1959 and the Office of the Deputy Chief of Civil Affairs in the 1960s. USCAR was placed under the Office of the Deputy Chief of Civil Affairs. After the GARIOA appropriations ended, the Office remained exclusively for USCAR, funded with part of the Congressional appropriations for USCAR. Thus, the history of the Civil Affairs Division, Army, indicates that the U.S. administration of Okinawa began as a continuation of the occupation of Japan and gradually transformed into an exclusive organization for Okinawa.

## Civil Intelligence during the Cold War

Civil intelligence was a new concept introduced during the Cold War. While combat intelligence dealt with geopolitical information directly related to military operations, civil affairs intelligence or civil intelligence investigated ordinary civilians, including those living in allied countries. Because the Cold War was a total war, civil intelligence was adopted as a preventive formula against the outbreak of war. It directly targeted civilian populations to eliminate political, economic, and social factors that might trigger a war.[24] Intelligence officers were expected to collect information from local police, bureaucrats and civilians and to prevent espionage, sabotage and subversion.

The purpose of collecting civil intelligence was to plan a civil affairs control plan effectively supporting any U.S. military action. The field manuals granted executive authority to civil affairs officers for "screening, removal and appointment of local civil officials."[25] The manual further stated that civil affairs officers could reinforce strict speech control over residents and provide assistance for "measures to prevent local publication of information which is inimical to the military force." Civil affairs officers were officially permitted to intervene into local politics and mass media policy.[26] "Refugees, evacuees, and displaced persons" should be treated as information sources, the manual stated. The civil intelligence officers were also empowered to recruit personnel for covert operations.[27]

Civil intelligence was thoroughly collected in Okinawa. The Civil Intelligence Division, Ryukyu Command was the official civil intelligence organization, but USCAR supported the division as if it were the "thought police." A "Weekly Intelligence Summary," the official report of the Civil Intelligence Division, was filed in the USCAR Administration Office records, and was periodically circulated among American military and civilian employees in Okinawa. For instance, the Weekly dated June 11, 1969 indicates that the civil intelligence authorities had investigated political parties, Okinawa reversion groups and labor unions.[28]

The 526th CIC Detachment, stationed at Fort Buckner, in Okinawa, collected information about "communists," labeling them anti-American elements in Okinawa. The CIC had categorized the "danger levels" of Okinawan civilian groups in a five-level ranking,[29] closely watching not only political parties or labor unions but also women's associations, as well as small reading and study groups.[30] The Okinawan press such as the *Ryukyu Shimpo* and the *Okinawa Times* were also targeted under CIC surveillance. As discussed in Chapter 8, the Public Affairs Department monitored the content of Okinawan mass media. Once the Department pointed to an anti-American factor in the contents, the CIC and Ryukyu Command began investigation. Thus, the public affairs and civil affairs activities were closely related to civil intelligence activities of the military command.

The local intelligence officers in Okinawa seem to have categorized almost all anti-American elements as "communist." The United States defined Okinawa as "a showcase of democracy" against the Soviet's communist influences and decided to retain administrative authority over the islands. However, the purpose of maintaining the administrative authority over the islands seems to have undergone a subtle transformation, from promoting a democratic civil society to "merely" preserving the security of military personnel. Although the U.S. propagated fear of communism, the U.S. civil intelligence unit simply protected the military forces. Okinawans rejected military supremacy and the U.S. civil administration was unable to win the residents' support.

In the 1960s, civil affairs activities came to be described as a complex task including various elements "from military government to public affairs." In fact, the civil functions of the Army included a broad range of civilian control activities, from urging unarmed civilians to surrender during wartime to public affairs activities during peacetime. The U.S.

Department of the Army was responsible for the complex mission in Okinawa. The area unit was the United States Civil Administration of the Ryukyu Islands (USCAR).

## Chapter Summary

Chapter 2 briefly summarized the history of the Civil Affairs Division, Department of the Army and outlined its civil affairs activities. Civil affairs included a broad range of activities "from military government to public affairs." Congress officially assigned the mission to the Department of the Army, which had been charged with the postwar occupation of Japan. The mission was originally to comply with international laws, but gradually transformed into supporting military operations. In Okinawa, military supremacy penetrated the civil affairs activities. This is the dilemma of a military whose mission involves killing but is also obliged to protect unarmed civilians.

Civil functions were closely related to intelligence gathering for supporting the troops. The field manuals for civil affairs had decreed that theater commanders would be the senior-most officers for civil affairs. Throughout the U.S. administrative period in Okinawa, as the next chapter describes, the Joint Chiefs of Staff never compromised this policy.

Congress consistently approved budgets for the administration of Okinawa as a civil function of the Army. Although the U.S. Congress is the sole legislative body of the federal government and is expected to have oversight of U.S. government agencies and activities, it quietly acquiesced to the military rule of occupied territories in accordance with a quite different set of rules, drafted by the Army Judge Advocate in Charlottesville, Virginia.

# 3 U.S. Occupation Policy Defined in JCS 1231

## Introduction

Although the U.S. issued many martial laws to regulate Okinawa, the overriding administrative principles for the postwar occupation had been set out in JCS directive 1231, issued by the Joint Chiefs of Staff as a pre-assault directive on January 12, 1945 to Admiral Chester Nimitz, Commander in Chief, Pacific Fleet. Nimitz issued the first series of proclamations, called Nimitz Proclamations, concerning Okinawa and the surrounding islands, which detailed the U.S. occupation principles.

This chapter summarizes the content of the JCS 1231 directives, analyzes the background, and highlights transformations in the original directives from 1945 to 1950. JCS 1231 introduced the counterpart funding system and detailed policy regarding the U.S. political and economic administration of Okinawa. For example, the Financial Directive ordered the Okinawa military government to establish a commercial bank in the occupied area and authorized a *persona sui juris* to manage the bank account, which enabled investment in social infrastructure such as roads and bridges, as well as public corporations to build and operate petroleum storage facilities, electric power plants and water pipelines.[1]

## Directive to Admiral Nimitz

According to USCAR records, the first U.S. military government in the Ryukyu Islands was established on Kerama Island on March 26, 1945.[2] The military government aimed to establish a logistical support base for landing on Okinawa Island, the main island of the Ryukyu archipelago. It also aimed to control civilians, especially any disruptive actions that could be an obstacle for U.S. military activities against the Empire of Japan.

On August 15, 1944, four Army and fifteen Naval officers had started planning the military government at Scofield Barracks in Oahu, Hawaii. Among them was an anthropologist, Lt. Comdr. George P. Murdock of the Navy. By November, the group was incorporated into the Military Government Team after Brig. Gen. William E. Crist of the Army joined the group. Meanwhile, JCS 819/5 had determined that Navy Admiral Chester Nimitz would command the Army-Navy combined military team.[3]

On January 12, 1945, the Joint Chiefs of Staff issued JCS 1231 to Nimitz with orders to occupy the islands close to Japan, titled "Directives for Military Government in the Japanese Outlying Islands" targeted at Izu, Ogasawara, Chishima and the Ryukyu Islands. According to the Records of the Combined Chiefs of Staff (CCS) of the United States and Britain, Earnest J. King, Chief of Naval Operations, drafted the original directives. The Joint Chiefs approved the final draft and issued it to Nimitz.[4] A copy was sent to the Army Commander in Chief deployed in Continental China, but JCS 1231 was originated at the Navy's direction.

The JCS 1231 series is filed in the Geographic File, Records of the Joint Chiefs of Staff (RG218) in the U.S. National Archives as Pacific Ocean Area (POA) files, of which Nimitz was the commander-in-chief. JCS 1231 was declassified on August 25, 1950 but has not been well researched, probably because the Army replaced the Navy as the U.S. administrator of Okinawa after 1946 and Army historians were uninterested in Navy directives. The original JCS 1231 was repeatedly revised until the fourteenth amendment, JCS 1231/14, which directed MacArthur to establish USCAR. JCS 1231/14 was sent to the State Department and was included as a "memorandum" in "Foreign Relations of the United States" (FRUS), part of the official history of the State Department.[5]

On October 4, 1950, thus, JCS 1231/14 became a new directive issued to General Douglas MacArthur, Commander-in-Chief of the Far East Command (FEC) stationed in Tokyo. In accordance with the JCS directive, MacArthur issued an FEC directive to establish USCAR in December 1950. Subsequently, Major General Robert S. Beightler, Deputy Governor of the Military Government in Okinawa, issued Civil Administration Proclamation No.1 on December 15, declaring the establishment of USCAR.[6]

The JCS 1231 series was revised again and again and finally sent to the State Department on April 21, 1954, when the National Security Council advised Defense to revise the directives again according to the U.S.-Japan peace treaty of 1951.[7] Nevertheless, the wartime directive continued to provide the basis for the U.S. administration of Okinawa until Executive Order 10713 was issued in June 1957.

## JCS Directive 1231

Approved on January 12, 1945, JCS 1231 consisted of twenty-two pages, divided into three sections: political, economic, and financial directives. Page one is a cover sheet entitled "Memorandum." Three directives and an appendix were attached as follows:
 1. Memorandum for the Commander in Chief, United States Fleet and Chief of Naval Operations (p. 1)
 2. Enclosure A = Political Directive (pp. 2–6)
 3. Enclosure B = Proposed Economic Directive (pp. 7–11)
 4. Enclosure C = Financial Directive (pp. 12–17)
 5. Appendix to Financial Directive, Basic Accounting Instructions (pp. 18–22)

According to this memorandum, the State Department "concurred" with the political and economic directives. Of these, Section One of the Political Directive defined the targeted areas regarding JCS 1231. Section Two directed that military governments should be established in Japanese outlying islands as soon as the U.S. Forces achieved occupation. Section Three and the remaining sections presented principles for the military government. The political directive comprised twenty-nine sections which Nimitz addressed when drafting the Proclamations.

The Nimitz Proclamations began with a preface addressing the target audience, "to the people of the islands of Nansei Shoto and adjacent waters occupied by United States Forces," a well-known phrase to Okinawan people. By issuing these proclamations, Nimitz notified the residents that he, as the Military Governor, had established the military government. Proclamations One to Ten seem to retrace the contents of JCS 1231. For example, Section 9, Political Directive, JCS 1231, had directed Nimitz to suspend local power and laws upon establishing the military government. Nimitz Proclamation One duly suspended the authority of the Japanese and Okinawa prefectural governments. Section 13, Political Directive, directed the establishment of a martial court, after revoking the authority of the existing courts. These actions were proclaimed in Sections 5 and 6 of Nimitz Proclamation One. Section 18, Political Directive, determined basic policy on censorship and the suspension of civilian communications including publications, radio, and telephones, which was announced in Proclamation Ten.

The economic directive of JCS 1231 determined economic policy for the U.S. occupation. While the political directive was fully approved by the Combined Chiefs of Staff, the economic directive was simply a "proposal." Despite not having been approved by other departments, agencies, or by the British Chiefs, it was to have a tremendous impact on postwar Okinawa. Importantly, although it is usual practice for civilians to supervise economic matters in peacetime, the economic directive designated the theater commander – in this case, Chester Nimitz – as the highest authority regarding economic policy in occupied areas. It detailed basic policies regarding civilian employee salaries, price guidelines, and supervising principles toward local farmers and fishermen. The British Chiefs might not have agreed on the U.S.-centered economic supremacy. Nevertheless, the economic directive was sent to Nimitz as "an enclosure" to JCS 1231 and the "proposed" directive was executed in Okinawa as an economic principle which the U.S. took great advantage of throughout the occupation period.

The financial directive of JCS 1231 presented a more concrete fiscal management policy, especially regarding local currency administration. The financial directive, including a detailed appendix, comprised more than half of the pages of JCS 1231. It included a policy on supplemental military yen, type B, which had been approved by the U.S. Department of the Treasury.[8] The B yen was implemented in U.S.-occupied Okinawa. The military government was permitted by the Financial Directive to establish public corporations and a central bank in occupied areas and was required to report to the U.S. Department of the Treasury. The system of counterpart funds, as we have seen, had already been recommended in the earliest JCS directive issued during the war.[9] In sum JCS 1231 was a joint production of the Joint Chiefs and the U.S. Treasury Department.

## Political Directive

The political directive determined that Okinawa was under the direction of the U.S. Joint Chiefs of Staff. Admiral Chester Nimitz was the first Military Governor, the highest authority in the occupied area. The political directive clearly specified that military missions must have the highest priority. It is important that the JCS directive defined JCS's supremacy over Okinawa. This is the most probable explanation for why JCS 1231 was not revoked until the reversion of Okinawa.

Section One, the Political Directive, defined the targeted areas, described as "the Japanese Outlying Islands," as follows: 1) the Nampo Shoto or southern islands, consisting of the Izu, Bonin, and Volcano Islands, 2) the Nansei Shoto or southwestern islands, consisting the Ryukyus or Loochoo Islands, and 3) the Kurile Islands, northeastern islands of Japanese archipelago.

It is notable that JCS 1231 excluded former Japanese mandated islands in the Southwest Pacific such as the Mariana Islands, the Caroline Islands, and the Marshall Islands. Prior to landing on Okinawa, JCS issued JCS 1231 as special directive for Nanpo and Nansei Shoto and the Kurile Islands because greater resistance was expected from the local populations of these islands, which had been more strongly influenced by Japanese militarism. The special directive imposed a much stricter civilian administration policy in the islands closer to Japan than on the Marianas and other South Pacific Islands.

Section 19 of the Political Directive prohibited the Japanese outlying islanders from promoting political thoughts about Japanese militarism and ultra-nationalism. Section 20 ordered Japanese nationalist groups to disband and banned their activities. Section 21 prohibited Nimitz and his staff from publicly stating any opinions regarding the Japanese Emperor and his postwar status. It is interesting that the JCS directive not only restrained the speech of Okinawan people but also prohibited American soldiers from expressing their opinions of the Emperor. While the U.S. occupation forces in Japan used the Emperor as a national symbol to help reconstruct postwar Japanese society, JCS prohibited any discussion of the Emperor in Okinawa. As we have seen, JCS also ordered Nimitz to issue proclamations to notify the public of the military government's occupation policies.

The Joint Chiefs of Staff further ordered the commander to comply with international laws when dealing with non-militant civilians. JCS policy was to separate civilians from military personnel, confining them in U.S. civilian camps (Section 15) where they were interviewed about their political beliefs and thoughts. Civilian camp administration was to comply with the guidelines of the Geneva Convention 1929 (Section 16). Accordingly, JCS prohibited forced labor, directing that military government teams should recruit laborers on a voluntary basis to avoid any perceptions that they were running concentration camps. JCS 1231 was attuned to international public opinion.

Although the directive ordered the Military Governor to remove high ranking officials of the existing government in occupied areas (Section 10), it recommended utilizing local governmental organizations and residents in so far as they did not conflict with U.S. military objectives (Sections 11, 12). Koreans and Chinese in Taiwan, for example, should be accorded higher status than Japanese (Section 7), and Japanese government properties and public documents were to be liquidated (Section 26, 28). Religious freedom was permitted with the exception of Japanese militarism. The restoration of regional history and culture were encouraged but civilian publications, radio, and telephones were prohibited (Section 18). Schools and other educational institutions were temporarily closed. The Military Governor had exclusive authority to recommence education (Section 23).

The political directive of JCS 1231 was intended to set a basic framework for the U.S. occupation. The Joint Chiefs of Staff firmly believed that the military mission would depend on whether civilian populations were successfully controlled.

## Economic Directive

The military dominance indicated in the political directive was carefully continued in the economic directive, declaring the U.S. theater commander to be the head of economic policy in the Japanese Outlying Islands.[10] The economic directive effectively rendered postwar Okinawa "a military colony." Although, as mentioned, the economic directive was officially only a proposal, it significantly affected Okinawa in real and concrete ways.

Compared with Germany, which was jointly occupied by Britain, France, U.S. and Soviet Union after World War II, Japan and Okinawa were occupied by U.S. forces alone. The U.S. High Commissioner to Germany was responsible to the State Department. In Japan, General MacArthur governed through the State-War-Navy-Coordinating Committee (SWNCC). In contrast, the JCS governed Okinawa directly, relatively free of State Department influence.

The economic directive presented economic principles to develop an independent economy in occupied areas. Price setting guidelines for relief supplies and civilian wage rates were among the items seen as immediately necessary for the military government. The directive also included longer-term economic planning policies such as public corporation management, agricultural and fishing industry development, licensing corporations and obligations to report on the economic situation of occupied areas. This suggests that the United States had planned long-term economic development and a long-lasting occupation of Okinawa from the very beginning.

The economic directive consisted of a list of administrative policies for civil affairs teams. For instance, as we have seen, JCS 1231 specified a funding method in which the United States would sell relief supplies for local currencies and then invest those funds to develop the local economy. This was a prototype of the funding method that the Marshall Plan would dub the "counterpart fund." George Marshall, the Army Chief of Staff at the time, was one of the drafters of JCS 1231, and later proposed the Marshall Plan for European recovery, when he was Secretary of State. The JCS 1231 economic directive included detailed instructions regarding logistics and record keeping for the counterpart fund.

The basic policies the economic directive presented to support the local economy included: a) utilizing local resources as much as possible, b) preventing disease and social unrest, and c) providing the minimum supplies necessary to civilian populations. It clearly stated that relief supplies should be kept minimal to not burden the United States. Research on the local economy was a priority for the U.S. military commander, as was obtaining industrial output of sugar, vegetables, fish, and phosphate rocks – a raw material for ammunition.

Section 14 of the economic directive ordered the military governor to administer the production and logistics of private corporations. Section 15 ordered the governor to control incoming and outgoing foreign trade. Section 17 ordered the governor to control foreign trade and the local economy. Sections 18 and 19 stipulated that the military government should control public facilities such as ports, warehouses, ships, railroad, postal services, telecommunication and radio stations. Section 20 directed the military government to control public corporations for petroleum, electricity and water distribution. Financial officers of the

Army and Navy were permitted special authority to deal with foreign currency exchange in Sections 7 and 8.[11]

Thus, the Economic Directive, JCS 1231, indicates that the U.S. occupation of Okinawa had been carefully planned based on a long-term perspective of economic development, extending military domination into economic administration.

## Financial Directive and Appendix

In addition to the political and economic directives, JCS included a financial directive, which was approved by the U.S. Department of the Treasury. Sections 1 and 2 ordered the suspension of Japanese military yen, which had circulated in Japan's occupied areas during World War II, and stipulated that prospective proclamations should legalize the "supplemental military B yen" issued by the U.S. military government. Sections 3 and 4 prohibited the use of U.S. dollars and Hawaii dollars in the targeted areas except for emergencies. Section 10 ordered the suspension of local commercial banks and financial institutions and Section 11 ordered the establishment of a new bank supervised by the military government. An appendix to the financial directive provided detailed accounting instructions required for implementing the economic policy.

According to the appendix, military governments in the Japanese outlying islands should have corporate personhood and were permitted to manage a central bank account to accomplish the government's mission. The military governments were authorized to manage the accounting of Japanese yen, supplemental military bills and U.S. dollars as well as the counterpart fund. The military governors were required to report periodically to the U.S. Department of the Treasury, but the financial directive also permitted the military governments wide discretion to manage local currencies acquired by selling GARIOA supplies.[12]

As we saw in Chapter 1, the U.S. Congress did not officially legalize the USCAR special account until 1959, although the U.S. Department of the Treasury had approved the accounting of the wartime directive's GARIOA funds. In 1946, Congress formally appropriated GARIOA budgets for the first time. But the basic accounting guidelines in prospective occupied areas had already been prescribed by the issuance of JCS 1231 in January 1945. JCS had also prescribed detailed accounting instructions for selling supplies, local currencies and foreign currency exchanges to maximize

American advantage. In this regard, JCS 1231 was the most important document determining the basic framework of the U.S. occupation of Okinawa even prior to Congressional approval.

JCS 1231 seems to have been forgotten for a while after the war. However, as the next chapter describes, the nearly-dead directive was revived on October 4, 1950, following the advent of the Korean War. After being thoroughly revised, it succeeded the wartime directive's policy. The fourteenth amendment of JCS 1231, JCS 1231/14, established the United States Civil Administration of the Ryukyu Islands, USCAR.

## Chapter Summary

This chapter demonstrated that JCS 1231 established the principles for U.S. postwar occupation of Okinawa. The wartime directive from the Joint Chiefs of Staff to Admiral Nimitz, the theater commander, defined political, economic, and financial policies for a prospective occupation aiming to prevent civilian resistance to U.S. military actions in Okinawa. The political directive provided necessary instructions for the immediate suspension of Japanese laws and the establishment of a military government. Meanwhile, the economic and financial directives indicated a long-term U.S. economic interest, including an early version of the counterpart fund method that would be central to the Marshall Plan.

Most importantly, JCS 1231 designated the U.S. military theater commanders as the highest-ranking officers responsible for economic policy in Okinawa. Consequently, the U.S. military force extended its military dominance to political and economic matters. It is not certain how long JCS 1231 was in effect, but the military officer in charge continued to be the highest-ranking U.S. official in Okinawa until the reversion in 1972. As to U.S. military interest, JCS 1231 provided the U.S. military an enormous advantage in peacetime. Hence. Okinawa can be accurately understood to have been "a military colony."

# 4 United States Civil Administration of the Ryukyu Islands, Wartime Directive Revived

## Introduction

JCS 1231, the wartime directive described in the previous chapter, seems to have been forgotten in the U.S. capital. After World War II ended, civilian officers in the State and Defense Departments had attempted to transform the U.S. military occupation of Okinawa into a civilian administration to avoid anticipated international criticism. However, as the Korean War broke out, the wartime directive was revised and the fourteenth amendment of JCS 1231 was promulgated as the USCAR Directive[1] to establish the United States Civil Administration of the Ryukyu Islands on October 4, 1950. The U.S. armed forces insisted on maintaining JCS's direction over Okinawa until peace came to the Far East.

Records of the Civil Affairs Division of the Army Staff reveal that an original draft of USCAR Directives was revised into JCS 1231/14 and revised again into Executive Order 10713 of 1957, which set a new principle for the latter half of the U.S. administration of Okinawa. This chapter traces the process of revising the USCAR Directive, JCS 1231/14 and analyzes its transformation. Importantly, the USCAR Directive officially permitted USCAR to forcefully acquire land and other real estate in Okinawa. The land issue was central to the Okinawa situation, but it was not certain whether it was done by local authority or direction from Washington. This study clarifies that the forced land acquisition was executed in Okinawa based on the revised directive.

## The USCAR Directive

The military is a hierarchical organization. The priority for the Joint Chiefs of Staff was to maintain the chain of command from the Joint Chiefs to the lower echelons. Without the chain of command, they insisted, the military would not able to accomplish its mission. To maintain the command lines, JCS insisted that the military theater commander must be the governor of Okinawa.

As described previously, the USCAR Directive to establish U.S. Civil Administration of the Ryukyu Islands was approved by JCS on October 4, 1950, and sent to General Douglas MacArthur, Commander-in-Chief of the Far East Command in Tokyo on October 11.[2] The Far East Command (FEC) revised the directive and sent it to the Commander-in-Chief, Ryukyu Command, on December 5 as the USCAR Directive, Directive for the United States Civil Administration of the Ryukyu Islands.[3] Based on the FEC directive, on December 15, General Order Number 1 established USCAR, the United States Civil Administration of the Ryukyu Islands, which took over the role of the military government. General Order Number 1 was written by Brigadier General John H. Hinds, previously the Deputy Military Governor, who became the Civil Administrator for the newly born USCAR.[4] According to the directive, military government teams in Amami, Miyako, Okinawa, Ryukyu, Yaeyama, and Tokyo were reorganized into civil affairs teams.

General Order Number 1 simply ordered the reorganization of the military government into a civil administration. However, the process of revising the USCAR Directive indicates that the necessity of civilian control over Okinawa had been discussed in the Army Civil Affairs Division and the State Department. Behind the scenes there was conflict between civilian agencies such as the State and Defense Departments and the uniformed Joint Chiefs of Staff. The civilian agencies insisted that a new directive be based on NSC 13/3, the policy for Japan, and regarded the Okinawa issue as a subset of U.S.-Japan relations. However, as the previous chapter described, the Joint Chiefs of Staff took a hard line, insisting that the new directive should be an amendment of the JCS 1231 series.

JCS 1231 was a pre-assault directive issued prior to the landing in Okinawa.[5] Civilians in the Department of the Army considered it difficult to amend, due to its wartime authority, and proposed a new directive be issued based on Section Five, NSC 13/3, decreeing the separation of Okinawa from mainland Japan in unambiguous wording.[6] The Far East Command in Tokyo opposed this suggestion. Hence, the USCAR Directive was approved by the JCS and sent "informally" to the State Department as a "memorandum," which was later published in "Foreign Relations of the United States."

When the Korean War began in June 1950, it threw Okinawa back into a wartime regime. "Summations" were the official reports of the military government and civil affairs from 1946 to 1949.[7] A "Statistical Bulletin" replaced the "Summation" in 1950,[8] but the military government issued command reports in 1951 and 1952.[9] This indicates that the U.S. administration of Okinawa was directly under military command during those two years. The outbreak of the Korean War literally brought East Asia back into the wartime chain of command as the Joint Chiefs of Staff increased their influence on Washington policymakers. In sum, the USCAR Directive, which was originally drafted by an Army civilian, was transformed into an amendment of the dated wartime directive. JCS was determined to keep the Ryukyu Islands on a wartime footing to maintain its military chain of command.

## Origin of the USCAR Directive

The Civil Affairs Division, Department of the Army, had initiated a proposal for establishing a "civilian administration" immediately after the National Security Council approved NSC 13/3 on May 6, 1949, which decreed the separation of Okinawa from mainland Japan.[10] Specifically, George M. Pollard, Chief of the Economic Policy-Coordinating Section, Civil Affairs Division, proposed the original USCAR directive on May 5, four days prior to the approval of the NSC policy papers. Pollard's initiative named the administrative body "the Civilian Administration of the Ryukyu Islands" and urged the Civil Affairs Division to propose a plan for the U.S. administration. Pollard's draft was based on the First Hoover Commission's report on the reorganization of the federal government, which had been sent to the House of Representatives on March 26.[11]

The Hoover Commission, formally the Commission on the Organization of the Executive Branch of the Government, was named after its chairman, Herbert Hoover, the former President of the United States. In 1947, President Truman commissioned Hoover to research the reorganization of the federal government. Hoover made a series of recommendations, including the creation of an Overseas Affairs Administration. Hoover proposed establishing a civilian agency specializing in the economic development of areas occupied by the United States, following the Marshall Plan model for European recovery. The Economic Cooperation Administration (ECA) was established for European economic recovery, but the U.S. Army had sole responsibility for the occupation of Japan. The Hoover Commission Report had urged the Army to establish a "civilian administration" to replace the military government. The GARIOA appropriation for Korea, originally assigned to the Army, had been transferred to a civilian administration. The report indicated that the military government of Okinawa should have been similarly replaced.[12]

Pollard proposed a civilian administration in Okinawa based on his own research. He proposed:
1. to create a boundary between U.S. facilities areas and surrounding residential areas for local population
2. to establish an administrative body by civilians
3. to consider U.S. dollars as the local currency in the Ryukyu Islands. He proposed that the top-ranking official responsible for the administration of Okinawa should have a civilian-sounding title, such as the U.S. High Commissioner for the Civilian Administration of the Ryukyu Islands or Director of the Civil Government of the Ryukyu Islands.[13]

A U.S. High Commissioner had been appointed with Congressional approval for the Allied occupation of Germany. The policy for Germany was decided by a tri-national committee of the U.S., Britain and France. For the Ryukyu Islands, a High Commissioner had been proposed in 1949, but it was not implemented until 1957.

The Civil Affairs Division, Department of the Army, had recognized the benefits of establishing a civilian administration in Okinawa. Given the Hoover Commission's proposal, Congress had launched a study on the U.S. administration of Okinawa. The State Department delegated an anthropologist, Dr. Douglas Oliver, to the Ryukyus. The Hoover Commission's proposed Overseas Affairs Administration was to replace the Army's administration of the Asia-Pacific region.

On April 29, 1949, a joint conference of the State Department and the Department of the Army was held in Noel Hemmendinger's office at the State Department. According to the memorandum, they discussed an institution for the U.S. administration of the Ryukyu Islands that seamlessly cooperated with the proposed Overseas Affairs Administration. Accordingly, the senior official should be a civilian responsible for civilian administration and private enterprise in the Ryukyus and candidates for the post should be sent to Okinawa as soon as possible to explore an effective program for cultivating a favorable impression of America.[14]

The planning paper dated May 24 suggested that the Ryukyu Islands as well as the northwestern Pacific areas should be under United Nation's Trusteeship. The author's name is unknown, but the paper presented two versions of the Ryukyu governance:
1. U.S. Overseas Affairs Administration, a civilian controlled agency, would govern the Ryukyus under U.N. trusteeship.
2. The Commander, Ryukyu Command, would be the highest ranking military officer reporting to the Department of the Army, with a subordinate civilian administrator reporting to him.[15]

The subsequent document dated June 1 describes the above Ryukyu administration plan in detail. The first draft of the USCAR Directive was presented in this file of which the personnel budget needed for the administration was estimated at 40–60 American employees and 100 at the maximum.[16] According to the USCAR record as of 1960, though, it was found that the U.S. administration of Okinawa needed 400 employees including Ryukyuan staff.[17] The United States had estimated the administrative cost to be much lower than it was. The Civil Affairs Division was consciously attempting to downplay the centrality of the military regime and to promote the U.N. Trusteeship.[18]

The Civil Affairs Division recommendation was sent to Brigadier General Weckerling, Far East Command, and circulated throughout the military government in the Ryukyus. However, the proposal was dismissed in what Pollard referred to as a "vain dispute." Disappointed, Pollard wrote to Robert R. West, Assistant Secretary of Defense, Far Eastern Affairs, that civilians in a military-oriented organization were regarded as inferior to military personnel, and that was a problem.[19]

## The Far East Command, a Hard Line

On September 14, 1949, an early draft of the USCAR Directive was discussed at an Army conference. Attendees included Robert R. West, Assistant Secretary of Defense; General Eichelberger, General Weckerling,

Lieutenant General Hendricks, and others. General Hendricks contended that the prospective civil administrators should report directly to General MacArthur, following the chain of military command, and proposed revisions to the draft as follows:
1. Commander, Ryukyu Command would be the senior United States official.
2. Civil Administrator would be responsible for civil affairs activities in the Ryukyus.
3. Commander, Ryukyu Command, and Civil Administrator would coordinate military elements in civil affairs and civil elements in military activities, but if they were not able to reach the same conclusion, they would report to the Commander-in-Chief, Far East Command except in an emergency.[20]

The proposed revisions appear to have been based on the Army field manual described in Chapter 2. Hendricks pointed out that Major General Joseph R. Sheetz, Commander, Ryukyu Command, was a military officer with civil affairs experience in Korea and 68 civilian employees were working for the military government.[21] The USCAR Directive drafted in Washington D.C. attempted to replace the military government with a civilian administration, but the Far East Command dismissed it. The Far East Command had established the military government in the Ryukyus and never compromised on the principles presented in the field manual. General Eichelberger criticized the draft as unacceptable for the military mission and demanded further revisions.

However, the Defense Department needed the State Department's cooperation to acquire U.N. trusteeship.[22] On September 15, Army and State held a conference joined by West, Eichelberger, Weckerling, Hendricks and Hemmendinger of the State Department and anthropologist Dr. Douglas L. Oliver. Dr. Oliver had been researching the Micronesian economy and briefly visited the Ryukyu Islands. He presented three choices for the United States: 1) to include the Ryukyus as a U.S. territory or state, 2) to leave the Ryukyus as it was, 3) to cooperate with Japan while maintaining U.S. bases on the Ryukyus. The anthropologist recommended the third option because it would be less expensive to return the islands to Japan, contending that the administrative costs would become burdensome if they took the first option. The conference attendees did not reach a conclusion,[23] but the draft was sent to Douglas MacArthur and the Far East Command on January 3, 1949.[24]

## Civil Liberties Clause Deleted

The January 1949 version of the USCAR Directive had an independent clause titled "civil liberties" which would have allowed Ryukyuans the popular vote in selecting a chief executive. Furthermore, civil liberties principles such as freedom of speech, assembly, petition, religion, and press were permitted in Section 9, Article E.[25] However, after being circulated at the Far East Command, the civil liberties clause was deleted in the final draft of 1950.

The January 1949 version also included an item which placed a Ryukyuan representative in the civil administration. Hemmendinger of the State Department contended that there should be a Ryukyuan representative in the administration in support of the U.S. application for U.N. trusteeship.[26] However, Major General Carter B. Magruder, Chief, Civil Affair Division of Army Staff, objected to the policy, and it was deleted.

The USCAR Directive was based on NSC 13, but because it was in the process of being classified at the time, the State Department was unable to disclose its contents at the United Nations when applying for trusteeship.[27] On April 25, 1950, the draft USCAR Directive was finally sent to Dean Rusk, Assistant Secretary of State, Far Eastern Affairs.

The draft was further circulated among the Navy, Air Force, and Army and sent again to the Far East Command on May 24. The FEC added "Supplementary Instructions to the Governor-General" to the original draft.[28] According to *Foreign Relations of the United States*, the State Department had requested two revisions of JCS 1231/14. The first was to avoid the term "military governor." JCS accepted this proposal and the senior administrator in the Ryukyu Islands was to be called simply "governor." Another request was that the military governor not be given the power to appoint judges to martial courts.[29] JCS rejected this request. In the revision process, democratic factors of the original USCAR Directive were removed and the military's authority was strengthened. The final draft of the USCAR Directive was sent to the Joint Chiefs of Staff on September 9 and approved as JCS 1231/14 on October 4, 1950.

After the revisions, on October 11, the final draft of JCS 1231/14 was sent to General MacArthur, Commander-in-Chief of the Far East Command. The Far East Command changed the directive again into the

FEC Directive and sent it to the Ryukyu Commander on December 5. The FEC Directive established USCAR on December 15, 1950. Okinawans have therefore long believed that the Far East Command ordered the USCAR's establishment, as it was difficult to discern how the U.S. federal departments had directed the administration of Okinawa.

As we can see, the original draft included a democratic ideal which permitted civil liberties, but these clauses were deleted. The USCAR Directive developed through a series of negotiations and compromises between the State and Defense departments with the aim of acquiring a long-term U.N.-sanctioned trusteeship.

Although the State Department aimed to minimize the characteristics of a military occupation, in the end, both State and Defense agreed to maintain the vested interest in the Ryukyus.

## Constabulary and Comptroller

JCS 1231/14 was amended on November 8, 1950 and approved as JCS 1231/16, establishing the Constabulary and Coast Guard in the Ryukyu Islands. Although it is not clear what "the Constabulary" means, the Joint Strategic Plans Committee (JSPC) had proposed this amendment based on a recommendation of the Far East Command. According to JCS 1231/16, the FEC had proposed empowering the U.S. military police with the following justifications: 1) military attack and deployment from Okinawa was necessary for the Korean War; 2) information from Sakishima Islands (close to China) indicated communist brainwashing of Okinawans; 3) withdrawal of U.S. forces would leave the Ryukyus militarily vulnerable after the Japan Peace Treaty was enacted, 4) Ryukyu police were unable to counteract civil disturbances.[30]

Instead of the term "Constabulary," the State Department favored the term "police" because it sounds "less international," but the term Constabulary was used as the Far East Command originally proposed. Although the FEC's position was taken in the end, it is notable that the State Department had a consultative authority at the time. It remains unclear how USCAR was related to the Constabulary and Coast Guard established by JCS 1231/16, but there can be no doubt that the U.S. security police functions, including that of "thought police," were deeply embedded in the original establishment of USCAR.

The Office of Comptroller assumed responsibility for USCAR's budgetary matters on January 15, 1951. The Office of Comptroller played a central role managing Congressional appropriations from budgetary planning to execution.[31] The Office also controlled the GARIOA counterpart funds and invested the funds to construct social infrastructure and manage public corporations. The Office was a core component of USCAR until the reversion.

USCAR was quite unique in having its own comptroller's office. For instance, after Japan recovered independence in 1952, the Far Eastern Branch of the General Accounting Office (GAO), was established in Tokyo on July 1, 1956 to manage the budget appropriated for the U.S. Forces in Japan, including the Ryukyu Command, the "traditional" military part of the U.S. occupation of Okinawa.. The newly established GAO Tokyo managed almost all budgets for Asia-Pacific regions such as Korea, Taiwan, Philippines, Marianas, Vietnam, Thailand, and Pakistan.[32] Although GAO Tokyo managed the U.S. defense budgets for Asia, the Office of the Comptroller, USCAR, a civilian (non-military) part of the U.S. occupation of Okinawa, had a special status directly assigned by Congressional appropriations. Moreover, the U.S. Commander-in-Chief in the Ryukyu Islands was responsible for the management of the counterpart funds as described earlier. The Bureau of Budgets described USCAR as "unique"[33] in directly receiving the federal budget proposed by the Executive Office of the President. Why it enjoyed this unique status is unclear, but one possible explanation is that an important part of the USCAR mission was psychological warfare, which was under the authority of the Executive Office, as discussed in later chapters.

## Chapter Summary

This chapter analyzed the development of JCS 1231/14, the USCAR Directive. The original draft by civilian staff at the Department of the Army proposed transforming the military government into a civilian administration. Behind the scenes the U.S. was aiming for a United Nations trusteeship. However, the draft was strongly opposed by military hardliners. Finally, the USCAR Directive was incorporated into the fourteenth amendment of JCS 1231. The United States needed to acquire local and international support to maintain its vested interests in Okinawa.

# 5 Quest for Legitimacy: Army-Congressional Relations

## Introduction

Congress needed a legal basis for budgetary appropriations for the administration of Okinawa. This chapter analyzes the series of problems that the Department of the Army faced in its quest to legitimize the U.S. administration of Okinawa during the period between the Japan Peace Treaty of 1952 and Executive Order 10713 in 1957. The policy formation process can be traced through the revisions that transformed JCS 1231/14 and eventually lead to Executive Order 10713. What was the rationale for the U.S. administration of Okinawa?

Previous studies pointed to a fundamental cleavage between the State Department, pursuing diplomatic interests, and the Defense Department, defending military objectives. This cleavage was never mended within the inner circles of the federal government. While the National Security Council ostensibly determined U.S. peacetime policy toward Japan, including the separation of Okinawa, JCS's wartime directive continued to be effective. State opposed forced land acquisition, but it took more than two years to revise the forced acquisition clause of JCS 1231 due to Defense's resistance. Meanwhile, the Army Corps of Engineers forcibly acquired land using bulldozers and bayonets against local opposition.

## Wartime and Peacetime

After the United States and Japan signed the Peace Treaty in San Francisco on September 7, 1951, the premise for the USCAR Directive was undermined, as it had been based on the U.S. status as an occupation force after the Japanese surrender. Further revisions of the USCAR Directive were needed. The Far East Command in Tokyo requested revisions of the Secretary of the Army on October 2, 1951.

In anticipation of the peace treaty, a local administrative body, the Provisional Central Government, had been established under the authority of USCAR on April 1, 1951.[1] Part of this Provisional Central Government, the Ryukyu Legislature, petitioned President Harry S. Truman to end the occupation and return administrative authority to the local people. In a letter dated May 20, 1952, Chosho Goeku, chairman of the Ryukyu Legislature wrote to Truman that the USCAR Directive is obsolete and would be ineffective after the enactment of the Japan Peace Treaty because the occupation had ended. The political leaders of docile Okinawans did not make overt demands, but euphemistically petitioned for reversion to Japan. In response, the State Department proposed a new Executive Order based on Article 3 of the international treaty to legitimate the domestic administration of Okinawa.

Meanwhile, the Department of the Army had conducted a study reviewing GARIOA counterpart funds. The final draft, submitted on August 8, 1952, clearly stipulated that GARIOA funds should not be used for purchasing foreign land.[2] Adjutant General C. C. B. Warden of the Army, admitted that the term "occupation" was no longer appropriate and reluctantly began discussing amendments to the USCAR Directive.

However, the amendment process was extremely slow. The outbreak of the Korean War in 1950 had revived the military's waning authority. The official USCAR report was published as the Annual Command Reports for the years 1951 and 1952.[3] The first issue of Civil Affairs Activities in the Ryukyu Islands, USCAR's official report followed the military action reports on December 31, 1952. Thus, the wartime report and peacetime report were concurrently published in 1952 in Okinawa, indicating that military units and civilian units were concurrently deployed in the small islands.

It was not until February 17, 1953, a month after Eisenhower's inaugural Presidential address, that the first meeting about the USCAR Directive Amendment was held at the Civil Affairs and Military Government (hereafter, CAMG) Section, which had succeeded the Civil Affairs Division, Army. Among the attendees was Edward O'Flaherty, of CAMG, who was involved in discussions about the administration of Okinawa from 1953 until the reversion. He was one of the key figures in Army-Congressional relations and towards the end of the U.S. administration worked to privatize the public corporations that USCAR had invested in in preparation for the reversion.

Following this meeting in February 1953, CAMG proposed extensive amendments to the directive. The preamble of this proposal stated:

> In accordance with the terms of the Treaty of Peace with Japan The United States presently exercises full power of administration, legislation, and jurisdiction over the territory, inhabitants, and territorial waters of those islands…; (and) the United States is deeply and sympathetically aware of strong bond of culture and custom which link the people of the Ryukyu Islands and the people of Japan; and it is contemplated that in due course the people of the Ryukyu Islands and of Japan will be fully re-united in accordance with wither aspiration… However, until such time as conditions of peace and stability prevail in the Far East, the United States will be required to develop and maintain military facilities in the Ryukyu Islands… While the retention of this authority is not to be regarded as permanent, no date has been determined on which it might be possible to relinquish it.[4]

The revised directive continued the "blue sky position" which committed the U.S. to returning the Ryukyu Islands to Japan "when peace is secured in the Far East."[5] Peace in the Far East referred to securing the Korean Peninsula after the Korean War ended. At this point, however, the clause authorizing USCAR to forcefully acquire Okinawa lands was deleted and a new clause was added, authorizing USCAR to lease Okinawan lands when necessary.[6]

CAMG regarded the U.S. administration of Okinawa as a foreign relations issue at the beginning of 1953, based on NSC 125/2 signed on August 7, 1952, which placed the U.S. military bases in Okinawa under the U.S. policy for Japan. As a liaison office in the Department of Defense, CAMG functioned as a coordinator with the Far East office at the State Department and the Bureau of Budget in the Executive Office and proposed the Okinawa policy to the Secretary of Defense. The Secretary of Defense submitted the final decision to the National Security Council after the interdepartmental discussions. In Washington, CAMG functioned as an interdepartmental coordinating liaison. Secretary of Defense worked as a coordinator of civilian and uniformed staff in the Defense Department and the CAMG draft reflected the civilian perspective at the Department of the Army and State Department. Specifically, policy toward Japan and Okinawa was discussed at the office level between Department of the Army and State Department and proposed to the National Security Council.

In Okinawa, H. Earl Diffenderfer, director of the USCAR Civil Information and Education Department, took a different approach to revising the directive. Diffenderfer was a hard-line supporter of the military objectives of the occupation, maintaining that forced requisitions should be permitted when landowners rejected negotiations for land purchases. However, since the U.S. Congress drastically decreased the budget for USCAR in 1953, USCAR could not afford land purchase costs from GARIOA funds. Accordingly, Diffenderfer insisted that land costs should be paid for from military budgets of the Army, Navy or Air Force rather than the GARIOA counterpart funds, and stipulated that the U.S. should pay a reasonable price for private properties acquired after July 1, 1950.[7]

His revision also decreed that USCAR should supervise the Government of the Ryukyus, a local governmental body. Ultimately, USCAR was maintaining a hard line on the U.S. administration of Okinawa, defending the vested interests established during the Battle of Okinawa, while CAMG began to regard the U.S. administration of Okinawa as temporary after the Japan Peace Treaty came into effect in 1952.

## Theater Commander's Hard Line

Brigadier General David A. Ogden, Commander in Chief, the Ryukyu Command, arrived in Okinawa in January 1953. He had worked as an engineer during World War II and the Korean War and, based on his experiences in East Asia, insisted that the U.S. should maintain a long-term administrative authority over Okinawa. As a deputy governor of USCAR, Ogden wrote a nine-page letter to Lieutenant General W. K. Harrison, Deputy Commander, Far East Command, presenting a rationale for maintaining administrative authority over Okinawa.

The Governor of the Ryukyus must be an active military commander, Ogden contended, explaining the strategic importance of the Ryukyu Islands and the political situation in detail. The Yoshida Cabinet of Japan, he observed, was mostly pro-American. However, a prospective anti-American cabinet which might reject the U.S. administration of Okinawa could place the U.S. in a dangerous situation. Ogden also explained the divisions within the local legislature. Of the total of 31 legislators, he explained, eighteen were "pro-U.S. democrats" but the other thirteen were "communists." Although those he called communists never regarded themselves as such, the military commander's attitude was that all anti-American elements must be communists. If these anti-American legislators became the majority, he contended, the U.S position in the Ryukyus could be endangered. The U.S. would lose the authority to appoint local policemen, civil servants and the Chief Executive of the Government of the Ryukyus.[8]

The popular vote for the Chief Executive must not be allowed, Ogden insisted, contrary to the views of the civilian staff at both the State and Defense departments. Ogden warned that the U.S. counter intelligence unit's investigation of ordinary Okinawan people had found communists even among pro-American residents. But then again, he regarded anyone who was opposed to the presence of U.S. military bases to be "dangerous communists."[9]

## Double Standards: NSC Action 824-b

The State Department had proposed establishing a legal basis for the U.S. administration of Okinawa as early as possible by issuing an executive order asserting U.S. administrative authority based on Article Three of the Japan Peace Treaty. On September 16, 1953, Robert J. G. McClurkin, the State Department's Deputy Director of East Asia, sent a draft of the executive order to Charles Sullivan at the Office of the Secretary of Defense. The draft clearly states that the U.S. administration be based on the bilateral treaty and defines the Department of the Army as the executive agency of the United States while the State Department was responsible for foreign relations between the Government of the Ryukyus and other countries and international organizations.[10]

In response, Sullivan wrote to McClurkin on October 12, asking:
1. Does the U.S. formally admit the Army as the executive agency of the U.S. administration of Okinawa?
2. Does the U.S. intend to hold a long-term administrative authority based on the Peace Treaty?
3. Are the U.S. laws applicable to the Ryukyu Islands?[11]

These questions sought to confirm the basic framework of the U.S. administration of Okinawa. Politely interrogating the State Department, in fact, the Defense Department carefully avoided comment on the draft.

Nevertheless, discussions about the legal basis for the U.S. administration entered a new phase when the Army's repeated revisions of the USCAR Directives became an inter-departmental negotiation between State and Defense. The correspondence between McClurkin and Sullivan was quite different from previous discussions. The 1950 revision was finalized within the Defense Department, with the State Department being consulted and informally concurring with some of the revisions. However, the 1953 revision was initiated by the State Department and sent to the Office of Secretary of Defense. The State Department no longer initiated deliberations with the Department of the Army, dealing directly with the Secretary of Defense instead. Although the Joint Chiefs of Staff had significant influence on the administration of Okinawa from the beginning, the inter-departmental relationship between State and Defense gradually transformed the U.S. decision-making process in Washington.

The State initiative was in accordance with NSC 125 "Policy with respect to Japan" which stated that the U.S. administration of Okinawa was part of U.S.-Japan relations. On June 15, 1953, NSC Action 824-b rendered the Secretary of Defense responsible for USCAR and its policies in accordance with the NSC 125 policy papers. More importantly, NSC Action 824-b proposed a reduction of the Secretary of Defense's responsibilities for the administration of Okinawa and urged the Secretary of Defense to propose the reduction to the National Security Council. The Eisenhower administration had decided to drastically reduce the defense budget and USCAR was not exempt. In fact, NSC Action 824-b redefined USCAR as a temporary organization and specifically proposed reducing administrative costs. An important indicator of the different attitudes of the two agencies can be found in the NSC's spelling of the name of the administrative body. In Army documentation, USCAR had consistently been a proper noun spelled out as the "United States Civil Administration of the Ryukyu Islands" (all capitalized) but the NSC documents refer to the "United States civil administration" in lower case.[12] This suggests that the Executive Office was reluctant to accept the continuing military administration of Okinawa.

As described previously, the USCAR directive that established the administrative body in Okinawa had been issued by the Joint Chiefs of Staff prior to the Battle of Okinawa. Generally, the Joint Chiefs of Staff directives have priority during times of war. As a Presidential committee, the NSC decided a civilian secretary of Defense should be responsible for the administration to reduce JCS control. NSC Action 824-b launched another civilian initiative to give the executive directive control, authorizing the Secretary of Defense to represent the federal government's administration of Okinawa. This can be understood as an attempt to turn Okinawa's administration into a peacetime mode, while at the same time authorizing the Defense Department's administration of Okinawa instead of State, which is usually responsible for peacetime diplomacy.

On the same day that NSC Action 824-b was issued, the NSC Planning Board submitted a report to President Eisenhower, informing that the State and Defense Departments had agreed that the United States would not submit a proposal to place the Ryukyu Islands under United Nations Trusteeship. The NSC presumed that Japan would oppose the motion and the Soviet Union would veto it. Although the U.S. did not notify the local people of the decision, it had abandoned the possibility of placing Okinawa under U.N. Trusteeship as early as mid-1953.[13] The report also recommended redefining the role of the U.S. civil administration (in lower case) and further revising the USCAR directives. In keeping with the previously mentioned use of lower case when referring to civil affairs, this report did not refer to "USCAR Directives" but called them "Civil Affairs Directives" of the Army.[14] The NSC regarded the U.S. civil administration of Okinawa as civil affairs activities within the U.S. military's domain. Nevertheless, it was an important turning point which placed civilian control of the Secretary of Defense over the direct chain of command of the Joint Chiefs of Staff.

## Secret Presidential Directive

However, the process of revising the USCAR Directive did not proceed at all. During the early occupation period, the U.S. military government had issued numerous proclamations, directives, ordinances and orders in accordance with JCS 1231 and the field manuals to rule the local populations. Therefore, the Defense Department had to thoroughly reconsider all administrative protocols if the foundation policy underwent transformation. As described earlier, JCS 1231 functioned as the fountainhead of the enormous political and economic advantages of the United States in the garrison islands. The State Department proposed issuing an Executive Order as early as possible. However, Defense insisted on maintaining the USCAR Directive, JCS1231/14, to ensure the military retained administrative control.

Reluctantly, the Army's Civil Affairs and Military Government (CAMG) Division liaised between the State and the Defense Departments in the revision process. The revised USCAR Directive of October 6, 1953 comprised two parts:1) the permeable definition of the status of the Ryukyu Islands was available to the public and 2) the directives specifically describing the organizations and functions of USCAR remained confidential. The definitions of the role of the Chief Executive and the Government of the Ryukyus were included in the classified part of the document,[15] which became the official directive to the USCAR employees. It clearly stated that USCAR supports the U.S. military missions in Okinawa and supervises the local Ryukyuan government in order to ensure the U.S. security interests in East Asia.

This October 1953 version was endorsed by the JCS on November 18 and sent to the NSC the following day, where it was filed as an attachment to NSC 125 in the Records of the Special Assistant to the NSC.[16] However, Secretary of State John Foster Dulles urged the NSC to reconsider its contents. Accordingly, the NSC did not immediately accept the revised directive. At the final meeting of the year on December 23, 1953, the NSC deliberated on the reversion of Amami Islands to Japan and had no time to discuss the USCAR Directive. Thus, the next revision of the USCAR Directive was left as an agenda item for the following year.

Dulles' letter to the Secretary of Defense dated January 11, 1954 pointed to difficulties with the U.S. administration of 700,000 foreign people. Dulles contended that the U.S. administration of Okinawa must be thoroughly reconsidered to avoid becoming a target of international criticism. It would be appropriate, he argued, for a Bill of Rights to be issued as an Executive Order for the Okinawan people.[17] Dulles' proposal was based on McClurkin's draft, which Assistant Secretary of State Walter Robertson had sent to Dulles on January 8. Robertson's memorandum had warned Dulles that the U.S. would be criticized if the international community deemed the Government of the Ryukyus to be a "puppet" of USCAR. Robertson urged his boss to express concerns about the language in the USCAR Directives that might reveal the reality of the military regime.[18] Robertson also pointed out that the U.S. would need to establish a legal basis for the U.S. administration of Okinawa. On January 12, the Defense Department received Dulles' letter along with State's revised draft. The Defense Department began deliberations, but once again did not reach a conclusion. At Dulles' insistence, however, Defense had to respond to the NSC before its meeting scheduled for January 14.

Another hardliner at Defense was General John E. Hull, Commander-in-Chief, of the Far East Command. He argued that a Bill of Rights for the Okinawan people would fatally weaken the U.S. position in the Ryukyu Islands. He opposed Dulles on the grounds that the local population would never understand the U.S.'s military needs in the Far East.[19] One of the central arguments remained the question of who should appoint the military governor. The State Department proposed that the President should appoint the governor, but Defense disagreed, since such a move would compromise the chain of command. Defense insisted that command integrity was essential to military action. In response, State proposed sending a political advisor to the Ryukyus, but Defense rejected this suggestion, too.[20]

Meanwhile, the Army Chief of Staff revised the USCAR Directive, proposing to issue the revisions as JCS 1231/26 on February 2, 1954.[21] Another meeting of State and Defense department officials was held on February 15 to discuss this proposal. The attendees were General John E. Hull, Commander in Chief of the Far East Command, Assistant Secretary of State Robertson, and Dean Allison, Ambassador to Japan. After their deliberations, on February 17, the revised directive was sent to the NSC, where the directives were briefly discussed, but no conclusion was reached since Dulles was in Berlin. The NSC issued NSC Action 1047, which advised that the President should decide the basis of further discussions between State and Defense. After further deliberation between Defense and State on April 20 and 21, the Secretary of Defense Charles E. Wilson sent the revised directive to President Eisenhower as a top-secret document on April 23,[22] entrusting him with the final decision.

A two-page preface titled "Supplemental Instructions to the Governor, Ryukyu Islands" was attached to the April 1954 version of the USCAR Directive. The main texts of the directive were classified as "confidential," but the preface was "secret." Interestingly, the Supplemental Instruction is also filed in the records of the State Department, but the preface is placed with the endnotes.[23] The Supplemental Instruction defined the primary mission of USCAR as "to support and facilitate achievement of the military mission of the United States armed forces in and about the Ryukyu Islands, and to conduct its affairs in such a manner as to further the military, political, and psychosocial interests of the United States in the Far East." The directive also stated that USCAR should foster good relationships with influential Ryukyuans through consultation with and supervision of those key individuals. In so doing, the directive suggested, forced actions such as a veto could be carefully avoided. The classified instruction formally encouraged informal advice or supervision over the local government of the Ryukyu Islands.[24]

The usage of the GARIOA counterpart funds was targeted at the House hearing of the Subcommittee on Appropriations. On April 27, 1954, William Marquart, Director of Civil Affairs, Department of the Army, and Stuart Baron, Director of the Economic Division, USCAR testified regarding the accounting report of the previous year. A congressman asked Baron basic questions such as "what is USCAR?" The answers in the Congressional records are "off the record."

Baron testified about the usage of the GARIOA funds in the Ryukyu Islands. According to the testimony, using the GARIOA funds, USCAR constructed military facilities and roads, a weather forecast information network and the University of the Ryukyus. In addition, the Quartermaster had been acquiring local currency by selling petroleum and the Ryukyu Command owned the local electric power plants. Because USCAR had contributed to the U.S. national interests, he demanded the congressional appropriations for USCAR, in which 20 military persons and 130 civilians were working.[25] The U.S. Congress 1955 fiscal budget allocation for USCAR was considerably less than requested.

After Congress approved the budget, the revised USCAR directive was issued as a secret Presidential Directive on August 2, 1954.[26] The text was the same as the April 1954 directive discussed earlier. The controversial USCAR Directive, finally authorized as a Presidential Directive after the revisions, was sent to the Far East Command from the Civil Affairs Division of the Defense Department. Accordingly, the Far East Command remained the governing authority of the Ryukyu Islands and USCAR at the same time. Formally authorized by the President, the U.S. Commander-in-Chief of the Far East Command would continue to be the Governor of the Ryukyu Islands as well.

## Popular Election of a Chief Executive

One problem for the Joint Chiefs of Staff was that the Presidential Directive had permitted a popular vote for the top local representative in the Government of the Ryukyus. The top administrative post of the local populations was called the Chief Executive, not the Governor, as explained earlier, because the Governor of the Ryukyus was the U.S. Commander-in-Chief of the Far East Command. The Presidential provisions permitted the American Governor of the Ryukyus to appoint the Chief Executive from the elected representatives of the Ryukyu Legislature.

Given the situation in the Ryukyus, where a grassroots reversion movement was as persistent as ever, the Joint Chiefs of Staff and Far East Command regarded this "indirect popular vote" clause to be potentially as problematic as a direct vote. The Defense Department consulted Rowland Hughes, Director of the Bureau of the Budget in the Executive Office of the President (EOP), regarding the treatment of popular elections in U.S. Territories and Possessions. In a letter dated August 10, Hughes presented a case study in which the result of a popular vote became problematic in the U.S. Territories and Possessions and said it would be difficult to maintain the U.S. administrative authority with the introduction of a popular vote.[27] Ultimately, the discussions about the popular vote in the Ryukyus did not reach any conclusions in Washington.[28]

Finally, the Department of the Army decided to issue another Directive to USCAR, making the Presidential Directive confidential. Thus, the double standard was born. The Presidential Directive was necessary to persuade Congress to allocate the budget for the U.S. administration of Okinawa, but the Joint Chiefs of Staff did not approve the popular vote provisions introduced in the Presidential Directive because they wanted to maintain absolute administrative authority in the garrison islands.

The Army directive was sent to the Ryukyu Command on January 14, 1955. This was six months after the Presidential Directive was issued,[29] and two years after the initial deliberations on February 17, 1953. During those two years, a series of forced land requisitions was carried out in the Ryukyu Islands. Based on the original USCAR Directive, the Land Requisition Act, Ordinance No. 109 was issued on April 3, 1953. Based on this ordinance, Ogden ordered forced land acquisitions in Mawashi Village on April 10, Oroku Village on December 1953, Onna Village on April 23, 1954, Ginowan Village on August 3 and September 15. On October 4, 1954, two months after the Presidential Directive was issued, forced land requisition was carried out on Ie Island.[30]

The USCAR Directive stated that Okinawan land could be forcefully acquired only when negotiations for purchase were unsuccessful. In practice, however, most of the land was forcefully taken because no farmers were willing to sell or lease their land.

## Ryukyu Organization Act

A bill to permit the U.S. military command to issue martial laws such as the Land Requisition Act was introduced to the Congress on January 20, 1955. Titled the Ryukyu Organic Act or H.R. 2684, it was introduced by Congressman Carl Vinson of Georgia to the House Armed Service Committee.[31] The same bill was introduced as S. 935 to the Senate on February 4.[32] The bill included a statement authorizing Congressional appropriations for the Ryukyu Islands every year based on Article Three of the Japan Peace Treaty. The bill proposed to authorize the U.S. administrative, legislative, and juridical rights in accordance with the international treaty. The bill also stipulated that U.S. federal laws would not be applicable to the Ryukyus and its martial ordinances or regulations.

The U.S. Congress delegated a Congressional research committee to Okinawa[33] to investigate the provisions of this bill. In preparation for the Congressional delegation, Secretary of Defense Charles E. Wilson sent preliminary research delegates to Okinawa. The chairman was William Marquart, Director of Civil Affairs and Military Government, Department of the Army. The purpose of the Marquart delegation was to submit a report regarding public corporations owned by USCAR, as well as the pros and cons of the popular vote.[34] Secretary Wilson had decided to send the delegates on October 1954 after the Presidential Directive was issued, and the Assistant Secretary of Defense coordinated a detailed schedule with Far East Command.[35]

The Marquart delegation left Washington D.C. on February 11, 1955 and returned to Washington on March 2. The delegation consisted of Marquart and Howard Sacks (Staff, Office of Assistant Secretary of Defense), Dr. Harold Seidman (Bureau of Budget), Osborne Hauge and other civilians at the Office of Civil Affairs and Military Government (CAMG). The delegates met David Ogden, Deputy Governor of the Ryukyus Islands, Walter Johnson, Civil Administrator, and Shuhei Higa, Chief Executive, Government of the Ryukyus. The delegation report titled "Operational Plan for Civil Administration of the Ryukyu Islands" was submitted to Secretary Wilson on March 15.[36] The report dealt with the following items: 1) a popular vote for the Chief Executive, 2) the legal status of the Ryukyu Islands, 3) the organization of USCAR, 4) public corporation management, 5) Ryukyu Organic Act, 6) the issuance of the Army Directive, 7) foreign relations consultant.

In short, the delegates discussed the conflicts between militarism and democracy and how the U.S. could manage these in Okinawa. Dr. Seidman was the accounting officer at the Bureau of the Budget in charge of the U.S. Territories and Possessions. Based on his experience, Dr. Seidman concluded that the popular vote would not be desirable.

The Marquart report proposed establishing a legislative research committee appointed by the Secretary of Defense. Dr. Seidman, a member of previous legislative committees for other territories and possessions, recommended David Ogden to the legislative research committee.[37] Based on this recommendation, the Secretary of the Army appointed Ogden as a member of the legislative research committee and the committee launched a series of enquiries into the Ryukyu Organic Act.

With the Marquart report, the "Okinawa problems" gradually became visible, at least at the Civil Affairs and the Military Government Division in Washington.[38] Among these problems were the public corporations established by GARIOA funds. The report questions whether those public corporations could be acknowledged in the framework of U.S. laws. The GARIOA appropriation had originally been approved for the temporary administration of U.S. occupied nations, especially Germany and Japan. A portion of the GARIOA appropriation for Japan had been allotted to Okinawa and USCAR had used these funds to establish public corporations such as water and electricity companies. Although the Congress presumed that the occupation would be temporary, USCAR had managed and invested its own fund, and now possessed public corporations. Was this legal? USCAR had previously satisfied the Bureau of the Budget and Comptroller General that it was legitimate, but the question remained whether the Congress should permit it, since the GARIOA was a Congressional appropriation. Congress had to check whether the specifics of the appropriation were duly executed in the Ryukyus. In the Marquart report, as a federal budget specialist, Dr. Seidman specifically questioned the American housing construction funded by GARIOA.[39] Given these problems, the deliberation on the Ryukyuan Organic Bill had been suspended by the Armed Services Committee in both the House and Senate.[40]

With the Congressional legislative process at a standstill, the Defense Department reluctantly started drafting an Executive Order in April 1955. Dr. Seidman revised State's original draft.[41] Without congressional approval of the Ryukyu Organic Act, the Executive Order was necessary to legitimize the congressional appropriations for the U.S. administration of Okinawa.[42]

On April 9, 1955, the National Security Council proposed NSC 5516/1, a new policy toward Japan. Section 54 of the NSC policy papers stated that the U.S. should consider Japanese requests regarding the Ryukyu and Bonin Islands providing they would not deteriorate the U.S. security and interests.[43] As described earlier, the NSC had regarded the U.S. administration of the Ryukyus to be part of its Japan policy. It is obvious that NSC 5516/1 further advanced the policy and demanded the Department of the Army to carefully administer the Ryukyus, specifically to not let the Okinawa problems become major obstacles for U.S.-Japan relations.

In accordance with Section 54, NSC 5516/1, Secretary of State Dulles and Secretary of Defense Wilson exchanged a memorandum on May 31 which determined the role of the State Department regarding the U.S. administration of Okinawa. It determined that State should maintain a consulate general office in Naha, the "capital" city of the Ryukyu Islands, and the Naha Consulate should be a U.S. diplomat reporting to the Ambassador's office in Tokyo and a foreign relations adviser to USCAR. The Defense Department should provide logistical support to the Naha Consulate.[44] The memorandum finally resolved a deadlock over dispatching a Consulate General to Okinawa.

## Price Delegation at Naha Hearing

Congress also sent delegates to Okinawa. Melvin Price of Illinois was the chairman of a delegation organized by the House Armed Services Committee. The Price Delegation visited Okinawa and other U.S. military bases in the Pacific from October 14 to November 23, 1955, on "an inspection tour of our military installations and missions in various parts of the world." The delegation of seven congressmen accompanied by six military personnel held hearings at Naha, Okinawa about the Okinawa land problems on October 24 and 25.

Shuhei Higa, Chief Executive of the Ryukyu Islands and four other Ryukyu Government staff members testified about the Okinawa land problem. Okinawan residents who had lost their land testified of their suffering. The witnesses testified about the low prices paid for the land, and petitioned against the economic suffering of the Okinawan farmers for whom the land had been their only source of livelihood. One witness argued that the forced land requisition was not legitimate in terms of international law because the land was forcefully taken after the Peace Treaty was enacted. The congressmen asked many questions to clarify the situation.[45]

The last witness was Darley Downs, an American who had been living in Okinawa. Downs identified himself as an old clergyman belonging to the National Council of the Churches of Christ in the USA (NCCCUSA) and eloquently described the suffering caused by the U.S. forced land requisition.[46] He criticized the expansion of U.S. militarism in Okinawa and Japan. The Congressional Records regarding the Naha hearings indicate the hearing sessions were successful because the facts of the suffering were fully exposed.

However, the Okinawan witnesses were disappointed when the Price Report was released the following year. The Price Delegation had submitted its report to the House Armed Services Committee in 1956, but the report excluded all of the Okinawan testimonies, discussing only the Army and Navy perspectives, which maintained that the U.S. Armed Forces required the Okinawan land for military bases.[47] Quoting Eisenhower's speech on January 7, 1954, the Price Report emphasized "military necessity" and recommended construction of a nuclear power plant in Okinawa.[48] Disappointed, the Okinawan people were ever more inclined toward reversion to Japan and anti-American public opinion became more apparent. The American Embassy in Tokyo reported the Okinawan reaction to the Price Report to the State Department and perceived that the land issue would emerge as a major problem in U.S.-Japan relations.

On June 22, 1956, Secretary Dulles wrote to Secretary Wilson that the U.S. should reconsider the means of land acquisitions in Okinawa.[49] As discussed, the State Department opposed land acquisition with GARIOA funds, but the situation did not change.

Meanwhile, Dr. Harold Seidman of the Bureau of the Budget wrote a letter to Norman D. King, CAMG on February 13, 1956. Seidman pointed out that the Executive Order must be consistent with the U.S. legal framework. However, the Ryukyu Islands were administered by martial law, without Congressional authorization, and those laws were never consistent with U.S. domestic laws.[50] Responding to Seidman's letter, King launched a project to realign the martial laws in the Ryukyus to comply with U.S. laws as much as possible.

After further revisions, on February 27, 1957, the draft of the Executive Order was sent to the Operations Coordinating Board (hereafter, OCB) for final deliberations.

## Executive Order 10713

During the Eisenhower administration, the OCB coordinated the U.S. federal government's actions and operations according to NSC decisions in the Executive Office. One working group of the OCB discussed the most appropriate timing for issuing the forthcoming Executive Order. Based on provisions of Section 54 of NSC 5516/1, it had been drafting an economic development plan for the Ryukyu Islands in collaboration with the State Department because the OCB regarded relations with the Japanese government to be crucial to maintaining the U.S. military status in the Ryukyus.[51]

As will be described in Chapter 6, the OCB had assumed the functions of the Psychological Strategy Board (PSB) established under the Truman administration. The PSB had prepared a "Psychological Strategy Program for Japan" (PSB D-27) and an Inter-Agency Committee in Tokyo had executed the program. In the Inter-Agency Committee, the Ambassador to Japan and the Commander-in-Chief of the Far East Command were working with and jointly coordinated the psychological, information, and cultural operations in Japan.[52] On September 2, 1953, however, President Eisenhower issued Executive Order 10483, which abolished the PSB and established the OCB as its successor. The OCB coordinated the information policy for Japan and worked to maintain the U.S. military bases in Okinawa in careful consultation with the Japanese government.[53]

Under the NSC's direction, the OCB discussed the most appropriate timing for issuing the Executive Order. The best timing was regarded as the date that would have the least negative effects on Japanese public opinion. The U.S. Embassy in Tokyo consulted Prime Minister Nobusuke Kishi prior to issuing the order, because Kishi was scheduled to visit

Washington in June 1957. Douglas MacArthur II, the newly appointed Ambassador to Japan and a cousin of the former Supreme Commander-in-Chief of Allied Powers, suggested to Kishi that the best date would be four to six weeks after his visit.[54] Meanwhile, the Far East Command had insisted that the Executive Order should be issued prior to Kishi's visit because it could be perceived as a failure in relations with the U.S., and the Kishi Cabinet would be subjected to criticism from the opposition parties in the Japanese Diet.[55] The U.S. expected Kishi to be a pro-American Prime Minister and wanted his Cabinet to continue as long as possible. However, the U.S. Ambassador did not consult on the pros and cons of the order, noting that its contents had been decided. He merely consulted with Kishi on the timing of its announcement. According to State Department records, Prime Minister Kishi told Ambassador MacArthur that he could not agree with the Executive Order because it might give the impression that the U.S. administration of Okinawa could last forever. Kishi requested some revisions and asked that the Executive Order be issued prior to his visit to Washington if its details had been already decided in Washington.[56]

Hence, President Eisenhower signed Executive Order 10713 on June 5, 1957,[57] prior to the Prime Minister's visit to Washington. The order revoked the classified Presidential Directive of August 1954.[58] The White House announced the Executive Order and disseminated a press release in Washington. On the same day, the text of the Executive Order was sent to the U.S. Embassy and the Far East Command in Tokyo and was scheduled for publication in the Federal Register.[59] Ambassador MacArthur showed part of the text of the Executive Order to Kishi in the afternoon on June 6, informing Kishi that he had asked Washington to revise the text as requested, and stressing his cordiality toward Kishi.[60]

Japanese newspapers such as the *Asahi*, *Mainichi*, *Nikkei*, and *Tokyo Shimbun* reported the issuance of Executive Order 10713 in the evening editions on June 7. The *Okinawa Times* reported the news based on the Japanese newspapers, but USCAR did not hold a press conference. On June 7, a signal officer at the Ryukyu Command urgently requested the final text from the Department of the Army.[61] On the same day, the Office of the Secretary of Defense sent a short message to the Far East Command and James Moore, Governor of the Ryukyu Islands. This brief message, however, simply stated that James Moore would be High Commissioner of the Ryukyu Islands from July 1, based on the new Executive Order. On June 8, USCAR released a short message to the Okinawan press, simply stating that James Moore, Commander in Chief, Ryukyu Command, was appointed as High Commissioner in the Ryukyu Islands with no reference to Executive Order 10713.[62] The details of the Executive Order were not made available to the Okinawan people.

Executive Order 10713 was issued to establish a legal basis for the U.S. administration of Okinawa defining the High Commissioner as the highest position representing the U.S. government and placing the Government of the Ryukyus under his authority. The High Commissioner was a new position defined by the Executive Order, but the real situation in Okinawa remained unchanged as the former military governor assumed the new position.

More important is that Executive Order 10713 formally referred to USCAR as "the United States civil administration" in lower case letters. As previously discussed, the Department of the Army had spelled it as a capitalized proper noun. Interestingly, even after the issuance of the new Executive Order, Defense continued to use all capital letters until the reversion in 1972, including in the copy of Executive Order 10713 filed in the Records of Legal Affairs Department of USCAR.[63] The Defense Department used the term as a proper noun, in contrast to the version printed in the Federal Register, a U.S. federal government publication, which suggests that "an alternative" Executive Order 10713 had been circulated within the Ryukyu Islands.[64]

What does this mean? One possibility is that the Executive Office did not acknowledge USCAR as a formal organization. Washington did not send the text of the Executive Order immediately to USCAR in Okinawa, perhaps because USCAR would object to this failure of the United States government to formally recognize it. President Eisenhower and the Executive Office agreed to sign the Executive Order to secure congressional appropriations for the Ryukyus. However, the Eisenhower administration may have carefully avoided the formal acknowledgement of the U.S. administrative body, using such a rhetorical technique. Since Japanese language expression is different from English, with no differentiation between lower case and capitalized letters, the Japanese translation of Civil Administration and civil administration is the same. This linguistic difference would have facilitated Washington's legal professionals camouflaging the distinction from Okinawan leaders.

With this Executive Order, the Defense Department finally established a legal basis for congressional appropriations for the administration of Okinawa. Congressman Melvin Price of Illinois proposed a bill to authorize the appropriations for the U.S. administration of Okinawa. Congress approved the so-called Price Act, "an act to provide for promotion of economic and social development in the Ryukyu Islands."[65] Twelve years after World War II ended, the U.S. Congress finally approved the U.S. administrative budget for the Ryukyus.

In fact, however, the Price Act merely legalized the special account of the U.S. administrative body as U.S. federal revenue based on the former Congressional appropriations of GARIOA. The Price Act also referred to "USCAR" as "civil administration" in lower case letters, in accordance with the Executive Order.

The passage of the Price Act legitimized the U.S. administration and USCAR's budget in the 1960s. However, the economic development of the Ryukyu Islands gradually undermined Congress's motivation to authorize further appropriations to promote "the economic and social development" of Okinawa. At the same time, the State Department had moved toward a policy of eliciting the administrative budget of Okinawa from the Japanese government. On February 27, 1958, the State Department submitted a document to the OCB which would render U.S. appropriations for USCAR unnecessary.[66] As the executive agency for the administration of Okinawa, the Department of the Army had continuously sought congressional appropriations, but could not satisfactorily answer congressmen's questions such as: "Why do we have to use American taxes for the Ryukyuan people?"

In 1965, the Japanese government aid to Okinawa surpassed the U.S. Congressional appropriations for Okinawa and the U.S. gradually lost its justification for maintaining administrative authority of Okinawa. Put briefly, the U.S. Defense Department desired to maintain the military bases in Okinawa but the Congress did not want to pay the expensive administrative costs for the Okinawan people. The State Department had insisted that the U.S. should return administrative authority to Japan and maintain only the military bases. Defense gradually had to accept State's position after losing the budgetary support from Congress.

## Chapter Summary

This chapter focused on the U.S. Army's search for a legal basis for the administration of the Ryukyus, examining Department of the Army documents from the enactment of the Japan Peace Treaty in 1952 to Executive Order 10713 in 1957. One important dispute was whether the U.S. should permit a popular vote for the Chief Executive, the head of the Ryukyuan government. If the U.S. did not allow the popular election, the international community might criticize the U.S. for not respecting the local population's right to self-determination. However, the U.S. administration of Okinawa would be at risk if they recognized these basic human rights because the leaders most likely to be elected would be anti-American. While the U.S. professed democratic ideals, the dilemma of U.S. militarism was revealed in the disputes regarding the pros and cons of popular election.

From the beginning, the State Department was reluctant to formally recognize the U.S. administrative body, regarding it as part of civil affairs activities of the Department of Army. The State Department's intention was to avoid international criticism, differentiating State's foreign relations concerns from Defense's military priorities. Meanwhile, the Defense Department was determined to maintain U.S. vested interests in the Ryukyu Islands by keeping the wartime directive in effect. The divergent positions of State and Defense were never reconciled, and revisions to the USCAR Directive were delayed. Forced land acquisition continued in Okinawa throughout these inter-departmental disputes.

The wartime and peacetime agendas co-existed in Okinawa. Congressional oversight functioned in a limited way in questioning the legal basis for the U.S. administration of Okinawa. Congress did not approve the Ryukyus Organic Act because the martial laws imposed in Okinawa were not consistent with U.S. federal law. At the same time, Congress tacitly accepted the legal framework of martial law. We might conclude that Congressional oversight was limited on foreign soil.

Furthermore, most disputes about the U.S. administration of Okinawa occurred within a closed circle of bureaucrats and political elites in Washington and were rarely open to oversight by the U.S. public. The most important policy decisions concerning the U.S. administration of Okinawa were not made by Congress, but by the Executive Office. The National Security Council played an important role in formulating the U.S. policy for Japan and Okinawa, and the Bureau of the Budget firmly supported the policymakers. Congress deliberated on budgets for Okinawa, but the core of the budgetary bills had been consolidated at the Bureau of the Budget. It appears that the expansion of the Executive

Office's authority reduced Congress's oversight responsibilities. The same could be said for U.S. policymaking for the administration of Okinawa.

The Executive Order was treated as supplementary legislation without Congressional authorization. Still it is important that the Executive Order was not completely classified[67] and that it did not formally acknowledge USCAR. The USCAR mission transformed into one of self-termination as it prepared to return Okinawa to Japan, according to an oral history interview with a public relations officer working for USCAR at the time.[68] However, this mission was kept in secret until the reversion.

After the Executive Order was issued, the Eisenhower administration developed psychological operations for Okinawa. The Operations Coordinating Board aimed to use soft power over the Okinawan people to effectively resolve the dilemma between democracy and militarism. The USCAR staff fully understood that anti-American sentiment could enflame reversion movements. USCAR's mission remained to undermine the local grassroots movements, as the Defense Department insisted on free usage of the American bases, regarding Okinawa as a necessary military base for the Vietnam War.

# Part II
# U.S. Foreign Information Policy for Okinawa

Part II discusses U.S. foreign information policy in Okinawa and its impact on the region. As well as the civil affairs activities of the Department of the Army, U.S. foreign information policy that originated in World War II was reorganized for the Cold War. Established by the National Security Act of 1947, the National Security Council (NSC) was the supreme policymaking organization coordinating U.S. information policy between federal departments and agencies, while the Central Intelligence Agency (CIA) coordinated gathering foreign information. As an auxiliary to the NSC, the Psychological Strategy Board (PSB) was established in April 1951 to coordinate psychological operations in foreign countries. PSB decisions were reported to the NSC for presidential approval.

The Secretary of State was primarily responsible for U.S. foreign information policy in peacetime, while the Secretary of Defense was responsible for foreign information policy in the theaters of war. As described in Part One, however, the U.S. administration of Okinawa was placed under the Secretary of Defense and the NSC regarded the U.S. information policy toward Okinawa as "psychological warfare" or "psychological operations." The PSB functioned as a coordinating organization subordinate to the NSC in the Executive Office. The Operations Coordinating Board (OCB) succeeded the PSB in September 1953 during the Eisenhower administration.

Established in 1953, the United States Information Agency (USIA) disseminated U.S. information policy guidelines to the United States Information Services, the foreign branches of the USIA. The civilian information post for peacetime was not established in Okinawa, which was under the wartime direction of Secretary of Defense. Instead, the Public Affairs Department of USCAR assumed the role of "USIS Okinawa." Thus, the wartime and peacetime characteristics of U.S. information policy oddly overlapped in Okinawa.

# 6 U.S. Foreign Information Policy

## Introduction

This chapter presents the basic U.S. foreign information policy framework from World War II until the establishment of the United States Information Agency in September 1953. The purpose of the study is to elucidate U.S. information policy for Okinawa. It is not possible to present a complete picture, however, as many central documents concerning the Okinawa policy remain classified, but an examination of the overall foreign information policy will help us to fill in some of the missing pieces, and thus provide a framework for the remaining chapters.

## World War II as Information Warfare

President Roosevelt launched a propaganda campaign against Germany as the European nations went to war in September 1939. At the time, however, the United States did not have a centralized, over-arching organization such as the German Propaganda Institute directed by Joseph Goebbels. U.S. federal agencies were each developing their own information strategies and disseminating bits-and-pieces here and there. To integrate these various activities, Roosevelt appointed William Donovan as Coordinator of Information (COI) in June 1941. In July, the Foreign Information Service (FIS) was established for monitoring foreign broadcasting and communications and in October the Office of Facts and Figures (OFF) was established in New York. After the Japanese bombed Pearl Harbor in December 1941, the U.S. went to war. However, the American public continued to resist government control of information. It was not until six months after Pearl Harbor, on June 13, 1942, that the Office of War Information (OWI) was finally established to coordinate all information going out of the United States.

Elmer Davis, a reporter for the New York Times and noted radio commentator, was appointed Director of OWI. OFF was abolished and integrated into OWI, but Donovan opposed the journalist's dealing with sensitive national security information which was under COI's control. In addition to OWI primarily dealing with information open to the public, Donovan, who was responsible for national security information, proposed establishing another agency to deal with secret information, the Office of Strategic Services (OSS). Roosevelt appointed Donovan as the Director of OSS.[1] As a result, during World War II, open information went through OWI, secret information was dealt with by the OSS, while military information remained the preserve of the Army and Navy.

OWI was divided into two branches: domestic and overseas. The director of the Domestic Branch was Archibald MacLeish, Director of the Library of Congress in which all available books, magazines, and newspapers – including Japanese American newspapers – were gathered and examined, and Japanese (foreign) language texts were translated into English.[2] A famous screenwriter, Robert Sherwood, was appointed director of the Overseas Branch. Collaborating with the Army and Navy information services, the Overseas Branch gathered foreign information and disseminated U.S. information to foreign countries under Sherwood's directorship. The former director of the United Press, London, Wallace Carroll, was appointed as Director of the London branch of the OWI.[3] In sum, the U.S. government mobilized journalists and writers for the information war.

After General Dwight D. Eisenhower began civil affairs activities in French North Africa in 1942, the Psychological Warfare Branch (PWB) was established as a division of the OWI. Brigadier General Robert A. McClure of the U.S. Army, who had engaged in radio broadcasting and other information services in Europe, was appointed chief of psychological warfare in North Africa. In early 1944, the Supreme Headquarters of the Allied Expeditionary Force (SHAEF) was established and the Psychological Warfare Division commenced information activities under its direction. McClure was later engaged in the psychological warfare conducted during the Korean War.

Roosevelt originally established OWI as a civilian agency, which worked in close collaboration with the psychological warfare divisions of the U.S. Army, Navy and OSS, which were all under the direction of the Joint Chiefs of Staff. Since the OSS radio broadcasters did not identify themselves, the

OWI was not able differentiate the OSS broadcasts from other foreign propaganda.[4] For instance, both OWI and OSS broadcast in China. However, the OWI could not figure out whether the radio waves they received had originated from the OSS or other Japanese propaganda broadcasts, as the OSS utilized Japanese prisoners of war for their radio programs. The Asian branches of the OWI collaborated with Britain and the Chinese Nationalist Party as well as the U.S. Army and Navy.[5]

Importantly, the OSS played a central role in planning the U.S. occupation of Japan. Especially, the Research and Analysis Division of the OSS gathered geopolitical and other information about Japan and surrounding areas and provided information to the Civil Affairs Division of the Department of the Army. The Research and Analysis Division seems to have had many Japanese-American translators fluent in the Japanese language; an enormous amount of information was translated into English from Japanese language sources. Based on the OSS information gathering activities, the Research and Analysis Division edited the volumes of "Civil Affairs Guides," which were used for planning the postwar occupation.

Compared with the covert mission of OSS, in which many Japanese language speaking staff engaged in information gathering in the Asia-Pacific theaters, the overt mission of OWI was not apparent until summer 1944 because it had been focused on the European theaters. After Roosevelt's visit to Hawaii in summer 1944 to meet with Nimitz and MacArthur, however, OWI Hawaii began to collaborate with the military intelligence services. After MacArthur's landing in the Philippines in 1944, OWI published "Free Philippines" and started broadcasting from Manila in March 1945.[6] Collaborating with the Psychological Warfare Division of the Military Intelligence Services, OWI conducted a series of psychological warfare operations in the Battle of Okinawa.

Navy Lieutenant Ellis M. Zacharias broadcast from the OWI branch in Saipan, urging Japan's unconditional surrender in 1945. This was one of the most important OWI psychological operations in the Pacific theater. Psychological warfare during World War II had not been regarded as a major weapon for the U.S. military operations. However, in the final stages of the war, the OWI and OSS psychological strategies gradually grew in importance as U.S. policymakers began to analyze Japanese suicide attacks, utilizing their behavioral scientists. Psychologists and anthropologists were mobilized to predict the behavior of Japanese soldiers, a practice that continued throughout the Cold War.

After Japan accepted the Potsdam Declaration on August 14, 1945, President Truman disbanded the OWI with Executive Order 9608, issued on August 31,[7] and disbanded the OSS with Executive Order 9621 on September 20.[8] The Psychological Warfare Division, however, was reassigned to the General Headquarters of the Supreme Commander for the Allied Powers (GHQ/SCAP), which was responsible for the U.S. occupation of Japan. According to Paul M. A. Linebarger, a psychological warfare planner for the Pacific theatre during World War II, the psychological warfare group was reorganized into the Civil Information and Education (CIE) section of GHQ/SCAP.[9] The CIE played an important role in the U.S. postwar re-education program for Japanese as well as similar programs in Okinawa, as described in the next chapter.

Prior to MacArthur's landing at Atsugi Airport on August 27, 1945, the Information Dissemination Section (IDS) was established as an advance group. Director Bonner Fellers was the Division Chief, Psychological Warfare Team in the Pacific, as well as MacArthur's military assistant. The CIE consisted of the former Army psychological warfare unit and OWI staff. On September 13, IDS was formally reorganized into the CIE after the requisition of NHK, Japan's national broadcasting network in Tokyo. On October 2, the CIE became a section of the Special Staff of GHQ/SCAP. During the Allied occupation of Japan, the CIE coordinated the Japanese mass media policies regarding newspapers, magazines, radio and television broadcasting, and movies.[10]

## From OWI to United States Information Agency

As the wartime information agencies were disbanded, Washington commenced reorganizing the federal government. The functions of the OWI were integrated into a new division of the State Department, the Office of International Information and Cultural Affairs. William Benton was appointed as its Director and as Assistant Secretary of State for Public Affairs.

However, public antagonism toward the government's control of information was rekindled. American mass media and professional organizations such as the American Society of Newspaper Editors opposed the U.S. government's attempt to control information.[11] From the perspective of defending freedom of speech, the American mass media believed that the dissemination of information in peacetime should be done by private enterprises, not the government. The Associated Press and United Press, both of which had provided free information to the OWI throughout World War II, announced that they would stop providing the U.S. government. Voice of America, a U.S. sponsored broadcasting service established during World War II, was in a difficult position without those news sources.

The State Department had taken over the broadcasting service after the OWI was disbanded, and Assistant Secretary Benton proposed to continue international broadcasting. He submitted a budget proposal for the Voice of America to the House Foreign Relations Committee in 1946. The House Appropriations Committee approved Benton's proposal for educational exchange, but only approved half of the proposed budget for publication of a magazine called "America" and international broadcasting.[12]

The State Department proposed the Smith-Mundt Bill (H.R. 3342) to secure congressional support for international broadcasting. The Senate approved the bill, but the House did not and, as a result, the bill did not pass the 1946 session of Congress. The following summer, Senator Alexander Smith and Representative Karl E. Mundt organized a subcommittee and the members visited Europe to research the European economic rehabilitation plan. They discussed Soviet propaganda and its menace with American businessmen in Europe and reported to the Congress that the U.S. should launch counter propaganda activities against the Soviet Union.[13]

After the congressmen's short trip to Europe, the bill proposed by Senator Smith and Representative Mundt was finally passed in the Senate and the House with revisions. President Truman signed the bill and the Smith-Mundt Act (P.L. 80-402) was enacted on January 27, 1948. It provided for the establishment of the Office of International Information and Educational Exchange (OIE), separated into two organizations: the Office of International Information (OII) for public affairs and the Office of Educational Exchange (OEX) for educational exchange.[14] One of the most important aims of the Smith-Mundt Act was to establish professional offices in the State Department to promote American ideals at the United Nations and other international audiences, combatting Soviet propaganda.

According to the Congressional Quarterly Service, OWI was a federal agency with 9,000 employees in 1945. Following the passage of the Smith-Mundt Act, the number of U.S. federal employees engaged in information activities increased to 12,167 by 1964. Of these, 8,885 employees were working overseas, of which, 7,368 were not Americans.[15] These figures show that U.S. foreign information organizations expanded after World War II.

U.S. public affairs policy originated in the OWI tradition. After World War II, the State Department and the USIA, established in 1953, succeeded in opening public information programs. The U.S. public affairs programs were transformed into public diplomacy in the 1960s. The Secretary of State was responsible for U.S. public diplomacy, but the Assistant Secretaries of State for Public Affairs were usually working professionals who promoted U.S. public relations to foreigners. The underlying concept of State's public affairs was to present fact-based information credited to the U.S. government. The U.S. government regards it as news, but some scholars call it "white propaganda."

## From OSS to Central Intelligence Agency

The functions of the OSS were absorbed into the War Department (former Department of the Army). When Truman ordered the dismissal of the OSS in 1945, General Carter B. Magruder and the War Department opposed the move, considering a secret intelligence service to be necessary even in peacetime. But others argued that functions such as moral and black propaganda and psychological operations were unnecessary in peacetime. As a result, the OSS was dismissed[16] and reorganized into the Central Intelligence Group (CIG), which was expected to collaborate with the Military Intelligence Services. Rear Admiral Sydney W. Souers was appointed as the Director of Central Intelligence (DCI).

In April 1946, General Hoyt S. Vandenberg, Chief of Army Intelligence (G-2) succeeded Souers and began to coordinate information gathered by a variety of federal departments and agencies. He established the Office of Research and Evaluation (ORE). ORE-1, the first research report of ORE into the national security policy of the Soviet Union, was prepared in July 1946. The ORE report was the predecessor of the National Intelligence Estimate (NIE), an important U.S. government report on international situations. CIG was reorganized into the Central Intelligence Agency (CIA) with the National Security Act of 1947.[17]

Integrated into the CIA, ORE prepared a four-page booklet about the Ryukyu Islands titled "The Ryukyu Islands and Their Significance" (ORE 24-48) on August 6, 1948.[18] The report was submitted to the NSC and circulated to the Executive Office, the Department of State, the Joint Chiefs of Staff and other departments and agencies. ORE 24-48 indicates that the CIA regarded the Ryukyu Islands as strategically important and probably contributed to finalizing the U.S. decision to keep Okinawa separate from mainland Japan.

ORE 24-48 stressed the threat of the Soviet Union and China and proposed to maintain U.S. military control over the Ryukyu Islands as a "watch post" to guard against seaward approaches by China and Korea. Specifically, the U.S. was afraid that China would claim sovereignty over the Ryukyus. Although the disposition of the Ryukyu Islands was not determined at either the Cairo or Potsdam Conferences, the report contended that the U.S. might "award" the Ryukyu Islands to Nationalist China. However, the report continued, given the possibility of the Chinese Nationalists losing to the Chinese Communists, such a resolution would result in the U.S. giving the Ryukyu Islands to Communist China. Therefore, the report concluded, it would be best for East Asian security for the U.S. to control the Ryukyu Islands. The U.S. administration of the Ryukyus would prevent these islands from being controlled by the communists.[19]

As discussed in Part One, the U.S. intention to maintain administrative control over the Ryukyus for the long-term had already been indicated in the JCS directive. Prior to the ORE 24-48 submission to the NSC, the NSC had approved NSC 13, Section 5 of which determined the U.S. policy of maintaining administrative authority over the Ryukyus.[20] The U.S. should obtain an international "sanction" to hold the Ryukyu Islands for the long-term. On May 6, 1949, the NSC policy paper for Japan was approved as NSC 13/3 after some revisions and sent to President Truman.[21]

Thus, the intelligence activities of the OSS were absorbed into the CIA. During World War II, the information gathering activities of the OSS had provided the basic resources for the U.S. policymakers regarding the occupation of Japan. The same could be said about the information gathering of the CIA for the U.S. administration of Okinawa.

## National Security Council as Information Policy Coordinator

The Military Intelligence Services of the U.S. Navy and Army also gathered information during World War II. As we have seen, the Army-Navy joint Psychological Warfare Division developed psychological operations. After the war, the problem was how these activities should be integrated and what role each organization should take. The State-War-Navy-Air Coordinating Committee (SWNACC) had coordinated the U.S. occupation policy of Japan and Germany, but it was a tentative committee. The NSC was originally established to succeed the SWNACC.

In the beginning, the NSC's role was not fully formed. President Truman attended the first meeting of the NSC but did not attend subsequent meetings to encourage free discussions among the attendees. The NSC gradually became the supreme decision-making organization directly proposing national policy to the President.

According to Robert A. Fearey who prepared the U.S. postwar occupation plan and worked as Civil Administrator of the Ryukyus prior to its reversion to Japan, the policy for Japan had been decided in deliberations between the State Department and the Department of the Army. In 1949, the working policy was coordinated between the Assistant Secretary of the Far East Bureau of the State Department, Assistant Secretary of the Army and the Far East Section of the Civil Affairs Division of the Department of the Army. Their decisions were submitted to the NSC,[22] which functioned as the coordinator of information policy between departments and agencies.

Information policy has two dimensions: gathering and disseminating information. NSC issued Intelligence Directive No. 2 on January 13, 1948 to define the role of each department regarding foreign information gathering. The directive ordered the maintenance of information gathering posts in foreign countries and defined the role of each agency: State to gather political, cultural, and social information; Army to gather military information; Navy to gather information regarding the seas; Air Force regarding the air. The directive said that gathering information concerning the economy, science and technology was to be jointly conducted.[23]

The NSC also determined information dissemination procedures. Prior to the NSC, the SWNACC had pointed out that psychological operations in peacetime would be necessary to support U.S. foreign policy, as it had received reports that Soviet propaganda was effective in Europe. The SWNACC had categorized "overt and covert propaganda" and "domestic and international information programs" and submitted a proposal to the NSC on November 7, 1947. SWNACC 304/11 had determined that the State Department should be responsible for both overt and covert information programs.[24]

The NSC held a meeting on November 14 to review the proposal. Secretary of State George Marshall was opposed to it, contending that State should only engage in fact-based broadcasting; it should not engage in "black propaganda." The NSC duly revised SWNACC 304/11.

Based on Marshall's opinion, on December 17, the NSC issued NSC4 and NSC4a policy papers regarding foreign information policy.[25] NSC 4 "Coordination of Foreign Information Measure" determined that the Secretary of State should be responsible for foreign information and the Assistant Secretary of State for Public Affairs answer to the Secretary of State. Meanwhile, NSC4a "Psychological Operations" determined that the Director of the CIA should be responsible for psychological operations. The CIA would not report details of covert operations, but must report a summary to the Secretary of State, since covert operations should be in accordance with national policy. Thus, U.S. information policy was divided into two dimensions: overt and covert information policy. During World War II, the OWI was responsible for overt or open information policy, while the OSS for covert. Similarly, in the postwar context, the State Department was responsible for overt public relations, while the CIA oversaw covert or psychological operations.

The Assistant Director for Special Operations was responsible for psychological operations under the CIA Director.[26] At the end of 1947, the Secretary of State was George Marshall; the Assistant Secretary of State for Public Affairs was George Allen; the CIA Director was Roscoe H. Hillenkoetter; and the Assistant Director for Special Operations was former OSS member Colonel Donald H. Galloway.

Following the issue of the NSC4 and NSC4a, an Interdepartmental Coordinating Staff was established[27] and State and the CIA discussed the procedural lines between the two organizations. On January 1, a Special Procedures Group (SPG) was established in the Office of Special Operations (OSO). The SPG was established in the CIA based on S.O. Directive 18/5 issued by General Galloway.

According to S.O Directive 18/5, SPG would conduct overt psychological operations overseas without revealing the U.S. as their source. A policy liaison officer was sent to State to coordinate psychological operations. S.O. Directive 18/5 detailed SPG's missions and procedures. According to the Directive, SPG would not only plan and execute psychological operations but also engage in research, analysis and evaluation. SPG policy liaison should contact the U.S. through a private person or corporation and could hire Americans and foreigners. The SPG liaison reported details of its operations only to the theater commander and the senior State Department official in the area.[28]

According to a memorandum by Thomas G. Cassidy, a former OSS member and the SPG chief at the time,[29] the SPG policy liaison received guidelines disseminated to information posts all over the world by "CIE (Voice of America) of the State Department." The memorandum also states that CIE (Voice of America) was the foreign branch of OIE under the Assistant Secretary of State for Public Affairs. The memorandum indicates that SPG policy liaison with the CIA was through CIE, the foreign post of OIE.[30] As discussed later, CIE activities began in Okinawa in 1948. CIE Okinawa reported to the military government, but may have been under the direction of the SPG policy liaison.

U.S. information policy was about to move toward the State Department initiative, but the Joint Chiefs of Staff were opposed to such a move. During World War II, OSS was under the direction of JCS and its activities were closely related to the intelligence services of the War Department. The Joint Chiefs of Staff did not like the emergence of the CIA, which would remove the former OSS missions from their control.

In August 1948, the NSC issued NSC 10/2, an information policy paper that revoked NSC4a. SPG was renamed the Office of Policy Coordination (OPC). Former OSS member Frank Wisner assumed the position of OPC Director.[31] From that time on, the OPC coordinated U.S. information policy with State, Defense and other departments.

In December 1949, NSC59 determined that the State Department should be responsible for overt psychological operations in peacetime. Further, on March 9, 1950, NSC 59/1 determined that the Secretary of State should be responsible for the information program in peacetime as well as immediately after the beginning of a war. Based on the concept that the continuity of peacetime and wartime policy was critical, the Psychological Operations Coordinating Committee was established as a coordinating organization.[32] After the Korean War broke out on June 23, 1950, the State Department established the National Psychological Strategy Board (NPSB) in August, confirming that State should lead the policy-making process regarding psychological operations. The NPSB members consisted of Assistant Secretary of State for Public Affairs, the CIA Director and the representatives from State, Defense, the Joint

Chiefs of Staff, the National Security Resource Board (NSRB) and the Economic Cooperation Administration (ECA).[33]

In the process of allocating duties in peacetime and wartime, on April 21, 1951, the Psychological Strategy Board (PSB) was established as a Presidential committee as the coordinating office. The PSB was headquartered at Lafayette Park north of the White House and consisted of four sections: the Director's Office, the Office of Planning and Policy, the Office of Coordination, and the Office of Review. The chairman was CIA Director Walter Bedell Smith. The board members were Assistant Secretary of State James Webb, Assistant Secretary of Defense Robert Lovett, Admiral Leslie Stevens, and former Secretary of the Department of the Army Gordon Gray. The Joint Chiefs of Staff was excluded from PSB membership.[34]

The Truman administration's Psychological Strategy Board was abolished and reorganized into the Operations Coordination Board (OCB) by the Eisenhower administration by Executive Order 10483 on September 2, 1953. Thus, the U.S. foreign information policy decision-making process was gradually consolidated in Washington. Meanwhile, the Department of the Army had opened the Psychological Warfare Center at Fort Bragg, North Carolina on April 10, 1952 to expand and advance research and training on psychological warfare operations, which were now regarded as an important part of military activities.[35]

Overarching information policy was decided at the NSC and the role of each department and agency was also determined by the Executive Office. American universities were utilized to research the effectiveness of psychological operations. For instance, the Operations Research Office (ORO) at Johns Hopkins University and the Human Resource Research Center (HumRRO) at George Washington University received grants from the Army for research on psychological warfare during the Korean War.[36] A notable mass communication scholar, Wilbur Schrum, received grants from the PSB. U.S. psychological warriors had been optimistic about using social scientific knowledge as an alternative weapon for the Cold War.

## Smith-Mundt Act as Principle Law for U.S. Public Diplomacy

The United States Information and Educational Exchange Act of 1948 determined the guiding principles of U.S. foreign information policy. The commonly called Smith-Mundt Act was signed by Truman and enacted on January 27, 1948. The Smith-Mundt Act underwent several revisions through a process that was thoroughly discussed as a matter of free speech for American citizens yet lacked any perspective on how U.S. federal law affected foreign peoples. It is important to discuss what was absent in the discourse regarding U.S. public diplomacy, since it had provided the legal basis for Congressional appropriations for public relations activities on foreign soils such as Okinawa. In other words, the discourse had provided a budgetary endorsement for American soft power.

Given the internet connected global audience of today, the Smith-Mundt Act was recently revised on January 2013 to revoke Section 501, which had banned domestic broadcasting of Voice of America and other government news services, as the clause became meaningless. Although the Smith-Mundt Act had been misunderstood in many ways, the original Smith-Mundt Act of 1948 did not prohibit domestic news dissemination by the U.S. government.[37] The domestic ban was introduced by the 1972 revision of Section 501 and the 1985 revision of Section 206. These domestic bans were revoked by Section 1078 of the National Defense Authorization Act (NDAA) of 2013 (P.L.112-239).[38]

Discussions of the Smith-Mundt Act among U.S. scholars has focused on the pros and cons of the domestic ban clauses and the prohibition of U.S. government propaganda within the U.S. but never discussed how the principle law of U.S. public diplomacy affected foreign audiences such as those in Okinawa[39] The debates tended to discuss the dated provisions of the Act, based on the fact that the Voice of America was now domestically available on the Internet.[40] Or that the Smith-Mundt Act did not comply with the free speech provisions determined by the First Amendment of the U.S. Constitution and Freedom of Information Act that determined free access to U.S. government information.[41] Seemingly, these debates were all concerned with U.S. domestic free speech and not concerned with the freedom of speech in foreign countries, which U.S. propaganda had been targeting.

The Smith-Mundt Act introduced many important provisions regarding the U.S. foreign information policy besides the domestic bans. The most important is the Act designated the Secretary of State as the top government official responsible for U.S. foreign information policy and that the foreign information programs under the Secretary of State were aimed at influencing the United Nations and international audiences. As described earlier in this chapter, the Secretary of Defense was responsible for wartime information policy. The Smith-Mundt Act enshrined the State Department as the leading peacetime representative of the U.S. government to the United Nations.

Section 603 of the Act decreed that the Secretary of State should establish two advisory committees: the United States Advisory Commission on Information and the United States Advisory Commission on Educational Exchange. The Act also stipulated that the President should appoint the chairpersons of the commissions, while the offices of the commissions should be established within the State Department. More importantly, the Act empowered the Secretary of State to utilize the human resources of other federal departments and agencies with Presidential approval.[42]

Meanwhile, the U.S. had proposed to UNESCO that the international trade of educational audio-visual materials, including American movies, should be free of tariffs. Delegates of twenty-one nations attended the third UNESCO conference in Beirut, Lebanon, and decided to lift the tariffs for audio-visual materials for education purposes. The resolution was named the Beirut Agreement. Assistant Secretary of State for Public Affairs, George Allen, argued at the conference that the re-education programs for Japanese would need audio-visual materials.[43] In effect, Allen was selling America and Hollywood at the UNESCO conference. The Beirut Agreement was a boon for the international marketing of the U.S. film industry.

The Smith-Mundt Act further supported the U.S. film industry to work with the government to sell American movies to foreign countries. The Act directed the establishment of an office within the State Department to promote the international sales of American films. Although American movies brought to U.S.-occupied Japan included entertainment movies, the Civil Information and Education Section of GHQ/SCAP occasionally highlighted the educational purposes of films and sent them to Japanese schools for audio-visual education.[44] These CIE activities were based on provisions of the congressional appropriations to re-educate postwar Japanese. The Beirut Agreement and Smith-Mundt Act were behind these programs.

Section 203 of the Smith-Mundt Act further prescribed that the U.S. should establish and maintain schools, libraries, information centers and community centers to promote American democracy overseas. Section 402 of the Act provided that the Secretary of State could utilize technical and professional services of other U.S. federal organizations. Section 702 provided that the Secretary of State could transfer the Smith-Mundt budgets to other federal departments and agencies. Although Okinawa was under the authority of the Defense Department, information and educational programs of the Smith-Mundt Act were executed. It seems likely that funds appropriated via the Smith-Mundt Act were transferred to USCAR to conduct information programs in Okinawa.

Furthermore, the act allowed the Secretary of State to use private corporations to execute information programs to minimize government expenditure (Section 502) and to maximize the usage of American newspapers, radio and movie studios (Section 1005). The Act also specified that employees of private corporations engaged for such purposes be provided with the same salaries and benefits as U.S. federal employees for the foreign missions (Section 302). For example, Radio Corporation of America (RCA) was contracted to build the communications network in Okinawa and RCA employees requested the same overseas benefits as the U.S. federal employees.[45]

Finally, Section 603 of the Act required that a quarterly report be submitted to the Secretary of State and a biannual report to Congress. Thus, the Smith-Mundt Act established the basic framework for the U.S. foreign information programs.

## The Marshall Plan of Ideas

Another important component of the U.S. foreign information policy was contained in the economic aid to promote a free economy in Europe and Asia. The Economic Cooperation Act of 1948 established the Economic Cooperation Administration, the central agency for economic aid in the Marshall Plan. To promote U.S. economic aid, an ECA information program was implemented to promote America's free economy and democratic ideals through advertising. According to ECA records, ECA produced radio programs in local languages and broadcast them on local radio stations.[46] Newspapers, magazines, movies, and exhibitions were used for public relations purposes. ECA information programs, called "The Marshall Plan of ideas," basically aimed to counter Soviet propaganda. The ECA was abolished in 1952, but the U.S. engaged in "ideological warfare" to promote U.S. values throughout the Cold War.

In Europe, USIS sponsored a series of movie screenings under the State Department's authority, while ECA sponsored similar screenings. To be precise, the State Department sponsored the movie events based on the Smith-Mundt Act to promote better understanding of the U.S., while the Economic Cooperation Act was for the promotion of the U.S. economic aid. However, similar American movies were frequently screened in the same city on the same date. To avoid duplication, it was determined that the Secretary of State should lead the information program in Europe and the ECA should support the State Department.[47]

In contrast, such duplication did not occur in Okinawa and Japan since the economic aid and information programs were administered by the Department of the Army. As previously mentioned, the Far East Command of the U.S. Army was referred to as "the ECA in the Far East."

## Psychological Warfare

As described above, U.S. foreign information policy was decided at the NSC and coordinated in the Executive Office. In August 1950, the State Department established the National Psychological Strategy Board (NPSB) to oversee psychological operations. When the Psychological Strategy Board (PSB) was established in April 1951, it assumed responsibility for formulating psychological operations for Japan. The PSB chairman was the Director of CIA. The U.S. information policy toward Japan was based on NSC 125 titled "Policy Toward Japan" in which State, Defense and the CIA were each allotted a role in psychological operations toward Japan.[48]

U.S. information policy toward Japan was based on the Psychological Strategy Program for Japan (PSB D-27) approved at the PSB on January 30, 1952. It included psychological, informational, and cultural operations.[49] Assistant Secretary of State for the Far East, John M. Allison, chaired the committee on PSB D-27 and planned the psychological operations related to Japan. Committee members included the Assistant Secretary of State for Public Affairs, the CIA Director, the Secretary of Defense and others. The details remain classified, but one of its purposes was to democratize the Japanese people.[50] The committee was dismissed when Japan recovered her independence on April 28, 1952, but its successor, the Psychological Operations Committee (POC), continued psychological operations in Japan.

The POC was organized in Tokyo on November 19, 1952. The public affairs officer of the U.S. Embassy chaired the committee, which included the Ambassador to Japan and the Commander-in-Chief of the Far East Command. The policy determined by the committee was reported to the International Information Administration (IIA), at the State Department.[51] Psychological operations toward Japan were deliberated at the local committee, where the military commander was of equal rank to the Ambassador.

The Okinawa situation was quite different. The NSC Planning Committee reported on June 15, 1953 that the U.S. should maintain its military bases in the Ryukyu and Bonin Islands and carefully influence Japanese public opinion since Japan might limit the use of the U.S. military bases in mainland Japan.[52] Thus, the U.S. information policy toward Japan and Okinawa were executed as psychological operations.

## Chapter Summary

This chapter discussed the basic framework of the U.S. foreign information policy from World War II to the early Cold War period. Such wartime organizations as the Office of War Information and Office of Strategic Services were abolished in 1945, but the functions of these information agencies were reorganized into the United States Information Agency and the Central Intelligence Agency. During the U.S. occupation of Japan, Civil Information and Education had carried on both the OWI and OSS traditions.

Generally speaking, the Secretary of State was the principal decision-maker for U.S. foreign information policy in peacetime. However, Okinawa was under the jurisdiction of the Secretary of Defense based on NSC Action 824-b. The wartime structure remained in the U.S. administration of Okinawa. The U.S. information policy toward Okinawa was in the same situation. Representatives from the State Department were in supportive positions under the military commander-in-chief. Accordingly, the State Department did not overtly engage in U.S. information policy toward Okinawa, but USCAR constantly received information policy guidelines from the USIA while the Public Affairs Department of USCAR functioned as USIS, the Okinawa branch of the USIA.

# 7 Civil Information and Education Programs 1945–1957

## Introduction

U.S. foreign information policy during the Cold War was decided by the National Security Council attached to the Executive Office in Washington. This chapter discusses U.S. information policy toward Okinawa, focusing on the role of the U.S. military government established in Okinawa in 1945 and the United States Civil Administration of the Ryukyu Islands (USCAR) which succeeded it from 1950.

After landing on Okinawa in 1945, the U.S. forces established a military government to administer the local population in accordance with the provisions of JCS 1231. Civil Information and Education (CIE) commenced public relations activities with the Okinawan people as early as 1948.[1] U.S. information policy was subsequently characterized as strategic public diplomacy in which the State Department determined foreign information policy. The first three sections of this chapter discuss the period from the U.S. landing on Okinawa in 1945 to the establishment of the CIE in 1948. The remaining sections discuss CIE activities from 1949 to 1957.

## Information Blockade during the Battle of Okinawa

Prior to the U.S. landing on the western coast of Okinawa Island on April 1, 1945, the Navy bombed NHK Okinawa in Naha, the local branch of the Japanese national broadcaster, disrupting local radio broadcasting.[2] Okinawan newspapers also suspended publication after the bombings on March 23. Choko Takamine and other newspapermen of the *Okinawa Shimpo* had taken their printing equipment into an underground cave near Shuri Castle. They continued to publish their "cave newspapers," secretly receiving Domei News Service from Tokyo. However, the publication ceased after the U.S. bombing of Shuri Castle. The group left the newspaper cave on May 26 and commenced their barefoot journeys to the southern part of Okinawa Island. Some died, while others surrendered and were interned in U.S. civilian camps.[3]

Okinawa suffered a media blackout. Mass media generally play a crucial role recording social events and history, but Okinawa lost the capacity to record history in their own narratives. The U.S. occupation of Okinawa continued for twenty-seven years after the war, during which time the U.S. administration restricted the freedom of speech and of the press in Okinawa. U.S.-perspectives dominated postwar Okinawan history. The U.S. national archives indicate that U.S. forces strategically blocked military and civilian communications in Okinawa. Combat plans for Operation Iceberg – the invasion of Okinawa – clearly state that the U.S. should destroy key facilities such as bridges, roads, warehouses, and radio communication facilities prior to the landing. The After Action Report of Operation Iceberg specifically recorded Naval airplanes attacking the radio communication facilities on April 1, the day of the U.S. landing.[4]

Military planners considered shutting down the Okinawan communication infrastructure to be essential for victory. As discussed in Chapter 3, the JCS 1231 Political Directive determined the censorship policy on civilian communications. On November 12, 1944, another JCS Directive ordered the theater commander to organize civilian press censorship in the Asia-Pacific Region based on the advice of Byron Price, Director, Office of Censorship, the civilian censorship office which oversaw the U.S. domestic press during World War II.[5] This provision of JCS 873/3 was adopted in JCS 1231/2, the Directive for the U.S. military government for Japanese Outlying Islands. The military unit censored the press under the direction of the theater commander. As described in Chapter 2, censorship during the U.S. occupation was integral to local intelligence gathering.

In the process of formulating JCS 873/3, a communication blockade was initially considered to be necessary against mainland Japan.[6] Ultimately, though, the U.S. did not blockade communication on the mainland, but blacked out all civilian communications on Okinawa Island, the main island of the Ryukyu archipelago. Admiral Nimitz, the Commander-in-Chief, ordered the suspension of all civilian communications in Okinawa in Proclamation No. 10.

The Joint Chiefs of Staff imposed stricter controls on the civilian camps in the Japanese outlying islands than in their counterparts, such as the Mariana Islands, suspecting that the Okinawan people would be more loyal to Japanese Imperialism and militarism than the populations of the southern Pacific islands. The primary objective of the blockade was to obstruct espionage and other subversive activities. The Joint Chiefs ordered the military government to control the civilians in internment camps. The Counter Intelligence Corps put the civilians into the camps and provided food and medical services, while interviewing them about their "views."[7]

Meanwhile, U.S. forces had established their own communications infrastructure as soon as they landed on Kerama Island on March 26, 1945 in preparation for the landing on Okinawa Island. Soon after the landing, the construction of roads, bridges, and airports as well as U.S. communications infrastructure and facilities had begun. Once the social infrastructure was ready for use, the U.S. psychological warfare team began producing content.

The *Ryukyu Shuho* was published during the Battle of Okinawa. It looked like an ordinary Japanese language newspaper, but was actually a series of U.S. psychological warfare leaflets. The weekly leaflets specifically aimed to disseminate news regarding the defeat of Germany and were published in Okinawa for six weeks starting on April 29. According to the operations report of the U.S. psychological warfare team, the *Ryukyu Shuho* was a handwritten series of newssheets jointly published by the Army, Navy and OWI. Similar newssheets published in the Marianas were regarded as effective.[8] Japanese speaking staff wrote the Japanese contents of the *Ryukyu Shuho* which were translated into English and delivered to the commander for checking. Japanese Americans and a Japanese prisoner of war, who had worked for a Japanese newspaper, were reportedly engaged in the production.[9] The English-speaking commander did not fully trust in his Japanese-speaking team members, who were U.S. citizens of Japanese ancestry.

On June 20, "The Buckaneer" was published and distributed among the U.S. troops. This was an English newsletter named for U.S. Commander Buckner, who had been killed in action. The U.S. Army radio WXLH began broadcasting in Okinawa with the tag-line, "A Stone's Throw from Tokyo."[10] According to Congressional records submitted to the Navy Committee on August 6, the U.S. communications cable network had been under construction in Okinawa Island prior to the Japanese surrender on August 14.[11] While the Okinawan press had been shut down, the U.S. forces disseminated information among the Okinawan people.

## Media Deprivation

The Battle of Okinawa deprived the Okinawan people of all mediated communications. The U.S. Proclamations announced that the U.S. had occupied Okinawa and the surrounding areas and suspended local laws. These proclamations had been prepared both in Japanese and English and were posted at community centers. They have been commonly called "Nimitz Proclamations" as they were issued in the name of Chester W. Nimitz, Commander-in-Chief of the U.S. Pacific Fleet. Army historian, Arnold G. Fisch, speculates on the effectiveness of the proclamations in his book *The Military Government of the Ryukyu Islands*.[12]

Proclamation No. 1 began with a preface targeted at the people of Nansei Shoto, the southwestern islands and surrounding waters. It proclaimed that the area was under U.S. authority and all administrative, judicial and police authorities of the Japanese government were suspended. Proclamation No. 2 was a set of wartime criminal laws prohibiting the possession of weapons, murder, espionage, rape and disturbances of U.S. communications. Any of these crimes would incur the death penalty.[13]

Proclamation No. 8 was important for its infringement on freedom of speech. The issue date was left blank, but it prohibited the possession of radio receivers, photography, printing, and publication of newspapers, magazines, books and pamphlets as well as the foreign trade of these items without the permission of the U.S. military government. Attending public meetings, movies and theatres was prohibited without an official permit from the military government.[14] Further, Proclamation No. 10 prohibited any civilian communications and information exchange with "enemies" through radio, telegraph, telephone, cables, and letters.[15] "Enemies" meant all Japanese, including those in Okinawa. The Nimitz Proclamations of 1945 ruled Okinawa until Special Proclamation No. 32 was issued on July 5, 1949, revoking the early military laws.[16]

The Nimitz Proclamations literally targeted civilian populations in Okinawa, but also were statements to the allied nations – Britain, China, and the Soviet Union – because the international community required that the occupation comply with international laws. International law permitted the occupation force to requisition the properties of local governments. Accordingly, JCS 1231 ordered the military government to be established upon commencement of the occupation, and the U.S. needed to announce that the occupation forces would acquire local assets in accordance with international law. According to the U.S. National Archives, the U.S. claims that the first military government was established on Kerama Islands on March 26, 1945. It was advantageous for the date to be as early as possible to legitimate the requisition of local properties by official announcements.

The U.S. occupation was defined at two levels; 1) assault phase, and 2) garrison phase. It is not clear in which phase the Joint Chiefs originally intended to establish the military government. Obviously, the military government at Kerama was established at the beginning of the assault phase as a base supporting the forthcoming landing on the main island. Meanwhile, a copy of Proclamation No. 1 filed in the records of the Legal Affairs Department of USCAR indicates that it was issued on July 1, 1945 when the battles were won and the garrison phase began.[17] It is not certain who wrote the date, but the U.S. occupation force officially announced the end of the war on July 2. Presumably the occupation force considered the garrison phase to have started in the beginning of July 1945. The Legal Affairs Department filed a series of martial laws which the U.S. military government issued in Okinawa.

## Newspaper Publication

During the media blackout, the U.S. military government supported the resumption of newspaper production. As described in Chapter 2, the field manual directed that the military government should re-establish mass media if the local media were destroyed. Okinawa was such a case. However, the purpose of newspaper publication was twofold: to gather local information and to disseminate the pronouncements of the military government to the local populations.

On July 26, the first issue of the *Uruma Shimpo*, a Japanese language newspaper, was published in the civilian camp at Ishikawa, on the eastern part of Okinawa Island. It was a U.S. supported two-page mimeograph of news sources obtained from the U.S. wire service receivers. Kiyoshi Shima was appointed as the "president" of the *Uruma Shimpo*. The first issue had neither a title nor a date, but the newspaper's name, the *Uruma*

*Shimpo*, headlined the second issue published on August 1.[18] The first to fifth issues were mimeographed, but from the sixth issue on they were printed using Japanese type recovered from the caves and broken-down printing facilities. Some welcomed the *Uruma Shimpo*, as they were hungry for information, but others criticized it as demagogy when it reported the Japanese surrender on August 15.

The U.S. regarded it as the official newspaper of the military government and censored the paper. Nevertheless, Shima later insisted that he chose the news to be printed and cordially regarded the *Uruma Shimpo* as his own newspaper for Okinawan readers. In fact, the early *Uruma Shimpo* contained hardly any local news, consisting mainly of foreign news stories. According to the U.S. National Archives, *Uruma Shimpo* was ordered to print only the U.S. military government's selection of news and any criticism of the military government was prohibited.[19] In other words, *Uruma Shimpo* did not have press freedom.

Kiyoshi Shima resigned from *Uruma Shimpo* on September 20, 1946 and relocated to Tokyo. Kamejiro Senaga succeeded him and proposed that the military government stop the pre-publication censorship and charge a fee for the paper. The new president intended to make the paper into a private enterprise.

As described in Chapter 2, censorship of civilian communication was central to the military government's civil affairs activities in Okinawa.[20] The U.S. resurrected *Uruma Shimpo* for intelligence gathering and disseminating propaganda, providing financial support until April 1947.[21] The newspaper was transformed into a private corporation as it began to charge subscription fees. It became a daily in November 1949 and changed its name to *Ryukyu Shimpo* on September 10, 1951. The U.S. supported mimeograph thus became one of the major dailies in Okinawa.

## CIE Okinawa

During the U.S. occupation of Japan, the Press Pictorial Broadcasting Division (PPB), a part of Civil Censorship Division (CCD), censored Japanese mass communications.[22] However, no media professionals had been dispatched to the military government in Okinawa. Instead, the *Uruma Shimpo* was censored by the Press and Publications Section, Public Information Office of the Philippines-Ryukyu Command.

A turning point came in 1948, after the Smith-Mundt and Economic Cooperation Acts were passed in Washington. In June, Congress approved the 1949 fiscal year Government Aid and Relief in Occupied Areas appropriations for the Department of the Army, although the State Department had originally proposed the bill as foreign aid appropriations. Subsequently, the distinctive characteristics of U.S. foreign information policy gradually took shape in the Ryukyu Islands.

In January 1948, the Civil Affairs Division of the Department of the Army established a field office in New York. Through this field office, the Office of International and Cultural Affairs of the State Department sent mass media materials such as movies, magazines, music and artworks to the Civil Information and Education section (the CIE) of GHQ/SCAP in Tokyo.[23] Some of this material was sent to Okinawa via Tokyo. However, the State Department did not directly instruct the CIE because the section was under the command of Douglas MacArthur. SWNCC 247, approved on February 7, 1946, determined that the OIC could direct the CIE but the final decision about whether to follow these directions was at the theater commander's discretion.[24]

The State Department, however, might have maintained other means of influence through SPG and, later, OPC political liaisons attached to the CIE Okinawa. According to the *Foreign Relations of the United States*, the CIE was a foreign branch of the OIE, a division of the State Department. The OPC, a political liaison of the CIA, coordinated with the theatre commander and the senior representative of the State Department in the region. The State Department did not direct the U.S. administration of Okinawa, partly because the theater commander represented the U.S. government in Okinawa. However, the CIE movies that arrived in Okinawa were those which the State Department's OIC had produced or procured.[25] These movies had arrived in Okinawa through the CIE Tokyo office as early as January 1948.

In April 1948, James N. Tull commenced CIE activities in Okinawa. Although the USCAR official report does not refer to him by name, Tull was a media professional transferred from the U.S. Armed Forces radio station WXLH in Okinawa[26] to establish AKAR, Voice of the Ryukyus, the first civilian Japanese-language radio station in postwar Okinawa. Etsujiro Miyagi favorably appraised Tull's contribution to Okinawa's broadcasting in the book *Okinawa Postwar Broadcasting History*.[27] Tull's main mission was a public relations campaign to promote American democracy and introduce the principles of elective government to the local populations.

After returning to the U.S. in 1951, Tull studied communications at the graduate school of the University of Chicago and then worked for USIA. As the Vietnam War began, he returned to Asia and worked as an information officer for the Joint United States Public Affairs Office (JUSPAO) in Saigon. Although what Tull was doing in Okinawa is not entirely clear, he was the first civilian professional who specialized in information policy.

His master's thesis, submitted to the University of Chicago, was titled "The Ryukyu Islands, Japan's Oldest Colony—America's Newest: An Analysis of Policy and Propaganda." In the preface, Tull described it as "a strategic intelligence document." It is an important primary source document on CIE Okinawa.[28] The 200-page thesis explains the historical background and political situation of the Ryukyu Islands in detail and stresses the strategic importance of the Ryukyus. Further, Tull proposed that a strategic public relations policy tailored for Japanese-language speaking audiences became necessary when the U.S. decided to administer the Ryukyus. Tull had proposed the policy and commenced it as he launched AKAR. Meanwhile, Tull's mission might have been to gather local intelligence in Okinawa and write a policy proposal based on first hand knowledge acquired among the local people. Tull's perspective is quite similar to that of the CIA document, "The Significance of the Ryukyu Islands," (ORE 24-48) discussed in the previous chapter.

While Tull called Okinawans friends, his mission was to use propaganda for the "political indoctrination" of the Okinawan people.[29] Tull criticized the military government's efforts to simply impose American values on the local populations, proposing to revise the U.S. information policy to reflect the cultural differences of the target population. Tull further criticized the military government's focus on the construction of the hard infrastructure without giving due consideration to the contents of communications. For example, he continued, the military government supported the *Uruma Shimpo* until April 1947, but did not discuss information policy after the financial aid ended. He complained that the military government's public relations people were not interested in information activities despite being dispatched as information specialists.[30]

The military government, Tull observed, had regarded information as something like education, regarding movie screenings as a form of adult education,[31] consistent with the GARIOA budget, which was appropriated for "information and education programs" in occupied areas. The same could be said for the ECA appropriations. The U.S. Army and the military government of Okinawa emphasized the educational purposes of CIE films, even though they were not specifically educational films, including American entertainment movies.[32]

Tull stayed in Okinawa from 1948 to 1951, the period in which the ECA and related appropriations were approved by the Congress and allocated to the Far East Command headquartered at Tokyo. During this period, "Governor" Joseph R. Sheetz strategically distributed economic aid to Okinawa in preparation for the expected separation of Okinawa from Japan. As an information specialist, James Tull appears to have gone to Okinawa to psychologically prepare the local populations for this separation.

The relationship between CIE Okinawa and CIE Tokyo is unclear. However, CIE Okinawa was formed shortly before August 1, 1948 when the Ryukyu Command was detached from Philippine Command and attached to Far East Command in Tokyo. On September 6, the Ryukyu Military Government Section was established in Tokyo, with Brigadier General John Weckerling as its chairman. Weckerling had testified before Congress regarding the Economic Rehabilitation for Occupied Areas (EROA) appropriations as described in Chapter 1. Representing the "ECA in Far East," Weckerling controlled the budgets of the Ryukyu Military Government Section from Tokyo because the military government in Okinawa did not have an accounting office. Congressional records indicate that EROA appropriations for Okinawa and Korea were formally separated from the Japan budget in 1949 and thereafter.[33]

Soon after the Ryukyu Military Government Section was established in Tokyo, the Department of Public Information and the Education Department of the military government were abolished and reorganized as the Civil Information and Education Department or CIE.[34] In January 1949, Tull was appointed as Chief, Information Division, CIE.[35] CIE Okinawa received movies and newsreels dubbed with Japanese in Tokyo and planned a series of screening sessions using mobile units and NATCO projectors recycled from military entertainment programs. Although no movie theaters or hall remained in the war-devastated islands, in 1949, movies were shown five times a week with these projectors[36] and an Audio-Visual Radio Section was established within the CIE. In 1950, CIE established the University of Ryukyus and five information centers in Naha, Nago, Ishikawa, Miyako and Ishigaki. Student exchange programs were begun, and local leaders and students were dispatched to the United States.

The information and education programs for the Okinawan people closely resembled those of the Smith-Mundt programs, while the economic aid resembled the Marshall Plan. In effect, the information and education programs for Okinawa were an Asian version of the Marshall Plan of ideas. It aimed at educating the local population against Soviet propaganda to be pro-American. The ECA information programs started under the Truman administration and OCB succeeded it during the Eisenhower administration.[37]

## Supervising Newspapers

After local mayors were elected on February 1, 1948, Okinawan politics were gradually revived during the period of 1948–1951.[38] In early 1949, CIE launched a public relations campaign for the coming gubernatorial election of September 1950. The campaign was highly political.[39] Interestingly, the U.S. had promoted the popular vote for the gubernatorial election. The U.S. policymakers appear to have been optimistic about the power of public relations campaigns and mass communications. Also, the U.S. needed to present a favorable image to the United Nations, if it intended to seek a U.N. trusteeship for the U.S. administration of Okinawa.

The Office of Censorship during World War II had censored the U.S. press, but it was soft censorship without pre-publication checks. It educated editors and reporters to self-censor in accordance with their own patriotism. The U.S. censorship office faced a dilemma, as the First Amendment of the U.S. Constitution prohibited Congress from making any laws restricting free speech. The Department of Justice had censored Japanese language newspapers published in Japanese-American internment camps during the war. The censorship officers continuously monitored the Japanese-American press. But it was done in a relatively soft style in which the officers contacted, warned, and supervised the editors only when they found problematic expressions.[40]

In Okinawa, the Nimitz Proclamations had prohibited any criticism of the U.S. military government. Therefore, U.S. policy makers were optimistic about controlling political speech in Okinawa through education programs for newspapers and voters. The *Uruma Shimpo* was the only newspaper in Okinawa until 1947, but CIE permitted other publications from 1948 to 1951. First, the CIE permitted the publication of a second newspaper, the *Okinawa Times*, on May 15, 1948. Second, the *Okinawa Mainichi* was permitted to publish in Nago City, commencing July 12. Finally, the *Okinawa Herald* in Ishikawa started publication in 1949 and the *Ryukyu Nippo* in 1950. After the CIE was established in Okinawa, as we have seen, four newspapers started publication with CIE's approval.[41] CIE seemed to have different policies than the military government, encouraging newspaper publication under its supervision.

Meanwhile, on February 14, 1949, the military government issued another directive requiring a permit for mass media corporations to produce film, dramas, photographs and other paper publications. The directive does not have an English version or numbering, so it might not be an Army directive.[42] The military government permitted newspaper publications, primarily for the purpose of disseminating propaganda information to the local populace. The *Okinawa Mainichi* was a messenger to the residents in Nago and the *Okinawa Herald* for Ishikawa.[43] The military government regarded the newspapers as their watch posts.

## Information and Education Programs

The GARIOA and EROA appropriations peaked in fiscal year 1950, funding the rapid construction of social infrastructure throughout the small islands. On January 21, 1950, Voice of the Ryukyus or AKAR began regular broadcasting. The opening ceremony was held on February 1. On March 4, the Ryukyuan Communication Administration (RCA) was established to coordinate all communications and navigation systems, including weather forecasts. The weather forecasting service began on April 1.[44]

Thus, the information infrastructure had been prepared for the forthcoming separation of Okinawa from mainland Japan. On May 10, 1950, General Order No. 24 directed the reorganization of CIE and its functions and responsibilities were redefined as to educate the local population and to supervise the local press.[45]

In June, the construction of an information center at the library building of the University of Ryukyus was completed and a collection of English books and magazines was opened to the public. CIE also collected Japanese books in Okinawa at the time. The center also provided a rental service of sixty NATCO projectors and American movies dubbed with Japanese. CIE trained the technical staff to use the recycled NATCO projectors.[46] The localization process was similar to ECA information programs in Europe.[47] The USCAR official report proudly states that American movies were so popular that 50,000 local people watched the CIE films.

Managing the information centers was an important part of the CIE mission. According to the USCAR report, the information centers were established to "propagate" American democracy and encourage cultural exchange between the United States and the Ryukyus. Six information centers established in Naha, Nago, Ishikawa, Miyako, Ishigaki, and Amami had public libraries and conducted music concerts, lectures, and American movie shows. The explicit purpose of the information center was to teach American democracy to "the average Ryukyuans." At the same time, the centers were regarded as local posts for gathering information from average Ryukyuans. The USCAR official reports named these facilities "information centers," but later they were euphemistically renamed "cultural centers."

Meanwhile, it was CIE policy to use exchange programs to educate people who were regarded as prospective leaders. In June 1950, the CIE launched the first national leaders program in which Ryukyuan political leaders visited U.S. government organizations. In 1953, the CIE ran a GARIOA funded program, sponsoring 96 Ryukyuans to the U.S. for three months to prepare them to become pro-American leaders.

The student exchange program sent young leaders to U.S. high schools and universities to educate them as prospective English translators and interpreters needed by USCAR to interface with the local Ryukyuan government. Contracted with the Department of the Army, the Institute for International Education supervised the exchange students during their stays in the United States, intentionally sending them to small colleges to increase opportunities for communicating with "ordinary" Americans. Initially, it was a one-year exchange program, but the returning students did not speak English fluently enough to work at USCAR. So, the CIE extended the period to two or three years, and it eventually became a GARIOA funded program to provide university degrees.[48] The CIE also sent students to universities in mainland

Japan, since the islands had no professional institutions to educate medical doctors and pharmacists. The CIE initially ran the program using GARIOA funds, but after the Government of the Ryukyu was established in 1952, the exchange program with Japan was funded by taxes collected by the local Ryukyuan government.[49]

As well as the information and education programs, CIE launched a series of public relations campaigns targeting the forthcoming Ryukyuan gubernatorial election in 1950. Tatsuo Taira, Seiho Matsuoka, and Kamejiro Senaga ran as candidates. None formally stated that Okinawa should belong to Japan. Taira was elected as the first governor by popular vote. He later wrote in his memoirs that it was taboo to criticize the U.S. administration or to suggest reversion to Japan.[50] The CIE public relations campaign controlling political speech might be deemed successful, since the elected candidate confessed he was unable to speak freely during the campaign. While promoting American values through Hollywood movies, the CIE continued to suppress the Okinawan press.

## CIE Mission Statements

In July 1951, seven months after U.S. Civil Administration of the Ryukyu Islands (USCAR) was established, the CIE took over the English translation of the Okinawan press which had been performed by the Ryukyu Command Public Relations Division. The CIE mission was redefined in General Order No. 11 on February 25, 1952 as follows:
  1. To support the rehabilitation of mass media at the least necessary level to disseminate information about the U.S. administration and to make the democratic procedures understandable.
  2. To supervise education policy in so far as the economic resources are available.
  3. To translate the Ryukyuan press and edit the summary.[51]

In other words, the CIE missions gradually changed from education to information control. To this end, CIE sponsored "Newspaper Week" in October 1951 for the Okinawan press. It aimed to improve communications between USCAR and the local press through a series of seminars and meetings. As a social gathering for understanding each other, USCAR continued the Newspaper Week throughout the administrative period. One of CIE's central missions was to educate members of the press about American journalism and its norms.

USCAR's official report in 1953 redefined the CIE missions as follows: 1) to supervise and encourage the democratic newspapers, 2) to establish, maintain, and supervise Ryukyuan radio networks; and 3) to manage the Ryukyuan-American Cultural Centers.[52]

## Controlling Speech

"Civil Affairs Activities in the Ryukyu Islands," the official report of USCAR, stated that the U.S. needed to gather intelligence to plan information and education programs specifically tailored to the Ryukyu Islands. The Plans Branch was established at CIE in July 1951 to examine the information programs of the State Department and other agencies and to propose specific programs appropriate for the Ryukyuans. The Plans Branch conducted a series of research projects such as public opinion polls, radio listeners' surveys and a readers' survey of the *Ryukyu Koho*, the public relations newsletter of the provisional government.[53] From 1951 to 1953, a research team from the Pacific Science Board – including anthropologist George P. Murdock, historian George H. Kerr, and zoologist Harold J. Coolidge – visited Okinawa and gathered information for administrative planning. Scientific Investigation for the Ryukyu Islands (SIRI) also studied Okinawa in collaboration with CIE staff. Anthropologist Alan Smith, a former counter-intelligence officer in the postwar civilian camps, returned to Okinawa as Chief of the Plans Branch, CIE and conducted a survey on Ishigaki Island,[54] supposedly continuing Tull's preliminary research with more depth.[55] These research projects, however, were conducted after the NSC's decision on the U.S. long-term administration of the Ryukyus. The research reports therefore never challenged national policy, but simply proposed more effective means for the administration of Okinawa.

On April 28, 1952, the Japan Peace Treaty effectively separated the Ryukyu Islands from Japan. CIE regarded half of NHK radio programs to be inappropriate for Okinawa and began providing U.S. news sources such as USIS news releases, wireless bulletins, and FBIS daily reports. CIE selected the news from Tokyo and restricted the Okinawan press's access to Japanese news services such as Kyodo and Jiji. Fewer and fewer news sources became available to the Okinawan press. On September 19, 1952, CIE started providing a bilingual news service to the Okinawan media. This was an important mission of the CIE Information Division.

On October 1, CIE contracted with American Newsreel Company and Zanier Brothers Production in Tokyo to make films exclusively targeting the Okinawan people.[56] Jean Zanier and Ian Mutsu established the film companies in Tokyo.[57] With the support of a Japanese consultant, CIE also launched a series of exhibitions introducing American culture.

After Japan's independence in 1952, USIS Tokyo took over the functions of CIE/SCAP, maintaining contact with the CIE in Okinawa. Receiving USIA information policy guides and radio programs through USIS Tokyo, CIE Okinawa played the role of policy liaison for USCAR. For instance, USIS Tokyo conducted public opinion polls in conjunction with CIE Okinawa.

Civil Affairs Activities of the Ryukyu Islands placed USCAR as a lower echelon of SCAP rather than part of the Far East Command. General MacArthur was appointed as Commander-in-Chief, Far East Command as well as Supreme Commander for the Allied Powers. While the military government was formally placed under the Far East Command, its successor, USCAR was placed under SCAP. The difference indicates that USCAR represented not only the military but also, to some extent, the State Department. It is interesting that the first issue of the USCAR official report carried the United Nation's logo above the front-page headline. It was not present in subsequent reports, though.

During the occupation of Japan, CIE supervised information dissemination to the Japanese press, while CCD censored the mass media.[58] CIE Okinawa consisted of five Americans who also had other jobs, engaged in both censorship and public relations simultaneously.

The Press Division, CIE, routinely translated the Okinawan press into English, producing summaries of the local news, disseminated to American military and civilian stationed in the Ryukyus. The division's mission was to guard against anti-U.S. speech in the Okinawan press.[59]

## Chapter Summary

The Battle of Okinawa imposed a media blackout on Okinawan society. The U.S. landing forces had planned a communication blockade and attacked radio and newspaper facilities. *Uruma Shimpo*, the first handwritten mimeograph, was published in the civilian camps established by the U.S. forces. Based on directions prescribed in the Army and Navy field manual, the military government supported newspaper publication as a convenient tool for gathering local intelligence and a necessary channel for disseminating information.

In 1948, the military government established the CIE, which supervised the Okinawan press. In December 1950, after USCAR succeeded the military government, CIE was reorganized into a department of USCAR. CIE public relations activities included intelligence gathering from newspapers and radio broadcasts. Closely collaborating with the military powers, CIE activities attempted to propagate American democracy against Soviet and other communist countries. This was the official U.S. information policy throughout the Cold War, and CIE was tasked with the mission in Okinawa.

In December 1956, the Information Division, CIE, was separated from the education section and reorganized into the Office of Public Information. When the Research and Analysis Division was established in April 1957, the CIE was abolished and reorganized into the Public Affairs Department, as described in the next chapter.

# 8 Public Affairs Department, USCAR: 1957–1972

## Introduction

This chapter discusses the organization and functions of the USCAR Public Affairs Department and related information organizations in Okinawa from 1957 to 1972, when Okinawa was returned to Japan. The previous chapter discussed the CIE information and education programs prior to Executive Order 10713 and the fact that CIE focused on education rather than information programs as the local mass media was destroyed during World War II.

This chapter deals with the latter half of the U.S. administration of Okinawa. In December 1956, the education division was detached from CIE and the Office of Public Information (OPI) was established. OPI was reorganized into the USCAR Public Affairs Department, establishing a Research and Analysis Division in April 1957. Accordingly, the Public Affairs Department specialized in public relations with the Okinawan people through the press and in coordination with other information gathering agencies in the Ryukyu Islands. The radio station supported by the CIE was privatized in 1954 and commercial television broadcasting started in 1959. Thus, the Okinawan mass media appeared in full bloom by the end of the 1950s.

## From Occupation to Diplomacy

After Executive Order 10713 was issued, Okinawa continued to be under the administration of the Department of the Army. However, the Executive Order specified that the U.S. President was ultimately responsible for the administration according to the Japan Peace Treaty of 1952. Prior to the Order, NSC policy papers treated the Okinawa administration as part of

U.S. foreign policy toward Japan, but the Executive Order only partially concurred. The Order clarified that the U.S. had to formally acknowledge that Okinawa was not a domestic matter, but a matter of foreign relations. As described in previous chapters, the authors of the Ryukyu Organic Act at the Department of the Army had attempted to situate the Ryukyus in the same status as U.S. territories and possessions like Puerto Rico and the Virgin Islands and had lobbied the Bureau of the Budget to persuade Congress. In contrast, the Executive Order defined it as a matter for which the Secretary of State as well as the Secretary of Defense should take responsibility.

In accordance with the Executive Order, a High Commissioner succeeded the Governor as the highest-ranking officer of the United States within Okinawa. But, in fact, Lt. Gen. James Moore, Commander-in-Chief of the Ryukyu Command, and therefore the former Governor, was appointed as the first High Commissioner of the Ryukyu Islands. So, in effect, the military theater commander continued to hold the highest position in the administrative body. What changed was that the military personnel had to be appointed by the President, rather than the Secretary of the Army or the JCS. The President of the United States had assumed ultimate responsibility for the administration of Okinawa.

The Executive Order strengthened the role of the U.S. Ambassador to Japan and the Secretary of State who was responsible for U.S. foreign relations. Under the Kennedy administration's foreign information policy from 1961, the Operations Coordinating Board was abolished, the Executive Office was reorganized, and the Secretary of State was given responsibility for foreign relations.[1] Kennedy also gave plenary powers to the U.S. Ambassadors, as representatives of the State Department, placing them in a superior position to the theater commanders and the CIA mission chiefs in their respective countries.[2] As discussed in the next chapter, Edwin O. Reischauer, Ambassador to Japan under the Kennedy administration, was empowered by this policy to take the initiative on the Okinawa problem in Tokyo.

However, the establishment of the U.S. Consulate General Office in Naha did not resolve the Okinawa problem, because Okinawa remained under the direct control of the Department of Defense. The United States Information Agency, established in 1953, launched a series of public diplomacy programs targeted at the foreign public throughout the Cold War. Public diplomacy was a new idea, but it was soon regarded as an essential component of U.S.

foreign relations. The public affairs officers of the Defense Department were expected to support State Department endeavors. At the same time, information technology had transformed the state of warfare even as nontraditional warfare such as guerrilla warfare emerged as the new norm in conflicts. That transformation quietly began to penetrate Okinawa.

During the Eisenhower administration (January 1953 to January 1961), the U.S. foreign information policy toward Japan and Okinawa was coordinated at the Operations Coordinating Board. When the Kennedy administration (January 1961–November 1963) abolished the OCB, the Executive Office continued to function as a coordinating hub between military and diplomatic matters. Under Kennedy's leadership, the Carl Kaysen Task Force was dispatched to research the Okinawa problems. Based on the Kaysen Report, Kennedy announced a new Okinawa policy on March 19, 1962, which formally acknowledged Japanese government aid to Okinawa. However, Japan's aid was limited in economic and technical scope while the U.S. military dominance in Okinawa appeared to remain unchanged.

## Transforming the Civil Administration

After the Executive Order was issued in 1957, the High Commissioner was appointed by the President, rather than the Secretary of Defense. The U.S. administration of Okinawa remained unchanged, though; USCAR remained subordinate to the Secretary of Defense. Nevertheless, the State Department's responsibilities for providing diplomatic support for the military bases gradually expanded. In the process, USCAR was transformed, as federal employees were dispatched from the State Department, and other agencies, as well as the Defense Department.

Official USCAR records (USCAR REG 10-1) document the organization and its functions, redefining its purpose. REG 10-1 was originally issued to USCAR staff to clarify the role of each department. According to its mission statement, USCAR's purpose was as to put U.S. national policy into practice and to encourage voluntary support from the Ryukyuan people. It also stipulated that USCAR should support the Ryukyuans to:
 1. Encourage and strengthen democratic tendencies in governmental, economic and social institutions of the Ryukyu Islands.
 2. Encourage the development of an effective and responsible government, based on democratic principles and supported by a sound

financial structure, the administration of which considers, among other things, the cultural and educational ties between the Ryukyu Islands and Japan.
3. Assist the Ryukyuan people in achieving a viable economy which will permit the maintenance of a standard of living, education, public health, and public safety requisite to the achievement of the objectives noted above.
4. Assist the Government of the Ryukyu Islands and the Ryukyuan people in achieving those standards of living, education, public health, and public safety requisite to the achievement of the objectives above.[3]

The first point had been included in the original GARIOA appropriations for the Ryukyu Islands: to make the occupied areas politically stable in compliance with international laws and to ensure the safety of the occupying forces. The second point, however, permitted educational and cultural ties with Japan that had not been included in the earlier policy. The third and fourth points must be seen as attempts to legitimize the U.S. administration of Okinawa through prospective legislation such as Price Act, encouraging certain types of U.S. aid with Congressional approval. To realize these objectives, USCAR's role was redefined to nourish social conditions in the Ryukyu Islands, while supporting U.S. foreign policy and the military mission.[4]

The executive order defined the duties of the High Commissioner, but did not specify USCAR's mission, probably because USCAR's mission had been defined by a classified army directive. REG 10-1 was issued to reiterate the duties of USCAR employees within the Department of the Army but, crucially, it redefined USCAR's duties to include supporting the foreign relations objectives of the State Department, in addition to the military objectives of the Defense Department.

USCAR's mission had been originally specified in the fourteenth amendment of JCS 1231 and subsequent revisions. Although the wartime directive was not revoked by the Executive Order, USCAR's mission was significantly transformed.

## Public Affairs Department

As described in Chapter 1, Congress approved budgets for USCAR's information and education programs throughout the U.S. administration of Okinawa. The budget for these programs was not as large as economic aid, but were consistently appropriated.[5] This indicates that psychological factors were regarded as important for the administration, euphemistically described as "information and education programs" in USCAR records. The CIE was basically in charge of the congressional appropriations as well as the GARIOA counterpart fund. The Office of Public Information (OPI) succeeded the CIE in 1957 and the Public Affairs Department had succeeded the OPI by 1961. However, the Public Affairs Department continued to identify itself as the OPI, which was how it was known to the Okinawan people. For example, USCAR periodically published *Today's Ryukyus* or *Konnichi no Ryukyu*, identifying the publisher of the monthly magazine as the OPI until 1964.

According to personnel records, as of 1960, USCAR employed about 400 people including Ryukyuan assistants. The OPI employed the largest number 122, including one military officer, 12 civilians, and 109 Ryukyuans – the majority of Ryukyuans employed by USCAR.[6] Basically, a military officer took the highest position in each department as a liaison to the Ryukyu Command, and U.S. civilian employees supervised local Ryukyuan employees. On September 11, 1958, a "psy-ops war officer," Captain Sam L. Amato, came to the OPI to administer the Federal Foreign Fund Campaign of 1958.[7] Other OPI staff were civilians, called Department of the Army Civilians (DAC).

REG 10-1 defined the duties of the Public Affairs Department as follows: 1) to inform Ryukyuans of U.S. policies; 2) to conduct public relations to support U.S. military activities in the Ryukyu Islands; 3) to maintain friendly relationships between the U.S., Japanese, and the Ryukyuan media; and 4) to execute USIS programs in the Ryukyus in collaboration with USIS in Tokyo.[8]

These duties confirm that USCAR supported both the Defense and State Department missions. For example, while the second point explicitly refers to Defense objectives, the first and third points were State Department responsibilities. The fourth objective was to support the USIA. In fact, the Public Affairs Department received information policy guidelines from USIA and conducted mass media research sponsored by USIA. It also supported the $7^{th}$ Psychological Operations Group, as discussed later.

The Chief of the Information Division worked concurrently as chief information assistant to the High Commissioner, as well as the public relations adviser for the U.S. forces in Okinawa. He also reported on

Ryukyuan public opinion to Washington and proposed U.S. information policy for Okinawa. The Director of the Public Affairs Department worked to promote cultural exchange between Americans and Ryukyuans. The Public Affairs Department, as of 1969, consisted of three divisions: 1) the Information Division, 2) the Research and Analysis Division, 3) and the Cultural Affairs Division. There had previously been two more divisions: Publication and Audio-Visual; but they were merged into the Information Division.

## Information Division

The Information Division was responsible for disseminating information. The Chief of the Information Division frequently assumed the role of Acting Director of the Public Affairs Department during the Director's absence. The division was further separated into a Press Branch, a Publications Branch, and an Audio-Visual Branch. The Chief of the Information Division coordinated the three branches, prepared press conferences and drafted the High Commissioner's statements. He also planned events when necessary, including the public relations strategy for media events. His duties included promoting a favorable image of the United States and U.S.-Ryukyuan cultural exchange. For example, when USCAR conducted a public relations campaign for the Japanese Prime Minister's visit to Okinawa in August 1965, the Chief was responsible for planning the project, as described in the next chapter. In accordance with USIA's information policy guidelines, he was assigned to promote public diplomacy and was basically responsible to the State Department.

The Press Branch prepared USCAR press releases for the Okinawan press. The press releases were prepared both in English and Japanese to inform about U.S. activities in Okinawa. The Press Branch also wrote news releases, such as announcing the High Commissioner's statements. Photographers were attached to the Press Branch, providing USCAR photos for the Okinawan media, in part to ensure control of photo-shooting activities.

The Publications Branch supervised local publishers and printers. It owned a photo lab and filed film negative for the records. It produced biweekly photo news and posters as well as two monthly magazines, *Today's Ryukyus* and *Shurei no Hikari*. These periodicals were published to nourish favorable attitudes toward the United States.

Sponsored by USIS, *Today's Ryukyus* had initially been pitched at Okinawan intellectuals. Therefore, university professors and newspaper reporters were asked to contribute articles to the Japanese language publication, but some were translated into English for censorship purposes. An unstated objective of the publication might have been to monitor the thoughts of Okinawan intellectuals. For instance, Kazufumi Uechi, Editor-in-Chief, the *Okinawa Times* wrote an essay titled, "Loving Freedom" in the inaugural issue of *Today's Ryukyus*.

In summer 1958, a survey of readers was conducted. Respondents participated by returning a postcard attached to the August issue of *Today's Ryukyus*. A total of 251 responses were collected. Some answered positively but most responded negatively. Among the positive comments were, "I am impressed by the U.S. democracy," and others calmly criticized, "You will have a negative effect if you have too much propaganda."[9] At the time of the survey, the circulation of *Today's Ryukyus* was 15,000, distributed to junior high and high schools, the University of the Ryukyus, and Ryukyuan-U.S. Culture Centers. But the number of individual subscribers was as low as 102.

Another monthly magazine, *Shurei no Hikari*, sponsored by the 7th Psychological Operations Group, was pitched as the "Voice of the High Commissioner." The inaugural issue of 1959 was printed in the U.S. Army printing facility near Yokohama. It targeted average laborers rather than intellectuals. Although the Public Affairs Department produced the two magazines for ostensibly different purposes, the contents of each looked similar. As of 1969, *Shurei no Hikari* had a circulation of 92,000, while *Today's Ryukyus* had 22,000. Hence, the latter ceased publication at the end of 1969.[10] The Publication Branch also published calendars and almanacs featuring messages from the U.S. High Commissioner, mainly targeted at farmers and fishermen.[11]

The Audio-Visual Branch aimed to fulfill U.S. information policy objectives with radio and television programs and movies. The Branch maintained recording studios, produced audio-visual materials, and circulated American commercial and USIS movies for the Okinawan audience. Collaborating with U.S. Armed Forces Radio Network, it sponsored a series of local radio and television programs for local broadcasters. The Audio-Visual Branch maintained a close relationship with the 7th Psychological Operations Group and Far East Broadcasting Corporation (FEBC), a U.S. private broadcaster.

The Public Affairs Department also provided USIS radio programs to FEBC.[12]

## Research and Analysis Division

As the Information Division disseminated information, the Research and Analysis Division collected local information. The Research and Analysis Division monitored the Okinawan media daily, and collected local intelligence from open sources. It also sponsored public opinion and mass media research, reporting the results to Washington.

"News morgues," a collection of English translations of local news clips, comprise the major part of the records of USCAR's Public Affairs Department. As of 1969, although the Press Branch of the Information Division produced the news morgues, the Research and Analysis Division also engaged in news clipping activities. It monitored the Okinawan media, translated articles into English, and filed them in the news morgue. These news morgues were circulated among USCAR employees and other Americans to share what was happening in Okinawa. Some of the news morgues were sent to Washington for further examination.

The *Ryukyu Shimpo* and the *Okinawa Times* were monitored by the Research and Analysis Division. Sometimes every word of an article was translated, but at other times the article was only summarized in English. For example, reports of an incident in which a B-29 exploded after taking off for Vietnam from Kadena Airport in 1969, or Red Hat Operations removing poison gas from Okinawa prior to the reversion in the newspapers which supposedly were critical of the U.S. military bases were translated in detail and sent to Washington. They also carefully surveyed news reports of elections and political activities.

The division also conducted a series of research studies of public opinion and mass media. Since some of the reports are filed in the United States Information Agency records, the research was probably done in collaboration with USIS Tokyo and reported to the USIA in Washington.

In November 1969, the Division researched public opinion about Prime Minister Sato's visit to President Nixon and the U.S.-Japan joint statements. Perhaps the survey was intended to examine the Okinawan reactions to the possible reversion of Okinawa to Japan. Under the direction of USIS Tokyo, a Japanese research company collected samples in Okinawa. The report states that the research was done in Okinawa with no indication that USCAR was the research sponsor.[13]

The Division also conducted a series of research projects examining the mass media in Okinawa. The media audience research of 1951 was probably the first media research after World War II. The questions asked what radio programs they were listening to, or what newspapers or magazines they were reading. The 1951 survey was specifically prepared to investigate the radio listening habits of the local populations, suggesting that the U.S. public affairs planners intended to use radio broadcasts for promoting U.S. policy.

Globally, the Central Intelligence Agency has researched mass media, annually publishing a World Fact Book. In Okinawa, the Research and Analysis Division researched the Okinawan mass media and periodically reported it to Washington.[14]

Frank S. Tanabe, a Japanese-American civilian, worked for the division from 1959 to 1972. When Japan attacked Pearl Harbor, Tanabe was a student at the University of Washington. He was forced into a Japanese American internment camp at Tule Lake, California, and later volunteered to fight against Japan. Tanabe went to the India-Burma-China theatre after briefly studying Japanese in Minnesota. As a member of the Military Intelligence Services, Tanabe worked under General Joseph Stillwell and went to Tokyo after the war, where he worked as a translator at Allied Translators and Interpreters Service (ATIS) and as a reporter for International News Service (INS). He was transferred to Okinawa without a break.[15] In his memoirs, Tanabe wrote that he regularly attended informal meetings of the Okinawan press, commonly called "*Uechi* School," named after Kazufumi Uechi, president of the *Okinawa Times*.[16] Tanabe was briefly mentioned in the memoirs of Miyagi Etsujiro, a reporter for the *Stars and Stripes*.[17] Tanabe stayed in Okinawa until 1974 and lived in Hawaii afterwards. He died in Honolulu in 2012.

## Cultural Affairs Division

The Cultural Affairs Division managed five Cultural Centers in the Ryukyu Islands. Of the Public Affairs Department, the largest numbers of Ryukyuan employees belonged to the Cultural Affairs Division. As of 1960, seventy-nine local Ryukyuan employees were working under the management of two U.S. citizens. USCAR was tasked with promoting

American culture and politics and had established the Cultural Centers as "advertising posts" in the Ryukyus. The libraries had many English language books, but English books were not popular among the Okinawan people, so the numbers of Japanese books and movies were gradually increased.[18] Cultural Centers were originally called "Information Centers" but became "Cultural Centers" after John Rockefeller III proposed emphasizing the cultural exchange aspects rather than the political dimensions of U.S. information policy.[19]

Dr. Richard Sakakida, an American citizen of Japanese ancestry, was the manager of the Cultural Affairs Department. Another Japanese-American working for the Public Affairs Department was Sam Kitamura. When USCAR raised some concerns about the content of local newspapers and broadcasts, Kitamura was dispatched to "advise" the editors of the Okinawan press. The Public Affairs Department records contain memorandums which indicate that USCAR frequently supervised the local press.[20] Translations were always a problem. Supposedly speaking both Japanese and English languages, Kitamura was dispatched to confirm the Japanese translations. Clarence K. Tatekawa at the Comptroller Department and Ronald Ota at the Legal Affairs Department were also American citizens of Japanese ancestry working for USCAR. USCAR utilized them to interface between the different cultures.

When Okinawa was returned to Japan, the Ryukyuan employees working for Cultural Centers became librarians or civil servants in the cities of Naha, Nago, Ishikawa, Miyako and Ishigaki based on the provisions agreed upon between USCAR and the local mayors. The public libraries continued lending books and American films.

## Other U.S. Information Services

The USCAR Public Affairs Department contacted information officers representing other U.S. organizations stationed in Okinawa, acting as liaisons between the U.S. organizations and the Okinawan people. USCAR and Army records document the relationship between USCAR and other U.S. information services in Okinawa during the Cold War. Paul Caraway, High Commissioner during the Kennedy administration, clearly stated that several federal departments and agencies were incorporated into USCAR. The following organizations had some relationship with the Public Affairs Department: 1) USIS (United States Information

Service), 2) 7th Psychological Operations Group, 3) FEBC, the Far East Broadcasting Corporation, 4) VOA (Voice of America), 5) FBIS (Foreign Broadcasting Information Services) and 6) CSG (Composite Service Group). USCAR records also indicate that they shared some employees. These U.S. information services disseminated information from Okinawa to neighboring countries, while the Public Affairs Department was responsible for public relations directed at the Okinawan people. However, their duties were duplicated in some cases. The U.S. Army, Navy and Air Force in Okinawa each had their own information and public relations specialists as well.

Many information agencies were crammed into the small islands. The following sections discuss those directly related to USCAR.

**USIS**

The Public Affairs Department was part of USCAR but functioned as the USIS Okinawa branch. Reporting to the High Commissioner, the Department was not formally identified as "USIS Okinawa" but telexed messages from the United States Information Agency to the Department were addressed to "USIS Okinawa." In fact, it was an "open secret" that the Public Affairs Department was the USIS post in Okinawa. The Public Affairs Department records include reams of USIA guidelines and press releases received from Washington. It would be reasonable to conclude that the Department's Information Division operated under the directions of the USIA in accordance with policy which made the Secretary of State responsible for U.S. foreign information policy.[21]

The relationship between the USIA and USCAR was not visible before late 1965. However, the linkage became obvious after the Public Affairs Department collaborated with USIS Tokyo in the public relations campaign for the Japanese Prime Minister's visit to Okinawa in August 1965. Subsequently, USIA dispatched directors to the Department. For instance, USIA delegated Joseph S. Evans to be Director of the Public Affairs Department at the end of 1965. The former counselor for public relations at the U.S. Embassy in Tokyo had executed a series of surveys on the participants of Atoms for Peace exhibitions sponsored by USIS.[22] Monta L. Osborne, Evans' predecessor, came to Okinawa after working for the CIE in Tokyo and the CIE of the United Nations Commands during the Korean War. After completing his mission in Okinawa, Osborne was transferred to USIS Saigon during the Vietnam War. Robert Kays, Evans' successor, was also dispatched from USIA. In sum, the directors of the Public Affairs Department were assigned by USIA. According to the USCAR Comptroller Department records, USIA reimbursed USCAR for the directors' salaries.

### 7th Psychological Operations Group

The 7th Psychological Operations Group was a psychological warfare unit countering communist propaganda which was attached to the U.S. Army, Pacific, in Hawaii. In Okinawa, the Group comprised two detachments, the 15th, responsible for psychological operations, and the 14th, responsible for staff training. The broadcasting division of the 15th detachment broadcast Korean language radio programs on the Voice of United Nations Commands (VUNC).[23] The publications division printed psychological warfare leaflets during the Vietnam War.[24]

USCAR records also include propaganda analysis reports on thorough examination of radio broadcasts from the Soviet Union, China, North Korea, and Vietnam. The reports called these broadcasts "propaganda." Content analysis was one of the duties of the 7th Psychological Operations Group.[25] The Group was established in October 1965, reorganized from the U.S. Army Broadcasting and Visual Activities in the Pacific. As a black operations organization, the Group, headquartered in Camp Kinser, dispatched operatives to mainland Japan, Korea, Taiwan, and South Vietnam.[26]

While the 7th Psychological Operations Group targeted the Asia-Pacific regions, the Public Affairs Department of USCAR was responsible for public relations with the people of Okinawa. However, the Public Affairs Department moved into the area at Camp Kinser where the 7th Psychological Operations Group was headquartered. According to USCAR documents dated February 25, 1970, the Group "supported the High Commissioner's civil information programs," that is, the Public Affairs Department's remit, including the publication of *Shurei no Hikari* and almanacs, as well as the production of radio programs broadcast through the Far Eastern Broadcasting Service. As of February 1970, the purpose of the psychological programs was explicitly to prepare the Okinawan people psychologically for reversion to Japan, while maintaining the U.S. bases on Okinawa.[27]

The Group produced Japanese language television programs in "support" of USCAR. USCAR had sponsored a series of 15-minute programs titled "TV Weekly" for Ryukyu Broadcasting Corporation and 30-minute programs titled "Man, Time, Place" for Okinawa TV.[28] According to USCAR documents dated February 22, 1971, the 7th Psychological Operations Group had created these Japanese language programs, but was determined that the programs be credited as products of the Public Affairs Department, USCAR.[29] The Department's name was apparently used as a "cover" for the covert psychological operations.

Officially, the 7th Psychological Operations Group and the Public Affairs Department were separate organizations, but they shared staff for some activities. An USCAR spokesperson explained that the Audio-Visual Branch was financed by the 7th Psychological Operations Group because USCAR budgets were limited.[30] Of the Americans working at the Public Affairs Department, at least two were identified as members of the 7th Psychological Operations Group, Alexander Liosnoff and Sam Kitamura. Liosnoff formally identified himself as Chief of Information Division, Public Affairs Department, USCAR.

**Far East Broadcasting Corporation (FEBC)**

FEBC was a non-profit religious broadcasting organization established in Manila in 1948 to promote Christianity in China. Colonel John C. Broger, advisor to the Joint Chiefs of Staff, proposed "Militant Liberty" programs against communist propaganda through radio broadcasting. Under the Eisenhower administration, the Operations Coordinating Board dismissed Broger's proposal, but Admiral Arthur W. Radford, who chaired the Joint Chiefs of Staff, adopted the "Militant Liberty" programs and carried out the idea as "Project Action" in Japan and Latin America.[31] However, the details of "Project Action" are unknown.

In Okinawa, FEBC began broadcasting programs through KSAB in February 1958 in both Japanese and English. In March 1959, KSDX began broadcasting exclusively in Japanese. Another broadcasting organization, KSBU for China, was launched the same year.[32] The 7th Psychological Operations Group produced daily 50-minute radio news programs targeting the Okinawan people, which were provided to the FEBC channels. The Director of the Public Affairs Department coordinated the program policies for the Ryukyuan audience.[33] The Public Affairs

Department also provided USIS radio programs to KSDX, a Japanese broadcasting station of the FEBC.[34]

**Voice of America (VOA)**

USCAR records do not include many documents about Voice of America (VOA), so it is difficult to clarify their relationship. However, some documents indicate that the Public Affairs Department shared USIA information guides with VOA. USCAR records do, however, include the VOA radio reception report in the Far East, South East Asia and Oceania regions. The report indicates that the VOA transmitting station targeting the Korean Peninsula was located in Okinawa. If the abbreviation "OKI" in the report meant the radio waves were emitted from Okinawa, then English, Chinese, Korean, and Russian language radio channels were broadcast from Okinawa.[35]

George V. Allen, Director, USIA, proposed budgets for mass media services in foreign posts on February 24, 1958 at the Congressional hearing into the proposed budget to establish and maintain VOA transmitting stations in Okinawa and Manila.[36] According to Congressional records, at least five USIA employees had been dispatched to Okinawa as of 1957.[37] Also, the question of whether the U.S. would remove the VOA transmitters from Okinawa or not became an important issue prior to the reversion.[38]

**FBIS**

FBIS (Foreign Broadcasting Information Service) was established during World War II to receive foreign radio broadcast communications. Until 1945, Federal Communication Committee (FCC) had operated the service, but it was incorporated into the Central Intelligence Agency (CIA) when it was established in 1947, as an open source intelligence gathering organization. USCAR records include FBIS reports which were English translations of Okinawan press reports.[39] As described earlier, the Public Affairs Department monitored the Okinawan press and sent the English translations to Washington. These Public Affairs Department duties were almost the same as the FBIS missions. FBIS Daily Reports were open to the public and circulated among university libraries and newspaper offices.[40] As well as translations of the Okinawan press, FBIS Daily Reports also include English translations of radio news from North

Korea, China, Mongolia, Vietnam, Laos and other "communist" nations. The 7th Psychological Operations Group analyzed these radio broadcasts. In short, the FBIS routinely monitored radio communications and the 7th Psychological Operations Group analyzed the FBIS reports.

FBIS had posts around the world. FBIS Tokyo periodically monitored *Akahata* or Red Flag, the official newspaper of Japan Communist Party. It is not clear specifically what radio channels FBIS Okinawa monitored, but at least periodically, it monitored radio broadcasts from Moscow and Vietnam. According to testimony of the technical staff at FBIS Okinawa, there were Chinese, Indonesian, Vietnamese, Koreans and Russians working there, as well as fifty Ryukyuans.[41] In August 1965, the FBIS Daily Report carried a detailed translation of Prime Minister Sato's press conference when he visited Okinawa, as discussed in the next chapter.[42]

**Composite Service Group (CSG)**

According to USCAR records, the Composite Service Group (CSG) was introduced to Okinawa as a classified unit. USCAR documents do not provide details, but CSG deployed missions from Camp Chinen, in the southeastern part of Okinawa Island. According to an article in the *New York Times* of July 1, 1971, CSG was a paramilitary support asset under the CIA tasked with preparing for unconventional warfare, such as guerrilla warfare.[43]

The CIA financed the Civil Air Transport (CAT), a commercial air carrier established in Delaware by Claire L. Chennault, formerly a member of the 14th Air Force of the U.S. Army, who had fought against Japan in cooperation with Chinese Nationalist Chiang Kai-Shek. After World War II, CAT transported UNRRA (United Nations Relief and Rehabilitation Administration) aid supplies to Japan and Korea, as well as transporting CNRRA (Chinese National Relief and Rehabilitation Administration) aid to China. The latter was a special project of the Office of Policy Coordination, supporting the CIA's covert actions based on NSC 10/2.[44] Under the direction of Frank Wisner, OPC, and the State Department, CAT conducted psychological operations using information sources such as newspapers, leaflets, and radio as well as disseminating rumors. CAT airplanes carried media materials and human beings under the OPC guideline.[45] In Japan, flying as Air America, CAT carried a Japanese language version of the *Stars and Stripes* from Tachikawa

Air Base to Seoul under its "Booklift" contract with the CIA. Based in Wakkanai, Misawa, Iwakuni, Itazuke, Okinawa, Taiwan, and Hong Kong, Air America planes transported a variety of things such as goods, human beings and animals. From 1957, Air America was based in Camp Chinen, Okinawa, from where it supported Tibetan guerrillas resisting the Communist Chinese invasion.[46] Okinawan employees working at Camp Chinen testified that Chinese, Korean, and Vietnamese people were living in the highly restricted residential district called "Z area" of Camp Chinen.[47]

The treatment of these people from third nations became a problem prior to the reversion. It is not certain what they were doing in Okinawa, but radio broadcasting would have required third country nationals who could speak the languages of the target populations. There is some evidence that a Russian language radio station called Radio Baikal broadcast from Okinawa.[48]

Many things remain uncertain, but it is clear from the USCAR records that Okinawa was an important base for U.S. foreign information activities, both overt and covert. The Public Affairs Department served as a liaison with these information services.

## Stateless Psychological Warriors

Alexander Liosnoff was a psychological warrior at the Public Affairs Department of USCAR. He arrived in Okinawa in 1957 and took a position at the Publication Branch, Office of Public Information. He returned to the United States when Okinawa was returned to Japan. Liosnoff's personal papers are filed at the Hoover Institution, Stanford University. This remaining section explores the mysterious profile of a "psy-ops" specialist based on oral history interviews and other documentation.

Liosnoff was born in 1920 in Qiqihar near Harbin, in northeastern China, near the Russian border. His parents were Russians of Jewish ancestry. He went to the American high school in Shanghai and studied journalism at the University of Missouri from 1939. During World War II, he was drafted and returned to Asia, initially to the Philippines. He told an interviewer from the Hoover Archives that he was not assigned to important missions because he was "stateless" since his parents were defectors from Russia. After the war, he became a radio announcer in Oakland, California, but when the Korean War began he was re-enlisted.

After FBI interviews, Liosnoff returned to Asia for the third time. He began his career as a psychological warrior in Tokyo, producing radio programs for the Voice of United Nations Commands, targeting Korea and China. He wrote radio scripts, interviewed prisoners of war, and recorded radio interviews.[49] Liosnoff wrote the script for a program titled "Behind the Iron Curtain," which was broadcast on the VUNC on June 5, 1952. It depicted the Romanian situation under Russian influence, stoking fears of communism. Liosnoff also wrote a series of radio scripts for the Weekly News Review.[50]

During the final days of 1950, Liosnoff went to Pusan, Cheju, and Koje Islands, in the southern part of the Korean Peninsula, and broadcast a series of psychological operations programs with Korean-American assistants. Liosnoff interviewed prisoners of war in Koje Island and broadcast the recordings on the VUNC.[51] Although he claimed that he was not fluent in Russian language, according to the FBIS reports of Radio Moscow and other Russian broadcasting stations, he had analyzed Soviet propaganda from 1953 to 1954.[52] In 1954, Liosnoff was Chief of the News Room, Army Psychological Warfare Detachment, 8239th Army Unit.[53]

In 1957 Liosnoff was assigned to USCAR in Okinawa. He launched *Today's Ryukyu*, a Japanese language monthly magazine because, he said, there were no appropriate public relations organs in Okinawa.[54] It is not certain that he was continuously engaged in the VUNC broadcasting during his stay in Okinawa, but he identified himself as a radio announcer in his job descriptions. Furthermore, a series of letters from Korean friends indicates that he had continuing connections with the "Korean radio people" who were supposedly "stateless" under the U.S. administration of Okinawa.[55]

Liosnoff became the last director of the Public Affairs Department prior to the reversion. He attended the final ceremony to dismiss USCAR on May 10, 1972. The last High Commissioner, James B. Lampert, and the last civil administrator, Robert Fearey, also attended the ceremony to mark the completion of USCAR's mission.[56] The psychological warrior informed the oral historian who interviewed him that it was his mission to close USCAR and return Okinawa to Japan.

Later Liosnoff lived in San Francisco and worked at the Bank of America. He donated his personal documents to the Hoover Institute in 2005, stating that he was deeply concerned about the future of the United

States, which had started yet another war in Iraq; another conflict in a different culture. Liosnoff died at his home in Reno, Nevada, in 2008.

## Chapter Summary

The U.S. foreign information policy toward Okinawa gradually transformed into a softer public relations strategy after the Executive Order was issued in 1957, although the Department of Defense and Joint Chiefs of Staff maintained the same military objectives. The U.S. regarded Okinawa as integral to U.S.-Japan relations and exerted careful control of the Okinawan press. The Public Affairs Department monitored Okinawan newspapers, public opinion, and anti-American sentiments. It was basically an anti-communist campaign, which would remain the hallmark of U.S. foreign relations and information policy throughout the Cold War. Many aspects remain uncertain, but it is clear that Okinawa was an important information gathering and dissemination base for the United States in the early Cold War period. Although previous studies have discussed the hard power of U.S. militarism, the soft power policy must be considered to have been an important factor in maintaining U.S. administrative authority over Okinawa.

# 9 U.S.–Japan's Operation Friendship

## Introduction

The preceding chapter discussed the role of USCAR's Public Affairs Department. As a case study of public relations activities, this chapter analyzes Operation Friendship, USCAR's public relations campaign for Prime Minister Eisaku Sato's visit to Okinawa in 1965. USCAR considered the first postwar visit of a Japanese prime minister to Okinawa to be an important media event and carefully prepared for it in coordination with Washington and Tokyo. This event and the associated propaganda campaign was named Operation Friendship.

Forty-six years later, after an earthquake struck northeastern Japan in March 2011, the U.S. forces stationed in Japan launched a disaster relief operation, also named Operation Tomodachi (Operation Friendship) in Japanese, appealing to the continuing close relationship between the U.S. and Japan.

Previous research has focused on U.S.-Japan foreign relations and the negotiations over the return of Okinawa to Japan.[1] Takuma Nakajima established that a group of Japanese Cabinet assistants and diplomats had prepared Prime Minister Sato's speech in Okinawa,[2] in which he stated, "the post-war period is not over for Japan unless and until Okinawa's return to its home country is realized."[3] Sato's famous speech stimulated Japanese nationalist sentiments about the reversion. Yoshiharu Fukui argues that Sato's firsthand experience of Okinawa motivated him to push for the reversion.[4]

However, the U.S. perspective on the Prime Minister's visit has received less research attention. While the Okinawa reversion was a political issue appealing to Japanese nationalism, Nicholas E. Sarantakes described it as simply a matter of bureaucracy for the United States.[5] The Japanese mass media reported Okinawa problems daily, but the American media rarely reported them. Accordingly, the American public had very little idea of what was happening to the Okinawan people under the U.S. administration. This chapter reveals that the Prime Minister's visit was a rare case reported by the U.S. media, which had important effects on the Washington bureaucracy.

## Prime Minister Sato's Visit as a Media Event

On August 19, 1965, Prime Minister Eisaku Sato landed at Naha Airport and stepped down the stairway of a Japanese national flagship plane which had been escorted by the U.S. military aircraft, "Friendship." Five hundred Okinawans welcomed Sato, along with a U.S. military marching band and an honor guard. Reporters and television crews had been waiting at the scene.[6] Sato made a short speech at the airport from a carefully prepared script, where he proclaimed that "the post-war period is not over for Japan unless and until Okinawa's return to its home country is realized."[7]

Both the U.S. and Japanese sides had strategically prepared the media event as an act of public diplomacy. The media event was named Operation Friendship after the U.S. aircraft escorting the Japanese national flagship carrier.[8] Although the U.S.'s approach was rather defensive, its accession to the Japanese premier's visit to Okinawa marked a turning point toward the reversion. The U.S. public relations planners originally had sought to present an image of the Japanese government not only acknowledging the U.S. administration of Okinawa, but actually authorizing the U.S. military presence. In contrast, the Japanese took advantage of the opportunity to call for reversion, appealing to both Japanese public opinion and the U.S. government.

Generally, media events are meticulously planned, to control the imagery presented in the mass media. Dayan and Katz contend that a properly executed media event can have a coronation effect for the covered subject. Television coverage, in particular, can elevate the status of a subject presented to the mass audience. To this end, diplomatic protocols are usually planned prior to media events, seeking the best outcomes for public relations.[9]

For example, when MacArthur returned to the U.S. and triumphantly joined the parade after his Japanese mission was completed, the television coverage only showed those attendees who passionately welcomed the old general.[10] A pilot study of the media event indicated that an enthusiastic image was created, despite the fact that the majority of onlookers at the parade had looked on passively.

USCAR had experience with a similar parade, "Operation High-Switch," welcoming the new High Commissioner, Lieutenant General Paul Caraway, upon his appointment in 1961, attempting to achieve a favorable image.[11] Television broadcasting had begun in Okinawa in 1959. A microwave connection to Okinawa Island was established in time for Japanese television to broadcast the Tokyo Olympics in September 1964.[12]

Seeking positive effects from the television coverage of Sato's visit, the five hundred participants at Naha Airport had been carefully selected from among Okinawans who were not critical of the U.S. administration. Twelve hundred people attended a lunch at Kokueikan movie theatre in Naha City. They were probably also selected to promote a favorable image. Prime Minister Sato had also carefully prepared for the media event. Being conscious of the television camera, Sato proudly announced that the Japanese microwave connection would reach the southernmost islands of Miyako and Ishigaki, so children there could soon watch Japanese programs, too.[13]

For the U.S. public relations planners, however, it was difficult to control this media event because the diplomatic situation was wrought with political complications: Okinawa remained under the U.S. administration, although Japan held residual sovereignty.

## Kennedy's New Policy

The Kennedy administration decided that the State Department should lead U.S. foreign relations, rather than Defense or the CIA. During this period, U.S. policy toward Japan was determined by senior staff of the State and Defense Departments and submitted to the Secretaries of State and Defense for approval. In Washington, Secretary of State Dean Rusk and Secretary of Defense Robert McNamara were co-responsible for coordinating Japan policy. In Japan, the U.S. Ambassador to Japan and the High Commissioner began discussions about the Okinawa problems.

Edwin O. Reischauer, Ambassador to Japan during the Kennedy administration, warned that the Okinawa problem was in a critical phase which could seriously undermine the U.S.-Japan relationship. Throughout his tenure from 1961 to 1966, Reischauer urged the State and Defense

Departments to move toward a solution. U.S. economic aid to Japan had been terminated in 1961 and military aid in 1964.[14] Meanwhile, Japanese aid to Okinawa had begun in 1962. The U.S.-Japan Consultative Committee was established in Tokyo to coordinate Japan's aid to Okinawa.[15] Reischauer was strongly of the view that the U.S. should return Okinawa to Japan, while maintaining the military bases in Okinawa.[16]

Meanwhile, Okinawan public opinion continued to demand a popular vote for the Chief Executive or their Governor. Chief Executive Seisaku Ota, appointed by the U.S. administration, had resigned in June 1964 and the Ryukyuans were without local leadership for a while, because no one volunteered to be the local face of the military regime. When Lieutenant General Albert Watson was appointed High Commissioner later that year, Robert Fearey and other Japan specialists at the State Department phoned Watson, a former soldier who had participated in the Battle of Okinawa, and lectured him about the Okinawa problem. The State Department asked for his support in foreign relations matters.[17] Watson visited Reischauer in Tokyo, promised his cooperation to the Ambassador, and went to Okinawa. In October, Watson finally, after an overnight discussion, persuaded Seiho Matsuoka to resume the position that he had once turned down and appointed him as Chief Executive. Matsuoka had been performing a liaison-like role between USCAR and Government of the Ryukyus but submitted his letter of resignation to the former High Commissioner as USCAR was too coercive. However, Watson regarded the U.S.-educated leader to be necessary for the U.S. administration of Okinawa. Watson's mission in Okinawa was to patiently persuade the Okinawan political leaders to accept U.S. military objectives.

On January 12, 1965, Prime Minister Sato visited President Johnson in Washington and requested permission to visit Okinawa. Johnson ordered the U.S.-Japan Consultative Committee to discuss the matter,[18] effectively expanding its functions, originally limited to economic matters, to diplomatic matters as well. A diplomatic memorandum was exchanged on April 2, acceding to the Prime Minister's request.[19] Thus, the U.S. Embassy in Tokyo commenced preparing Prime Minister Sato's visit to Okinawa under the direction of the State Department.

The Kennedy administration, had appointed Shannon McCune as the first Civil Administrator in 1962 on the recommendation of the Kaysen Task Force. The Joint Chiefs of Staff accepted the recommendations and JCS 1231 was revised to incorporate the 50$^{th}$ amendment, JCS 1231/50, which permitted civilians appointed as civil administrators to be seconded for psychological warfare purposes.[20] The military had finally approved civilians participation in the "psy-war."

The second civilian administrator, Gerald Warner, arrived in Okinawa on February 6, 1965. Warner launched a political campaign to influence attitudes toward Americans in preparation for the forthcoming election of Ryukyuan Legislature, scheduled for November 1965. On April 2, Warner handed a $455,000 U.S. check to Chief Executive Matsuoka as a U.S. gift for Ryukyuan education, welfare, security and the construction of water pipelines.[21] In return, Warner periodically received political situation reports from Matsuoka, indicating how candidates were polling in each electoral district based on research conducted by the Ryukyuan Legislature. Warner submitted these reports to Washington.

In Washington, covert action for the November election was discussed with the NSC in July. Reischauer returned to Washington and advised that direct political action in Okinawa would be dangerous, arguing that the U.S. would do better to support Japanese conservative politicians to intervene in the Ryukyuan election. John N. Steadman, Assistant Secretary of Defense for International Affairs, disagreed, insisting on directly supporting conservative Okinawan politicians. Covert action was discussed on July 22 at the 303 Committee,[22] which had been established by the NSC to ensure that CIA covert operations complied with U.S. national policies. The Committee's records are classified, and thus not available to researchers. Operation Friendship was an overt operation undertaken concurrently on the islands.

## The Secretary of State's Initiative

The State Department took the initiative to prepare for the Japanese prime minister's visit to Okinawa. On June 22, Secretary of State Dean Rusk sent a telegram co-signed by the Secretary of Defense to the U.S. Embassy in Tokyo and the Consulate General in Naha instructing them to prepare for the first diplomatic event in Okinawa. The message read that the State and Defense Departments would jointly support Sato's visit to Okinawa and the Embassy was to arrange the date and timing in consultation with the Japanese government and High Commissioner. The Secretaries' message ordered that details be reported to Washington. Further, the message explained that the purpose of the prime minister's visit to Okinawa was to promote a favorable image of the U.S.-Japan alliance and the importance of the U.S. military bases.[23]

On June 29, the Embassy discussed the schedule with the Prime Minister's Office and decided that August 19 to 21 would be convenient for all parties. On this occasion, Sato's representatives told Reischauer that Sato would like to discuss Japanese aid to Okinawa for education and social welfare. Although the provision of education and social welfare in Okinawa was a responsibility of the U.S. administration according to its own policies, the schools and hospitals remained poor.

Japan's Foreign Ministry requested a joint press conference scheduled on July 3 with the U.S. Embassy, but the Embassy was not able to arrange permission from the Secretary of the State in time, due to being given only short notice. As a result, Sato's announcement of his visit to Okinawa was made with no representative of the American perspective.[24] On July 9 the Embassy received a message from Washington, stating that Rusk was disappointed that the U.S. and Japan had not jointly announced the event. The Secretary directed the Embassy to arrange for a joint announcement that the U.S. High Commissioner had formally invited the Japanese prime minister to Okinawa.[25]

In Okinawa, Watson and USCAR were reluctant to respond to the message, although it had been co-signed by the Secretary of Defense. Edward O. Freimath, Director of USCAR's General Affairs Department, coordinated the schedule with the Embassy.[26] In early July, USCAR established a Control Committee for the forthcoming event. Russell Stevens, information officer for the Ryukyu Command, chaired the Committee. Eight subcommittees were established, including public relations. Alexander Liosnoff chaired the public relations subcommittee and was thus responsible for coordinating public relations activities with Tokyo and Washington. He thought that meetings between USCAR, the Embassy and the U.S. forces in Japan were required as early as possible.[27]

The public relations objectives for Sato's visit were to create the impression that the Japanese government accepted the U.S. administration of Okinawa and that the administration was legitimate – not due to its victory in war, but by the terms of the Peace Treaty.[28] Although Rusk requested that Japanese aid to Vietnam be discussed, Liosnoff did not think that was a good idea, believing it would have a negative effect on Okinawan perceptions of the U.S.

On July 5, Watson sent a telegram to Tokyo and the Department of the Army about his logistical concerns. As High Commissioner, Watson promised to do his best for the prime minister's visit and asked to pay for Sato's hotel rooms, pointing out that it would look better for Sato to stay in a civilian hotel rather than in U.S. military facilities.[29] The High Commissioner required Washington's permission to use the diplomatic budget. As we have seen, Congress appropriated huge budgets for the U.S. forces, but the budget for USCAR was separate and limited. On July 22, the Department of the Army responded that it would pay for civilian accommodation for Sato and other Japanese visitors.[30]

## Public Relations with the Press

Problems were piling up in public relations with the press.

First, what should be the High Commissioner's statement? The July 12 draft read that the "High Commissioner, representing the U.S. government," will welcome the Japanese prime minister. But the July 14 draft stated that Sato would visit Okinawa following a formal invitation from the High Commissioner.[31] The problem here was that if the High Commissioner were to extend the invitation as the representative of the U.S. government, he would appear to have equal or higher status than the Prime Minister of Japan. But this was not the case, so the phrase "representing the U.S. government" was not used in the final version.

Another question was whether the Japanese flag should be hoisted or not. Under the U.S. administration, Civil Affairs Ordinance No. 144 had prohibited hoisting the Japanese flag at public buildings. The chairman of the Control Committee, Russell Stevens, asked Eisenstein, Director of USCAR's Legal Affairs Department, for an interpretation of the ordinance. Civil Administrator Gerald Warner insisted that the High Commissioner should decide on the Japanese flag issue. Ultimately, the question was sent to Washington, where the Joint Chiefs decided that Japanese flag could be flown during the three days of Sato's visit. Watson received the decision on July 23.[32]

How to manage the press was another issue. The Public Relations Subcommittee held a meeting with Okinawan media representatives to provide direction for their coverage. The five attendees included two from the *Okinawa Times*, two from the *Ryukyu Shimpo* and one from Ryukyu

Broadcasting Corporation (RBC). According to an USCAR memorandum, the press agreed to report on Sato's visit respectfully, as befitted a Head of State, even though local public opinion about the visit might vary. Shui Ikemiyagi, President of the *Ryukyu Shimpo*, responded that his employees fully understood the situation. After the meeting, Liosnoff reported to Washington that the Okinawan press understood USCAR's policy from years of daily supervision.[33]

Kiyoshi Kabira, RBC, asked USCAR for permission to conduct a 30-minute interview with Prime Minister Sato and High Commissioner Watson. The Public Affairs Department agreed, but not as an exclusive; the RBC could conduct the interview as a representative of the other press on the condition that USCAR would review the scripts. The Public Affairs Department, High Commissioner, and the Embassy each carefully examined the questions prior to the interview.[34]

The press was kept under USCAR's strict control. The Public Relations Subcommittee established a Joint Press Center at the Ryukyu Tokyu Hotel, where Sato was staying. The Control Committee planned to supervise the event with many escort personnel. Only pre-approved newspaper reporters and television crews were permitted to cover the media event.[35] Photography was strictly monitored. Watson demanded that Sato's press conference be scheduled for the second day, not the first. The later timing, he thought, might give him an opportunity to develop some degree of friendship with Sato after the first night's reception.[36]

## Prime Minister's Speech Censored

The joint announcement of Sato's itinerary was prepared in Tokyo. The Chief Secretary at the U.S. Embassy was John K. Emerson, former second secretary to General Joseph Stillwell in the Indo-Burma-China theatre during World War II.[37] Emerson was in charge of preparations for the visit as Reischauer was in the U.S. at the time. On July 13, Emerson informed the Japanese that Secretary Rusk was disappointed by Japan's independent announcement of the prime minister's visit without U.S. approval. The Japanese responded by proposing a joint announcement of Sato's itinerary on July 28 after the election of the Tokyo Metropolitan Government, concerned about negative repercussions if the announcement preceded the election. The Embassy in Tokyo again sought approval from the Secretary in Washington and the High Commissioner in Okinawa.

During Sato's stay in Okinawa, the Japanese asked the Embassy for permission to publicly announce the following three points: first, Japan shall provide financial aid for education in Okinawa; second, Japan shall aid the agricultural and fishing industry through the provision of a long-term low-interest loan program; third, the ordinance prohibiting the Japanese flag shall be revoked. The embassy did not immediately concede to these requests but all three materialized after the prime minister's visit. The Prime Minister's Office also requested permission for Sato's government airplane to land at Naha (civilian) Airport rather than at the U.S. (military) Air Base. On July 22, Emerson finalized Sato's itinerary and sent it to Watson. The U.S-Japan joint press conference was scheduled for noon on July 28 as Sato's representatives had requested.[38] Thus, the preparation proceeded as the Japanese side negotiated with the Embassy in Tokyo. The Embassy and Japan's Foreign Ministry seem to have agreed that the Japanese government should increase education and economic aid to Okinawa. The State Department would have embraced an opportunity to reduce the U.S. budget for Okinawa, but USCAR and the Defense Department were concerned about the Japanese government expanding its influence in Okinawa.

Following the announcement, however, Japan's opposition parties in the Diet criticized Sato, pointing out that U.S. B-29 aircraft were using Okinawan airfields as a base for bombing raids on Vietnam. On July 30, Prime Minister Sato replied that Japan supported the U.S. involvement in Vietnam. Sato had secretly promised President Johnson that Japan would provide medical services, transportation of supplies, and dam construction in South Vietnam.[39]

On August 1, U.S. and Japanese public relations professionals visited Okinawa. Public relations staff from USIS Tokyo and the U.S. Forces Japan arrived at Naha Air Base and met with the USCAR public relations staff. On the same day, Japanese public relations staff from the Prime Minister's Office and Foreign Ministry arrived at Naha Airport and held a meeting at the Japanese Government Liaison Office (JGLO) in Naha.[40]

On August 13, the Department of the Army decided to exclude reporters from communist media such as the Soviet Tass News Agency and *Akahata* (Red Flag), the official newspaper of Japan's Communist Party. On

August 16, though, the High Commissioner's Office made an exception for reporters from Japan's Socialist Party, considering the forthcoming election for the Ryukyu Legislature in November.

On August 17, a draft of Prime Minister Sato's statement was translated into English at the Foreign Ministry of Japan and sent to the State Department for approval. "My Fellow Citizens," Sato's statement began, addressing the Okinawan people as Japanese citizens "the post-war period is not over for Japan unless and until Okinawa's return to its home country is realized."

Rusk strongly reacted to this phrase and directed Emerson to revise the scripts, claiming that this statement directly contradicted the agreed purpose of the U.S.-Japan joint announcement. Rusk ordered Emerson to pressure the Japanese government not to undermine or diminish the U.S. status in the Ryukyus. He did not, however, specify which phrases needed to be revised.[41] Emerson notified the Japanese Foreign Ministry of Rusk's message, requesting further revisions. As the revised scripts were sent to Rusk again, Emerson opined that Sato's speech would say nothing disrespectful towards the U.S., but also noted that cancelling the visit at this point would negatively impact Japanese public opinion.[42]

On August 19, Sato read the prepared statement at the Naha Airport immediately after his landing. "My Fellow Citizens. As my long cherished desire to visit Okinawa is here realized, and deeply moved by seeing you all here, I am at loss to find fitting words to express my feelings... I am most well aware that the post-war period is not over for Japan unless and until Okinawa's return to its home country is realized," as per the original draft of the speech. He continued, "this is one belief that all the people on the mainland share. I have decided to make this visit above all to convey to you this thought of ours on behalf of the people living on mainland Japan."[43] English and Japanese press releases were handed out to the press. According to Public Affairs Department records, sixty reporters and television crews came to Okinawa from Tokyo along with a group of Japanese conservative politicians and government staff. Sato's caravan was carefully escorted by USCAR employees from the airport to a lunch reception at the Kokueikan movie theatre in Naha. Prime Minister Sato met High Commissioner Watson and Chief Executive Matsuoka in the USCAR building. After the lunch, the group visited war memorials in the southernmost part of Okinawa Island and participated in a U.S. Force sponsored dinner reception at Kadena Air Base.[44]

## Okinawa in U.S. News

On the evening of August 19, there was public turmoil in Okinawa. The public relations committee was not expecting it. Thousands of demonstrators surrounded Sato's hotel, demanding to see the prime minister in person. The demonstrators clashed with local police. Sixteen were arrested, including six university students. According to Watson's letter to the Department of the Army that day, "the politically important" were not among those arrested. Since the demonstrators were not dispersed until after midnight, Sato was unable to reach his hotel in Naha, and stayed at facilities inside Kadena Air Base. The Japanese Prime Minister did not directly address the Okinawan demonstrators, whom he had called "My fellow citizens." After negotiations between a representative of the Prime Minister's Office and the leaders of the demonstration, the demonstrators quietly dispersed. Details of the negotiations are unknown.[45]

The demonstration was a goldmine for the newspaper reporters who had packed into the press center. The press generally favors the unexpected to the peaceful proceedings of diplomatic protocols. While Japanese mass media reported Sato's visit to Okinawa in detail, the U.S. media, which rarely reported on Okinawa, made the turmoil into a small piece of news.

The *New York Times*, *Washington Post*, and Associated Press had come to Okinawa to cover the diplomatic event, along with television crews from ABC and NBC. The *New York Times* reported Sato's visit on August 19 and 20. On the first day, the *Times* not only quoted Sato's prepared statement, but also reported that the Okinawan demonstrators were unable to get into Naha Airport.[46] The next day, the *Times* reported the protests in which the local police arrested some demonstrators. However, the AP news service was perhaps most influential in the United States. The report quoted in many local newspapers described the demonstrators as "leftists" or "mobs." Quoting the AP news, the *Los Angeles Times* headlined: "Sato protected by US as Okinawa riot flares."[47]

No follow-up stories were reported, but the American public had finally been informed of the Okinawa problems, which had been long discussed within the closed circles of Washington bureaucracy. USCAR public relations aimed to present a favorable image of the U.S-Japan alliance, but failed. Sato's visit highlighted some of the problems with the U.S. administration of Okinawa. For the Okinawan demonstrators, the publicity was quite successful.

After Sato's caravan returned to Tokyo, Liosnoff reported that the main problem had been that the joint press center was unable to receive information at night.[48] Although the public relations professionals had intended to control the dissemination of information through the press center, Watson and the USCAR event organizers had not properly understood this, and did not send them the information.

Douglas Kellner is critical of Dayan and Katz's media event theory, arguing that media events are frequently disturbed by unexpected happenings or incidents. Kellner called these unpredictable incidents "media spectacles,"[49] and notes that the press generally prefers to report media spectacles rather than the carefully planned event by public relations people. The Okinawan demonstration was such a media spectacle. USCAR had attempted to control the public sphere in the small islands, but the fact that there were demonstrations on the islands indicates that USCAR was not able to control public opinion and the American press.

## Internal Effects on Washington Bureaucracy

Meanwhile, Sato's visit to Okinawa had internal effects on the Washington political elites who had planned the event. As described earlier, the Departments of State and Defense had never agreed upon the Okinawa policy. However, the Embassy and USCAR cooperated on Operation Friendship and began to develop a closer relationship. Liosnoff wrote to Reischauer that USCAR could build a closer relationship with Tokyo through Operation Friendship. Reischauer, in turn, advised Washington that the most fruitful result of Sato's visit was the development of a cooperative relationship between the Embassy and USCAR.[50]

Various changes became apparent the following month as the Japanese government formalized its proposal for economic aid to Okinawa for the coming fiscal year. The Embassy received the fifty-page proposal and forwarded it to the State Department unchanged. The Embassy and State Department both supported the proposal, as it would reduce the financial burden on the U.S. Meanwhile, Watson had requested additional security units be deployed to Okinawa in anticipation of further agitation by "leftist mobs." The Army complied, while continuing to monitor the reversion movement.[51] Warner continued to report the political polling data to Washington. On November 14, the election for the Ryukyu Legislature was held and the pro-U.S. conservative party won the majority.

Operation Friendship was not as beneficial as the public relations people had anticipated. It did not emphasize the positive aspects of U.S.-Japan friendship, but rather highlighted the fact that there were conflicts in Okinawa. It did, however, have important internal effects on the Washington bureaucracy, forcing them to recognize the Okinawa problem.

Dayan and Katz argued that a media event has both external and internal effects. In general, media events are aimed at the impact on the audience – the external effects – but Dayan and Katz contended that organizers are also affected by the outcome of the event – the internal effects.[52] Washington policy makers were affected by the unanticipated turn of events which thrust the latent problems in Okinawa into the public sphere. An interdepartmental Ryukyu working group was established in Washington, which produced a report titled "Our Ryukyu Base" in June 1966.The report reiterated that Okinawa belonged to the U.S., but another research project to examine the merits of reversion began in the same month.[53]

Prime Minister Sato and President Johnson discussed the Okinawa reversion in November 1967 but did not reached a conclusion. Sato insisted the return was contingent upon the removal of nuclear weapons from Okinawa but Johnson did not accept this condition, insisting that the U.S. needs to use the bases freely without consulting prior to their military actions. The diplomatic negotiation regarding the Okinawa reversion was stuck.

## Psychological Operations toward the Reversion

President Nixon succeeded Johnson in January 1969. In November 1969, President Nixon and Prime Minister Sato announced their agreement regarding the reversion of Okinawa. The joint statement said that "the war in Viet-Nam would be concluded before the return of administrative rights over Okinawa to Japan." The United States and Japan agreed "to expedite the consultations with a view to accomplishing the reversion during 1972" and Japan agreed to "gradually assume responsibility for the immediate defense of Okinawa as part of Japan's defense effort." After the announcement, the Public Affairs Department of USCAR started a psychological operation toward the reversion supported by the 7th Psychological Operation Group. During the pre-reversion period, although the USCAR annual budget decreased, financial support from the U.S. remained necessary. USCAR's psychological operations were called "civil information programs" under the direction of the High Commissioner's office. The civil information programs were sponsored by the 7th Psychological Operation Group, but broadcast through Okinawan commercial television stations, and credited to "Public Affairs Department, USCAR."[54]

The style is quite similar to the CIA covert operations in which the U.S. government funded the production of television programs by local corporations or private professionals. Some programs overtly acknowledged U.S. sponsorship, but others did not, to avoid being dismissed as American propaganda. The CIA conducted these operations through corporations and religious organizations in Asia and Africa.[55] It is not certain whether the televised civil information programs were CIA operations or not, but documents exist which indicate that some funding was transferred from the CIA budgets to the Department of the Army.

According to a memorandum on February 25, 1970, there were psychological operations aimed at preparing the Okinawan people for the forthcoming reversion to Japan. To this end, the psychological operations propagated fear of communism and sought to foster an understanding of the benefits of the U.S. military presence in Okinawa. USCAR produced a series of television programs in cooperation with the 7th Psychological Operation Group.[56] In February 1971, the Public Affairs Action Committee was established to pursue an additional objective: to prepare the people for Japan's Defense Forces coming to Okinawa.

According to USCAR records, the 7th Psychological Operation Group produced a series of 15-minute radio programs, which were broadcast through Radio Okinawa, Far Eastern Broadcasting Service and other local stations. At the same time, a series of 15-minute programs for Ryukyu Broadcasting (KSAR-TV) and another series of 30-minute programs for TV Okinawa (KSDW-TV) were broadcast.[57]

At the completion of these operations, USCAR was quietly dismissed on May 10, 1972. High Commissioner James B. Lampert, Civil Administrator Robert Fearey and the last director of the Public Affairs Department, Alexander Liosnoff, attended the ceremony. The Director of the Administration Office read the Deactivation Order to the U.S. Civil Administration and unveiled an USCAR Commemorative Plaque.[58] The area administration unit suspended its operation. That was the full extent of the U.S.'s acknowledgement of the reversion of Okinawa.

On May 15, 1972, the Japanese government lavishly celebrated the reversion at the Budokan, a martial arts stadium in Tokyo. Prime Minister Sato announced that Okinawa had returned to Japan and Emperor Hirohito followed with a message of joy, stating his appreciation of "the hardship and sacrifice the people of Okinawa Prefecture have taken during and after the previous war." The Japanese traditional "Banzai" was shouted three times in chorus. In Naha, another ceremony was held, and the Okinawa Prefectural Government was established. Chobyo Yara, the last of the elected Chief Executive's became the Governor of Okinawa Prefecture. Japan's Defense Forces were deployed to Okinawa. The United States viewed the reversion as the "transfer of civil administration"[59] from USCAR to the Japanese government, which relieved the U.S. of the financial burdens of administering Okinawa, while retaining the military bases as before.

Okinawa returned to Japan but many crimes committed by military and civilian service men affiliated to the U.S. military bases in Okinawa have not been prosecuted by Japanese courts. In 1995, three Marine service men raped a twelve-year old elementary school girl but the local police was not able to arrest those men immediately because of the Status of Force Agreement (SOFA) ratified in 1960 between the United States and Japan that had permitted extra-territorial judicial rights for the U.S. military personnel stationed in Japan. In 2016, a U.S. civilian contract worker affiliated to the base murdered a twenty-year old woman jogging on a street in Okinawa. A provision of the Status of Force Agreement was slightly modified after Japanese Foreign Minister Fumio Kishida protested Caroline Kennedy, U.S. Ambassador to Japan at the time. Okinawa Prefectural Governor Takeshi Onaga petitioned a drastic modification of the SOFA, but the dominant bargaining position of the U.S. Force stationed in Japan and Okinawa has not changed.

## Chapter Summary

This chapter portrayed the Japanese Prime Minister's visit to Okinawa as a media event and examined the internal and external effects on U.S.-Japan relations, the U.S. administration of Okinawa and the Okinawa reversion. Although the media event did not produce the effects the public relations planners had anticipated, it had unexpected effects on the policy making process in Washington, bringing the Okinawa problems to the fore.

# Conclusion
## Militarism Betrays Democracy: Camouflaging the Garrison State's Dilemma

The purpose of this research was to reconsider the U.S. occupation of Okinawa from a soft power theory approach. Specifically, it has discussed U.S. information policy which sought to control residents surrounding the U.S. military bases in Okinawa, focusing on the role of the U.S. military government and its successor, the U.S. Civil Administration of the Ryukyu Islands (USCAR). Based on documents in the U.S. National Archives, the study has examined how U.S. policy was executed in Okinawa from 1945 to 1972.

The research questions were as follows:
1. What was the U.S. policymaking process regarding the administration of Okinawa?
2. How did the Congress oversee the U.S. administration of Okinawa?
3. What was public affairs and mass media policy under the U.S. administration of Okinawa?
4. What is the historical legacy of the U.S. soft war policies?

The following sections present the conclusions of this research.

### U.S. Policymaking Process

U.S. administration policy for Okinawa was initially outlined in the plans for Operation Iceberg, the U.S. landing on Okinawa and surrounding islands in the final stages of World War II. Gathering intelligence and disseminating information among the local populations were central to the military operations. Administration policy was formalized in the wartime directives of the Joint Chiefs of Staff, JCS 1231, and the joint field manual of the U.S. Army and Navy. The wartime directives, which the U.S. Joint Chiefs of Staff regarded as the highest authority bar the

President, remained in effect until the reversion of Okinawa to Japan in 1972. As a result, the U.S. theatre commander had supreme authority over the residents regarding politics, the economy and mass communications, as well as military matters. That was the bases of military occupation for 27 years. The garrison island was a U.S. "military colony" based on the JCS directive.

Through "area administration units," the U.S. supervised politics, economics, mass media and grassroots organizations. The area administration units had been established to support military operations and were engaged in local intelligence gathering and public relations to persuade residents to accept the military occupation of Okinawa. In this sense, the U.S. administration of Okinawa became a prototype of U.S. soft power policy as the Cold War developed.

U.S. soft power policy was executed as psychological operations following the combat operations of World War II. The Civil Information and Education Department of the U.S. military government and its successor, USCAR's Public Affairs Department, were the executive agencies of the U.S. soft power policy in Okinawa. The Department of the Army was engaged in civil affairs activities, which included executing information policy. It was coordinated in Washington with the Defense and State Departments, the CIA, the National Security Council and other Executive Branch organizations. With the NSC ultimately responsible for peacetime information policy and the JSC ultimately responsible for wartime policy, the administration of Okinawa was an unusual situation, with these competing policy directions operating concurrently.

The U.S. administrative period can thus be understood as a transitional process as the military occupation based on the wartime directive gradually transformed into the diplomatic objectives of peacetime. NSC 13 determined that the U.S. administration of Okinawa was part of its policy toward Japan, while the Defense Department continued to pursue the occupation policy objectives set out in the JCS directive to directly control the Ryukyu Islands. The State Department advised the Defense Department about its concerns of international criticism against the U.S. military occupation in Okinawa, but "informally" accepted the occupation directive active in the garrison islands. The U.S. did not intend to abandon the economic paradise in which the military commander enabled American corporations, such as Caltex, to freely develop their business, controlling the foreign exchange and trading profits of the islands.

The odd mixture of these competing objectives kept the administration mired in double standards. Okinawans describe the situation as "a carrot and stick policy" or *ame to muchi* in Japanese. The JCS position was understood as the stick of military or hard power, while the NSC's approach to public affairs can be seen as "a carrot" to ameliorate opposition to the military domination. The double standards posed a dilemma for the United States, which professed democratic ideals while maintaining a garrison state. The U.S. promoted Okinawa as a "showcase of democracy" in its ideological struggle against communism but the garrison state betrayed its democratic ideals, suppressing freedom of speech and other fundamental rights of democratic citizens. In other words, the U.S. was caught in the contradiction of defending democracy by undermining their democratic ideals.

## Congressional Oversight

Congress was ambivalent in its oversight of the administration of Okinawa. It approved the budget for the administration of Okinawa as a "civil function" of the Army throughout the 27-year occupation. Although the budget was renamed in 1957, from Government Aid and Relief in Occupied Areas (part of the U.S. postwar occupation of Japan) to Appropriation for Ryukyu Islands Administration, Congress was consistent in regarding the appropriations as being for the Army's civil functions and distinct from traditional military expenditures. Nevertheless, the role of the area administration units funded by these appropriations was to directly support the U.S. military in meeting its objectives. The units were tasked with controlling the public sphere so that residents would not disrupt the U.S. military. Congress's perspective was thus strictly in accordance with the policy of military supremacy.

However, Congress did not pass the proposed Ryukyu Organic Act, legislation that would authorize the administrative budgets based on the wartime directive of the Joint Chiefs of Staff, because it could not provide a legal basis for the appropriations. Some congressmen did question the legality of public corporations under U.S. federal management, demonstrating that there was at least some functioning oversight of overseas military activities, but never enough to challenge the military actions that were "justified" by the oft-repeated phrase: "It is a military necessity."

Congressional oversight weakened as the powers of the Executive Branch expanded in the late 1940s. The NSC's establishment in 1947 has been seen as the beginning of the expanded reach of the Executive Office. The separation of Okinawa from mainland Japan was secretly decided in NSC policy papers in 1948. Military and foreign relations policy are often dictated by classified decisions without Congressional review. Congressional deliberations about such matters can reveal classified decisions to the public. In sum, congressional oversight of overseas military bases was quite limited. Although Congress claims to be the only legislative body sanctioned by the U.S. Constitution, in practice it has very limited influence when martial law has been imposed on foreign lands. Throughout the Cold War, Congress approved huge sums for foreign aid and military assistance but was not able to fully monitor or access the consequences on foreign soils.

## Public Relations and Propaganda

The soft power policy combined with the foreign economic and military aid made the contradictions difficult to observe.

The Battle of Okinawa destroyed all mass communications, including newspapers and radio stations, depriving Okinawa of any mass communications channels after the war. The U.S. established a military government immediately upon occupying the islands in 1945. Gathering intelligence and disseminating information were understood to be essential to the military mission. The military government supported re-establishing newspaper publication as an important instrument for information gathering activities. It concurrently issued a series of proclamations and ordinances restricting freedom of speech among the local population, specifically prohibiting any criticism of the occupation forces. Thus, the U.S. information policy specifically aimed to provide support for combat operations.

The establishment of the Civil Information and Education (CIE) Department in 1948 transformed information policy, gradually incorporating certain aspects of peacetime public diplomacy. It launched a series of American movie screenings in information centers and libraries as well as educational and cultural exchange programs with the U.S. universities. In the early years of the occupation, the U.S. military police had strictly controlled the speech and daily activities of the locals, but the CIE public relations staff gradually softened the restrictions on speech, using public relations strategies to "teach American democracy" to the Okinawan people. Pre-publication censorship of the newspapers did not continue for long, as the CIE increasingly encouraged the Okinawan media to self-censor, while maintaining the authority to issue press permits. CIE personnel frequently visited the editorial offices, asking for revisions whenever they found unfavorable expressions. CIE continued to monitor anti-American speech throughout the administration period.

From 1957 until 1972, the Office of the High Commissioner was caught between the occasionally contradictory objectives of the military and the diplomats. Although the civilian objectives were regarded as normal for peacetime, the U.S. administration of Okinawa was subordinate to the Defense Secretary's information policy, which exposed the double standard at the base of the U.S. administration. Beginning with the Kennedy administration, the civilian objectives increasingly came to govern information policy. In that sense, information policy was a driving force in transforming the U.S. administration of Okinawa from wartime to peacetime standards. It was under the expanding authority of the Executive Office during the Cold War.

## U.S. Foreign Information Policy toward Okinawa

This study has reconsidered the U.S. administration of Okinawa through the framework of information policy and soft power theory. The wartime directives of the Joint Chiefs of Staff represented the policy making authority of the U.S. military, while the soft power practices of information policy under the NSC's direction symbolizes the democratic policy making process. In Okinawa, however, the NSC's information policies did not function as a civilian check on the power of the military. Rather it served as a faithful supporter of U.S. military actions, shaped by its Cold War mentality, which was, in turn, a product of U.S. public relations domestically.

The National Security Council accepted the Secretary of Defense's control of Okinawa to maintain the freedom for military actions in Okinawa and surrounding areas. Although, the State Department anticipated international criticism of the continuing military occupation, it also accepted the JCS's arguments of military necessity. The State Department's activities in Okinawa informally supported Defense's administration of Okinawa from behind the scenes by endeavoring to ameliorate negative public opinion in Japan and Okinawa.

As the primary peacetime coordinator of U.S. information policy, the State Department indirectly shaped the information activities deployed in Okinawa, injecting a foreign relations perspective into the Defense Department's administration of Okinawa. The civilian policymakers contend that information policy should be a continuum from war to peace. Although the policy in Okinawa was an odd mixture of wartime and peacetime, it functioned to transition from the wartime framework to the peacetime one.

During the Cold War, Okinawa provided bases for the U.S. forces during the Korean and Vietnam Wars. To persuade the Okinawan people to support the U.S. military activities, public relations professionals developed psychological operations through the Okinawan press to assuage the residents.

In the process, U.S. militarism betrayed its democratic ideals. While the public relations professionals promoted their democratic ideals in presenting Okinawa as "a showcase of democracy" against communism, the U.S. psychological operations limited the freedom of the Okinawan press to criticize U.S. activities. The information policy toward Japan was also treated as psychological operations as part of the U.S. military development in East Asia rather than foreign relations or diplomacy. After Japan recovered independence, U.S. policy toward Japan continued to be dominated by wartime elements. The Okinawa case serves to highlight how U.S.-Japan relations had been dragged through the framework of military supremacy. As described earlier, more than 70% of U.S. military bases in Japan are concentrated in Okinawa Prefecture.

## Camouflaging the Garrison State's Dilemma

Harold Lasswell regarded propaganda as a necessity for the modern state which presents a fundamental dilemma to a democratic society. In his book *Propaganda Techniques of World War*, published in 1927, Lasswell pointed out that information was crucial during World War I. Comparing a democracy to a totalitarian state, he pointed out that a democracy requires propaganda because its leaders must persuade the people to voluntarily go to war.[1] After World War II, as this study has shown, the United States developed its public relations toward foreign countries and audiences ostensibly as a means to reduce the likelihood of another war. While it manifested democratic ideals and used "democracy" as an ideal to persuade the global audience throughout the Cold War, the nature of warfare changed, blurring the difference between war and peace. As Joseph Nye argued, soft power emerged as "the second force of power" and the U.S. and other nations including Japan poured large portions of their national budgets into public relations activities both domestically and internationally. Public diplomacy today is regarded as a tool to support the postwar peacekeeping operations and the reconstruction of regional governance. When the U.S. invaded Iraq in 2003, the reconstruction of Japan was pointed to as a prototype for postwar operations, but the case of Okinawa should be carefully analyzed. This study's discussion of the Okinawa case could highlight various problems with the U.S. soft power strategy.

Military actions involve inhumane activities, such as murders and genocides. When such things are exposed in the United States, the most vehement criticism is typically expressed by the American mass media. Freedom of the press is crucial in a democracy, and the mass media in democratic societies can be highly critical of the nation's military activities. To pursue military objectives, then, a democratic nation is often compelled to control the domestic media and public opinion. In this way, militarism betrays democracy. To camouflage this dilemma, after World War II and throughout the Cold War, the United State expanded its overseas public diplomacy and public affairs efforts. The garrison state euphemistically described its military policy as security policy, contending that military effort is necessary to defend American democracy, and disseminating propaganda to global audiences to rationalize its actions.

The U.S. military expansion was deeply intertwined with its foreign information policy. U.S. policymakers often had to conceal inhumane and undemocratic activities. The public affairs officers worked for the government and military forces, attempting to control domestic and foreign media. In this sense, the role of soft power was to support hard power and originated in hard power. As this study has shown, the endeavors of the public affairs officers were not always successful but they did succeed in making inconvenient facts for the government and military forces as invisible as possible. As a result, what was happening in Okinawa was not even reported in the mass media and U.S. political leaders did not know about the effects of U.S. military activities overseas. Specifically, the U.S. media did not cover the local people's voice expressed in non-English languages.

"Soft power is more difficult to wield," Nye admits, "because...many of its crucial resources are outside the control of governments, and their efforts depend heavily on acceptance by the receiving audiences."[2] However, Nye's argument on soft power is so optimistic that he did not analyze any discourses of "the receiving audience." Pointing out that the U.S. public relations campaigns during the Iraqi War failed, he probably understood that the soft power strategy has many defects but did not talk about how it was received in different cultures.

As a critical analysis of the Cold War impacts towards third world countries such as Guatemala and Ethiopia, Norwegian historian Odd Arne Westad stated, "the *cultural* violence was sometimes as bad as physical: millions are forced to change their religions, their languages, their family structure, and even their names in order to fit in with the progress."[3] Okinawans under the U.S. occupation did not necessarily change their religions or languages and are not regarded as a part of the third world. However, the U.S. interventions in the cognitive sphere of the local populations left irreversible effects on the culture.

Soft power not only functions to reinforce hard power, but also to cover up the intrinsically negative aspects of hard power. Therefore, soft power theory should be discussed independently of hard power and national security issues. However, the premise of Nye's argument is the fact that the U.S. had already developed the world's largest hard power. Nye's perspective ignored the negative impact of soft power; how the U.S. foreign information policy attempted to limit freedom of speech, and went so far as attempting to dominate the psychological domain of the people residing the American military colony.

The U.S. had already poured tremendous economic and human resource to soft power, making the negative aspect of hard power invisible. It could be said that soft power per se had contributed to the expansion of militarism. Therefore, it is rather necessary to examine the process of political communications: how soft power covers up various problems caused by military forces and; how militarism betrays democracy in the process of mass communications.

As a case study, this work has examined foreign information policy during the U.S. administration of Okinawa and how the pursuit of military objectives betrayed its own democratic ideals.

## Manufacturing Threat

A central problem of propaganda is that it tends to obfuscate public discourses with dubious claims. The long-standing debate over whether the U.S. actually "needed" military bases in Okinawa is a case in point. The issue has been discussed with no factual basis, since "military necessity" is always based on an analysis of the international situation. Not only are the "facts" of any situation difficult to determine, but the available information might well be manipulated to justify the annual budgets for military deployment.

Richard H. Lamb, a former first secretary at the U.S. Embassy in Tokyo, wrote a memorandum to James V. Martin, Japan Division Chief, State Department on December 17, 1957, in which he raised the following questions regarding a draft of NSC papers.

> Must we always accept without question Defense's estimate of the military necessity of Okinawa, of the need for the vast areas of Okinawa land that we have acquired, and of the "threat" to our position which a partial return of administration to Japan might involve? It seems to me that we should require a full explanation of these facts (if they are facts) – not simply accept Defense's statements that the islands are "essential," that US land use is being "kept at the minimum," and that a return of administration to Japan would make it impossible for us to carry out our mission.[4]

U.S. military officials continually relied on the claim of "military necessity" to justify maintaining administrative rights over Okinawa. However, Lamb raised some basic questions about this claim of "military necessity." First, what was the "threat"? This question should be subject to rational interrogation, but the "evidence" presented to support the claim is rarely composed of objectively verifiable facts. Rather, the "threat" is always "speculative," based on "estimates" of the military power and intentions of a foreign power. Moreover, since the foreign power is presumed to be an enemy for "us," estimates tend to maximize the threat. Hence, the estimated threat presented in public discourses slips across the surface of another country's military secrets with no concrete facts.

Lamb's memorandum continued to question the threat theory, citing Admiral Arthur W. Radford, Chairman of the Joint Chiefs of Staff during the Eisenhower administration, which he heard first-hand in Okinawa.

> The military briefing we received in Okinawa in May 1956 indicated that our bases as then constituted were sitting ducks – difficult if not impossible to defend, likely to be knocked out completely in a one-shot operation. From the offensive point of view, the island was considered "too vulnerable" to permit stationing heavy bombers. With missile development, things no doubt have changed, but at that time I gathered the military role of Okinawa was to serve as a part – a relatively minor part – of the Pacific Defense arc – really not much more than a forward warning station. I was also told that Admiral Radford for one thought that it had been a great mistake to make such a big operation out of our bases in Okinawa – that he thought the whole thing has just "grown" without careful strategic planning, and that he believed our bases there were of limited military value.[5]

American think-tank analysts have pointed out that U.S. bases in Okinawa were vulnerable to missile attacks from the Eurasian Continent. The memorandum indicates that a certain consensus had been reached among U.S. forces, the Consulate in Japan, and the Joint Chiefs recognizing the limited value of the U.S. bases in Okinawa as early as 1957. However, USCAR documents show that the public relations campaigns continued to seek to maximize "the fear of communism" and stressed the military necessity of maintaining the U.S. administration of Okinawa. Fear of communism was USCAR's underlying principle. USCAR's public affairs staff continued to run their anti-communism campaigns because that was their *raison d'etre*. In other words, the threat was a discursive construct entirely independent of factual matters. Similarly, the military would lose its justification for massive budget appropriations if the threat evaporated. In this sense, the propagandist's creation of threat is a central characteristic of militarism. Such propaganda undermines congressional oversight and the role of the media, although both are necessary for democracy to work.

The purpose of this book was not to assess the need for U.S. bases in Okinawa. Rather, it's aim has been to reveal how the claims of military necessity were presented, with the facts obscured in ambiguity throughout public discourse from Congressional assessment, from diplomatic negotiations and from the public sphere and mass media. U.S. Presidents receive a daily analysis of the world situation from the CIA. These analyses are secret and therefore not available for public assessment. Political decisions are made by an elite circle within the Executive Branch.

Accordingly, international policies are formulated and implemented without public discussion. The general public is unable to assess whether the correct political decision was made because they do not have access to the information upon which it was based.

From the Battle of Okinawa until its reversion to Japan, the most important decisions regarding the U.S. administration of Okinawa were made in the Executive Office. The separation of Okinawa from mainland Japan was determined in the NSC papers and the U.S. annual budgets for Okinawa were decided in the Executive Office and submitted to Congress for approval. Established in 1947, the NSC and CIA expanded the Executive Branch's authority and undermined Congress's oversight functions. "The 1947 system" contributed to expanding U.S. militarism and to maintaining overseas military bases, in the process, weakening the democratic institutions they claimed to be defending. The Okinawa problem was also a product of the expansion of the Executive Office; a problem concealed behind bureaucracy and never exposed to the public sphere.

Fear is manufactured by mass communications that often maximize the threat of an enemy. In an era when global public relations campaigns are ubiquitous, new democratic devices should be established to protect free speech and discourse. One such device may be investigative journalism that could uncover the rhetorical programming or propaganda employed by politicians, government and military leaders that spring from ideological or commercial self-interest.

# Appendix

*Table 1: JCS 1231 Revisions*

| Directive No. | Page | Date | Title | Targeted Areas |
|---|---|---|---|---|
| JCS1231/00 | 1–22 | 1945/1/12 | Directives for Military Government in the Japanese Outlaying Islands | Nansei Shoto Nanpo Shoto Kulile Islands |
| JCS1231/01 | 23–25 | 1945/1/17 | | |
| JCS1231/02 | | 1945/1/30 | | |
| JCS1231/03 | | 1945/2/6 | | |
| JCS1231/04 | | 1945/9/8 | | |
| JCS1231/05 | | 1945/9/17 | | |
| JCS1231/06 | | 1945/9/21 | | |
| JCS1231/07 | | 1946/1/31 | | |
| JCS1231/08 | 44–50 | 1946/3/15 | Revision of Civil Affairs Directives for Former Japanese Mandated Islands and the Japanese Outlaying Islands | Marianas, Caroline, Marshall, Izu, Bonin, Volcano, Marcus, Ryukyus |
| JCS1231/09 | 51–54 | 1946/3/20 | | |
| JCS1231/10 | 55–61 | 1946/4/2 | | |
| JCS1231/11 | 62–76 | 1946/9/20 | | |
| JCS1231/12 | | 1947/3/21 | | |
| JCS1231/13 | | 1947/7/25 | | |
| JCS1231/14 | 90–101 | 1950/9/9 | Directives for the United States Civil Administration of the Ryukyu Islands (USCAR Directives) | Ryukyus |
| JCS1231/15 | 102–103 | 1950/10/2 | | |
| JCS1231/16 | 104–108 | 1950/10/30 | | Ryukyus |

*Continued overleaf ...*

*Table 1:continued*

| Directive No. | Page | Date | Title | Targeted Areas |
|---|---|---|---|---|
| JCS1231/17 | 109–115 | 1951/4/20 | Location of Capital Site of the Trust Territory of the Pacific Islands | Saipan |
| JCS1231/18 | 116–122 | 1951/5/3 | | Saipan |
| JCS1231/19 | 123–129 | 1951/11/26 | | Ryukyus |
| JCS1231/20 | 130–132 | 1952/3/10 | | |
| JCS1231/21 | 133–137 | 1952/9/25 | | |
| JCS1231/22 | 138-146 | 1953/2/13 | | |
| JCS1231/23 | 147-151 | 1953/3/19 | | |
| JCS1231/24 | | 1953/6/16 | | |
| JCS1231/25 | 154-159 | 1953/11/18 | | |
| JCS1231/26 | | 1954/2/2 | | |
| JCS1231/27 | | 1954/2/12 | | |
| JCS1231/28 | 195-219 | 1954/3/9 | Discontinuance of Native Ryukyuans Coast Guard Protect, and Deployment of a U.S. Coast Guard Unit to the Ryukyus | Ryukyu |
| JCS1231/29 | 220-222 | 1954/4/29 | Coastal Patrol Forces in the Ryukyus | |
| JCS1231/30 | 223-225 | 1954/5/5 | | |
| JCS1231/31 | | 1954/7/27 | | |
| JCS1231/32 | | 1954/11/2 | Directive for U.S. Civil Administration of the Ryukyu Islands | |
| JCS1231/33 | 235-237 | 1954/11/30 | Assignment of a Political Advisor to the Governor of the Ryukyu Islands | |
| JCS1231/34 | | 1956/3/19 | | |
| JCS1231/35 | | 1956/5/22 | | |
| JCS1231/36 | | 1956/9/27 | | |
| JCS1231/37 | 247-248 | 1956/9/27 | | |
| JCS1231/38 | | 1956/10/4 | | |
| JCS1231/39 | 253-256 | 1957/1/23 | Civil Administration in the Ryukyus | |
| JCS1231/40 | | 1957/4/27 | | |

Source: RG 218 Records of Joint Chiefs of Staff, U.S. National Archives.

Appendix

## Table 2: Political Directive JCS 1231

| | | |
|---|---|---|
| 1 | Target Areas (Nanpo Shoto, Nansei Shoto, and Kurile Islands) | |
| 2 | Establishing Military Government | |
| 3 | Complying with international laws | |
| 4 | Military purposes supremacy | |
| 5 | Treatment of local civilians | |
| 6 | Proclamations | |
| 7 | Treating Koreans and Taiwanese more favorably than Japanese | |
| 8 | Reestablishing legal system | |
| 9 | Suspending local authorities and laws | Proclamation No. 1 |
| 10 | Eliminating local political elites | |
| 11 | Utilizing local civilians | |
| 12 | Utilizing local governmental organizations | |
| 13 | Suspending local courts | |
| 14 | Establishing court-martials | Proclamation No. 3 |
| 15 | Establishing civilian camps | |
| 16 | Compliance with 1929 Geneva Conference | |
| 17 | Detaining diplomats and consulates | |
| 18 | Censorship of publication and other civilian communication | Proclamation No. 10 |
| 19 | Prohibiting Japanese militaristic thoughts and propaganda | |
| 20 | Prohibiting Japanese ultra-nationalistic political activities | |
| 21 | Prohibiting speech regarding Japanese Emperor | |
| 22 | Permitting religious freedom excluding 19–20 above | |
| 23 | Suspension and reestablishment of educational institutions | |
| 24 | Treatment of Allied civilians | |
| 25 | Protection of Allied civilians and their assets | |
| 26 | Foreclosure of Japanese government assets | Proclamation No. 7 |
| 27 | Prohibition of drugs and controlled substances | Proclamation No. 6 |
| 28 | Foreclosure of public documents | |
| 29 | Protection of history, culture and religions | |

Source: Political Directive for Military Government in the Japanese Outlaying Islands, JCS 1231, 1945/1/12. RG218 Box170 Folder: CCS 383.21 POA Sec. 1.

*Table 3: Economic Directive, JCS 1231*

| 1 | Theater Commander as op authority for economic policy | |
|---|---|---|
| 2 | Economic policy | a) Maximizing usage of local assets<br>b) Preventing diseases and social unrest<br>c) Providing minimum necessary civilian supplies |
| 3 | Prevent inflation | Inflation prevention |
| 4 | | Providing rations and price controls |
| 5 | | Prohibiting black markets |
| 6 | Wages and Price | Wages policy |
| 7 | | Same wages for same labor |
| 8 | | Price policy |
| 9 | Civilian Supply | Civilian supply and store |
| 10 | | Policy for profit margin |
| 11 | | Logistics management |
| 12 | | Selling supplies in local currencies |
| 13 | Records | Obligation to record civilian supplies provided |
| 14 | Economic Control | Industry and logistic control |
| 15 | | Import and export control |
| 16 | | Rehabilitation of food production and self-help economy |
| 17 | | Business licenses |
| 18 | | Port, warehouse, ferries and ships |
| 19 | Public Services | Railroad, postal service, telephone, telegram and radio |
| 20 | | Rehabilitation of public services and traffic |
| 21 | Agriculture | Promotion of agricultural industry |
| 22 | Fishing Industry | Control and promotion of fishing industry |
| 23 | Labor | Control labor hours |
| 24 | | Hiring enemy aliens within international law |
| 25 | | Civilian labor hiring policy |
| 26 | Estimate | Submitting economic estimates to JCS |
| 27 | | Reporting local economic situation to JCS<br>(fish, sugar and other agricultural products) |

Source: Enclosure "B," Proposed Economic Directive for the Japanese Outlying Islands, JCS 1231, 1945/1/12. RG218 Box170 Folder: CCS 383.21 POA Sec. 1.

*Appendix*

## Table 4: Financial Directive, JCS 1231

| | |
|---|---|
| 1 | Usage of Supplementary Military Bill |
| 2 | Abolition of Japanese Military Bill |
| 3 | Usage of U.S. dollars in emergencies and military purposes |
| 4 | Condition for U.S. Dollars in necessity |
| 5 | Prohibition of U.S. Dollars in targeted areas |
| 6 | Tentative tariff rate |
| 7 | Prohibition of foreign exchange |
| 8 | Navy-Army Financial Officer control civil administration |
| 9 | Limited moratorium proclamation |
| 10 | Closure of banks and financial institutions |
| 11 | Restart banks and financial institutions |
| 12 | Requisition of enemy government assets |
| 13 | Military governor authorizing and managing local banks |
| 14 | Issuing financial directives |
| 15 | Maintaining accounting records and profits |
| 16 | Account management |
| 17 | Basic accounting instructions as annex |

*Accounting Instructions*

| | |
|---|---|
| 1 | Military government in Japanese Outlying Islands controlling and recording accounts |
| 2 | Military Government as a Corporate Status |
| 3 | Accounting record required |
| 4 | Receipts |
| 5 | Dollar and En accounts |
| 6 | En account |
| 7 | Receipts submission required |
| 8 | Accounting currencies other than En and Supplementary En |
| 9 | U.S. dollar account management |
| 10 | Account reporting obligation |
| 11 | Accountant's inspection |
| 12 | Monthly report obligation |
| 13 | Application for civilian supplies |

Source: Enclosure "C" = Financial Directive for Military Government in the Japanese Outlying Islands and Appendix to Enclosure "C" = Basic Accounting Instructions, supplemental to Financial Directive, JCS 1231, RG218 Box170 Folder: CCS 383.21 POA Sec. 1.

## Table 5: Chronological development – Ryukyu Islands 1947–1960

| Date | Document | Title |
|---|---|---|
| 1947. 7.26 | | National Security Act of 1947 |
| 1947.12.9 | NSC 4/4a | Coordination of Foreign Information Measures |
| 1948. 1.13 | | NSC Intelligence Directive No. 2 |
| 1948. 1.27 | | Smith-Mundt Act of 1948 |
| 1948. 4. 3 | | Economic Cooperation Act of 1948 |
| 1948. 6. 2 | NSC 13 | U.S. Policy toward Japan |
| 1948. 6. 18 | NSC 10/2 | Covert operations |
| 1948. 8. 6 | ORE 24-48 | The Ryukyu Islands and their Significance |
| 1948.10. 7 | NSC13/2 | U.S. Policy toward Japan revised |
| 1949. 5. 6 | NSC 13/3 | U.S. Policy toward Japan (separation of the Ryukyus) |
| 1949. 3. 9 | NSC 43 | Planning for Wartime Conduct of Overt Psychological Warfare |
| 1950. 3. 9 | NSC 59/1 | Foreign Information Program and Psychological Warfare Planning |
| 1950. 4.14 | NSC 68 | Cold War / total war |
| 1950. 8. | | NPSB = National Psychological Strategy Board (State Department) |
| 1950.10. 4 | JCS 1231/14 | (USCAR Directive) |
| 1950.12.15 | | United States Civil Administration of the Ryukyu Islands established in Okinawa |
| 1951. 4. 4 | | Psychological Strategy Board Directive |
| 1952. 1.30 | PSB D-27 | Psychological Strategy Program for Japan |
| 1952. 8. 7 | NSC 125/2 | United States Objectives and Courses of Action with respect to Japan |
| 1952. 11.19 | | Psychological Operations Committee (POC) established in Tokyo |
| 1953. 4.28 | NSC 125/5 | U.S. Policy toward Japan revised |
| 1953. 6.15 | NSC Action 824-b | Secretary of Defense responsible for USCAR |
| 1953. 9. 2 | E.O.10483 | Operations Coordinating Board established |
| 1953. 9. 2 | State Reorganization No.8 | United States Information Agency established |
| 1955. 4. 9 | NSC 5516/1 | U.S. Policy toward Japan (Section 54) |
| 1957. 6. 5 | E. O. 10713 | Office of High Commissioner starts |
| 1960. 5.20 | NSC 6008 | U.S. Policy toward Japan |

# Notes

## Introduction

1 Public affairs activities aim to influence the general public, using various means including interpersonal communications such as cultural exchange and mediated communication.
2 Lasswell, Harold D., *Propaganda Techniques in the World War* (New York: Alfred A. Knopf, 1927).
3 Nicholas N. Cull discussed five components of public diplomacy. See, Cull, Nicholas J. *The Cold War and the United States Information Agency: American Propaganda and Public Diplomacy* (Cambridge University Press, 2008), xviii.
4 USCAR was described as the "7244$^{th}$ DU (Distribution Unit)," or "7244$^{th}$ Area Administration Unit. See, General Orders Number 1 (1957/1/1). Office of the Deputy Governor, United States Civil Administration of the Ryukyu Islands, RG 260 Records of Administration Office (hereafter, AO) Box 11 Folder 11 National Archives College Park (hereafter, NA). For example, the following document says that "Civil Administration of the Ryukyu Islands, 7244$^{th}$ Administration Area Unit" was organized at Fort Buckner on May 1, 1956. See, AGPA-A 320.4 (24 Feb 56) DCSPER, Subject: Organization of the 7244$^{th}$ Administration Area Unit. Department of the Army, Office of the Adjutant General, (1956/4/11), RG 260 AO Box 180 Folder 2, NA.
5 For example, William J. Sebald, political adviser for Douglas MacArthur described himself as an "occupation diplomat." See, Sebald, William J., *With MacArthur in Japan* (New York; W. W. Norton & Co., 1965), 52–76.
6 "Civil administration" was referred to as "civilian administration" in the original draft of the Civil Affairs Division of the Department of the Army, but because the civilian administrator's position was to be subordinate to the military commander it was soon referred to as "civil administration." See Chapter 4 for details. Civil administration might be understood as short for "civil affairs administration."
7 The Naha Liaison Office of the Japanese Government called USCAR the "Civil Affairs Division.," rather than *Beimin-seifu*.
8 Nye, Joseph S., Jr., *Soft Power: The Means to Success in World Politics* (New York: Public Affairs, 2004), 5, 145.
9 CRS Report for Congress, U.S. Occupation Assistance: Iraq, Germany and Japan Compared, (March 23, 2006), Congressional Research Service, Library of Congress.

10 Roger Hilsman, *To Move the Nation: The Politics of Foreign Policy in the Administration of John F. Kennedy,* (New York: Doubleday and Co., 1967), 542–543; James M. McCormick, *The Domestic Sources of American Foreign Policy: Insights and Evidence.* (New York: Rowman & Littlefield, 2012), 158–159; Seigen Miyazato, *Amerika no Taigai Seisaku Kettei Katei* (Policy making process of U.S. foreign relations), (Tokyo: Sanichi Shobo, 1981), 29.
11 Samuel P. Huntington, *The Soldiers and the States: The Theory and Politics of Civil-Military Relations,* (Cambridge, MA: The Belknap Press of Harvard University Press, 1957), 437–440.
12 Gerald C. Stone, Mary K. O'Donnell, and Stephen Banning, "Public Perception of Newspaper's Watchdog Role," *Newspaper Research Journal*, Vol. 18, No. 1–2, (Winter/Spring 1997).
13 David Manning White, "Gate Keeper: A Case Study in the Selection of News," *Journalism Quarterly,* 27, (1950): 383–396.
14 Robert Entman, "Theorizing Mediated Public Diplomacy: The U.S. Case," *The International Journal of Press/Politics*, 13:2 (2008).
15 Article 3, TREATY OF PEACE WITH JAPAN. United Nations Treaty Series, No. 1832.
16 Seigen Miyazato (ed.), *Sengo Okinawa no Seiji to Ho* (Politics and laws in postwar Okinawa), (Tokyo: Tokyo University Press, 1975).
17 Miyazato, op. cit.; Seigen Miyazato, *Nichibei Kankei to Okinawa 1945–1972* (U.S.-Japan relations and Okinawa 1945–1972) (Tokyo: Iwanami Shoten, 2000).
18 Robert D Eldridge, *Okinawa Mondai no Kigen: Sengo Nichibei Kankei ni okeru Okinawa* (The origins of the bilateral Okinawa problems), (Nagoya: Nagoya University Press, 2003).
19 Yasuko Kono, *Okinawa Henkan wo meguru Seiji to Gaiko* (Politics and foreign relations regarding Okinawa reversion), (Tokyo: Tokyo University Press, 1994); Takuma Nakajima, *Okinawa Henkan to Nichibei Anpo Taisei* (Okinawa reversion and U.S-Japan alliance), (Tokyo: Yuhikaku, 2012).
20 Masaaki Gabe, *Nichibei Kankei no naka no Okinawa* (Okinawa in U.S-Japan relations), (Tokyo: Sanichi Shobo, 1996), 59–63.
21 Nicholas J Cull, *The Cold War and the United States Information Agency: American Propaganda and Public Diplomacy* (New York: Cambridge University Press, 2008).
22 Yuka Tsuchiya, *Shinbei Nihon no Kouchiku* (Constructing Pro-U.S. Japan), (Tokyo: Akashi Shoten, 2009).
23 Yuka Tsuchiya and Shunya Yoshimi, *Senryo suru Me, Senryo suru Koe* (The occupying eyes, occupying voices: CIE/USIS films and VOA Radio in Asia during the Cold War), (Tokyo: Tokyo University Press, 2012).
24 Yasushi Watanabe, *Amerikan Senta* (American centers: U.S. international culture strategy), (Tokyo: Iwanami Shoten, 2008).
25 Etsujiro Miyagi, *Okinawa Sengo Housoushi* (Okinawa postwar broadcasting history), (Okinawa: Hirugi-sha, 1996); Masahide Ota, *Okinawa Senka no Nichibei Shinri Sakusen* (U.S-Japan psychological warfare during the Battle of Okinawa), (Tokyo: Iwanami Shoten, 2004); Naoki Monna, *Okinawa Genron Tousei Shi* (Okinawa speech control history), (Tokyo: Yuzankaku, 1996).

26 See past studies regarding USCAR. Miyazato, Seigen, *Amerika no Okinawa Touchi* (U.S. administration of Okinawa), (Tokyo: Iwanami Shoten, 1966); Ryukyu Bank Research Division, *Sengo Okinawa Keizaishi* (Postwar Okinawa economic history), 1984: Masaaki Gabe, op. cit.
27 USCAR was regarded as 7244th DU (Distribution Unit), 7244th Area Administration Unit. For instance, see General Orders Number 1 (1957/1/1). Office of the Deputy Governor, United States Civil Administration of the Ryukyu Islands, RG 260 Records of Administration Office (hereafter, AO) Box 11 Folder 11 National Archives College Park (hereafter, NA). (May 1, 1956), Civil Administration of the Ryukyu Islands, 7244th Administration Area Unit was organized at Fort Buckner, see AGPA-A 320.4 (24 Feb 56) DCSPER, Subject: Organization of the 7244th Administration Area Unit. Department of the Army, Office of the Adjutant General, (1956/4/11), RG 260 AO Box 180 Folder 2, NA.
28 For example, William J. Sebald, a political adviser for General MacArthur at GHQ/SCAP, represented the Department of State and referred to his position as "occupation diplomat." See William J. Sebald, *With MacArthur in Japan* (New York: W. W. Norton & Co., 1965), 52–76.

## Chapter 1

1 *Budget of the United States Government, 1946–1972*. Federal Reserve Archives.
2 Naruo Kabira, *Okinawa Kuuhaku no Ichinen* (Okinawa: one year after the Battle of Okinawa), (Tokyo: Yoshikawa Kobunkan, 2011).
3 Kent E. Calder, *Kichi no Seijigaku* (Embattled garrisons: comparative base politics and American globalism), (Trans. Yoichi Takeda, Tokyo: Nihon Keizai Shimbun Shuppan-sha, 2008), 35, 65.
4 Hearing before the Subcommittee on Appropriation, House of Representatives, 79th Congress, 2nd Sess., (May 8, 1946), 3–4, 10–11.
5 H.R. 6837, July 16, 1946, 70th Congress 2nd Session.
6 Government Aid and Relief in Occupied Areas, An Act Making Appropriation for the Military Establishment for the fiscal year ending June 30, 1947, and for other purposes (60 STAT. 560).
7 H.R. 6837, 122.
8 Hearing before the Subcommittee, May 8, 1946, op.cit., 9.
9 H.R. 6837, op. cit.
10 Hearing before the Subcommittee, May 8, 1946, op. cit., 321.
11 Hearing, Foreign Aid Appropriation Bill of 1950, 814.
12 Congressional Quarterly Service, *Congress and the Nation 1945–1964: A Review of Government and Politics in the Postwar Years* (Washington D.C.: Congressional Quarterly Service, 1965), 160–162.
13 B-114950, From Acting Comptroller General of the United States to the Secretary of the Army, (August 17, 1953). RG260, USCAR, CM, Box 211.
14 Hearings before the Subcommittee Foreign Affairs, House of Representatives, 89th Congress, 1st Sess., "Utilization of Excess U.S.-Owned Foreign Currencies in Certain Countries," 98, 196, 225.

15 History of Budget Program. RG 260, Records of USCAR (United States Civil Administration of the Ryukyu Islands), CM (Comptroller Department), Box 94. NA (National Archives).
16 Justification of Estimate, Fiscal Year 1960. RG 260, USCAR, CM, Box 84.
17 Okinawa Kyokai, *Nampo Douhou Engokai 17 nen no Ayumi* (17 year history of Southern Islands Friends Association), (1973), 97–98.

## Chapter 2

1 Arnold G.Fisch, *Military Government in the Ryukyu Islands, 1945–1950* (Honolulu, Hawaii: University Press of the Pacific, 1988), 12.
2 Harry L. Coles and Albert K. Weinberg, *Civil Affairs: Soldiers Become Governors* (Department of Army, 1964).
3 Hans Binnendijk, and Patrick M. Cronin (eds.), *Civilian Surge: Key to Complex Operations* (Washington D.C.: National Defense University Press, 2009).
4 Review of Civil Affairs Doctrine, (1964/9/23), 1. RG319, Records of Army Staff, DCSOP (Deputy Chief of Staff for Operations), Entry UD 110, Box 10.
5 United States Army and Navy Manual of Military Government and Civil Affairs (FM 27-5, OPNAV 50E-3). (1943/12/22), 1; FM27-5, United States Army and Navy Manual of Civil Affairs Military Government, (December 1947), 67–68.
6 Ibid., 17.
7 Ibid., 35–36.
8 Ibid., Section VI., 45–50.
9 Tentative Operational Plan No. 1–45, Iceberg, Annex 15, Military Government Plan. (1945/1/6). RG407, Entry 427, File 110-0.13.
10 Ibid., Tentative Operation Plan No. 1-45, Iceberg, 11.
11 XXVI-5, 10th Army Action Report, Chapter 11, Military Government. RG407, Entry 427, File 110-0.3.
12 Fisch, 16.
13 Masahide Ota, (2004), op. cit.
14 Report of Psychological Warfare Activities, Okinawa Operation, Appendix H, Joint Intelligence Center Pacific Ocean Areas. (1945/9/15). RG407, Entry 427, File: 110-39.
15 Psychological Warfare Development and Responses, United States Pacific Fleet and Pacific Ocean Areas, CINCPAC/CINCPOA Bulletin, No. 109-45, 13. (1945/5/15). RG407, Entry 427, File 110-39.
16 Strategic Map of the Nansei Shoto. RG 407, Entry 3688, Box 1669.
17 Review of Civil Affairs Doctrine, op. cit., 11.
18 Agenda of Research Requirements for Civil Affairs Administration of Japan (Report No. 1343), (1943/11/19). Research and Analysis Branch, Office of Strategic Service. RG 407, Entry 3688, Box 1658.
19 The Japanese Emperor and the War (R&A 2261S), (1944/9/8), Office of Strategic Service. RG 407, Entry 3688, Box 1660.
20 Civil Affairs Handbook, Japan, Section 2A: Government and Administration (Army Service Force Manual, M 354-2A). Headquarters, Army Service Force. (1944/7/3). RG 208, Records of Office of War Information, Entry 3708, Box 394.

21 Civil Affairs Handbook, Ryukyu (Loochoo) Islands (OPNAV 13-31). Office of the Chief of Naval Operation, Navy Department. (1944/11/15). RG260, USCAR, AO, Box 247, Folder 1.
22 Study of Pacific Base: A Report by the Subcommittee on Pacific Bases of the Committee on Naval Affairs, House of Representatives, 79th Congress, 1st Sess., (1945/8/6).
23 Organization and Functions, Department of Army, Office of the Chief of Civil Affairs and Military Government, (August 1952).
24 FM41-10, 167.
25 Ibid., 138. Civil Security. b(5), 170.
26 Ibid., 171–174.
27 Ibid., 172–173.
28 Weekly Intelligence Summary—Ryukyu Islands (WIS-RI) 69-23 (U). RG 260, USCAR, AO, Box 63, Folder 10.
29 Alphabetical Index of Leftist Organizations in Okinawa, 526th Counter Intelligence Corp Detachment, (1961). RG260, USCAR, PA (Public Affairs Department), Box 1.
30 Specific Intelligence Collection Requirement, To: 526th MI Det., (1968/8/9). RG 260, USCAR, AO, Box 56, Folder 10.

## Chapter 3

1 To General Twining from Wentworth, (1957/4/27). RG218, Records of JCS (Joint Chiefs of Staff), Entry UD4, Geographic File 1957, Box 14, Folder: CCS 383.21 POA Sec 8. National Archives.
2 Ryukyu Islands Facts Book, 25. RG260, Records of USCAR (U.S. Civil Administration of the Ryukyu Islands), CM (Comptroller Department), Box 128, Folder 2, National Archives.
3 Arnold G. Fisch, Military Government in the Ryukyu Islands, 1945–1950 (Honolulu, Hawaii; University Press of the Pacific, 1988), 15–20.
4 J.C.S. 1231, (1945/1/12), Directives for Military Government in the Japanese Outlaying Islands, 1. RG218, JCS, Entry UD2, Geographic File 1942–45, Box 170, Folder: CCS 383.21 POA Sec. 1.
5 794C.00/10-450, Memorandum Approved by the Joint Chiefs of Staff, Washington, (October 4, 1950), JCS 1231/14 Directives for United States Civil Administration of the Ryukyu Islands, *Foreign Relations of the United States (FRUS) 1950 JAPAN*, 1313-1319.
6 Civil Administration Proclamation No. 1, (1950/12/15). RG260, USCAR, LA (Legal Affairs Department), Box 39, Folder 5.
7 794C.0221/7-1554, Document No. 777, Secretary of Defense to the Secretary of State. *FRUS 1952–1954*, Vol. XIV, Part 2, China and Japan.
8 JCS1231, 12.
9 Masaaki Gabe, (1996), op. cit., 59–63.
10 JCS1231, 7.
11 Proposed Economic Directive for the Japanese Outlying Islands, JCS 1231, 7–11.

12 Appendix to Enclosure "C," Basic Accounting Instructions (supplemental to Financial Directives), JCS 1231, (1945/1/12).

## Chapter 4

1. JCS1231/14 is called "USCAR Directives" in the Records of Army Staff.
2. 794C.00/10-450, Memorandum approved by the Joint Chief of Staff, (1950/10/4), JCS1231/14, Directive for United States Civil Administration of the Ryukyu Islands). *FRUS*, 1950, Japan, 1313–1319.
3. AG 091.1 (5 Dec 50) RCA, Subject: Directive for United States Civil Administration of the Ryukyu Islands, From K. B. Bush, Adjutant General, General Headquarters, Far East Command to Commanding General, Ryukyu Command, (1950/12/5). RG319, DCSOP (Deputy Chief of Staff for Operation), PA (Public Affairs), Entry 100, Box 6.
4. General Order Number 1, (1950/12/15), RG260, USCAR, AO (Administration Office), Box 264.
5. Gabe, *Nichibei Kankei no naka no Okinawa*, 60–61
6. Memorandum for the Chief of Staff, United States Army, Subject: Directive for United States Civil Administration of the Ryukyu Islands, (1950/8/26). RG319, DCSOP, PA, Entry 100, Box 6.
7. Summation No. 1–35 (Nov 1946–Sep 1949). Summation No. 31–32 missing. RG 260, USCAR, AO, Box 1–3.
8. Statistical Bulletin No.1–No.12, (Jan–Dec 1950). RG 260, USCAR, AO, Box 3, Folder 13–19.
9. Annual Command Report 1952. RG 260, USCAR, AO, Box 6, Folder 1.
10. NSC13/3, A Report to the President by the National Security Council on Recommendations with Respect to U.S. Policy toward Japan, (1949/5/6) RG273, Policy Papers 11–18, Entry1, Box 2.
11. Civilian Administration of the Ryukyu Islands South of the 29th Parallel, (1949/5/2), Directive USCAR. RG319, DCSOP, PA, Entry 100, Box 6.
12. Harry Bayard Price, *The Marshall Plan and Its Meaning: An independent and unbiased appraisal of the entire record* (Cornell University Press, 1955), 195.
13. Civilian Administration of the Ryukyu Islands South of the 29th Parallel. (1949/5/2). Directive USCAR. RG319, DCSOP, PA, Entry 100, Box 6.
14. Memorandum for the Record. Subject: Government of the Ryukyu Islands. (1949/5/3). RG319, DCSOP, PA, Entry 100, Box 6.
15. Western North Pacific Trust Territory. (1949/5/24). RG319, DCSOP, PA, Entry 100, Box 6.
16. U.S. Administration of Civil Affairs and Civil Government in the Ryukyu Islands, (1949/6/1), 7RG319, DCSOP, PA, Entry 100, Box 6.
17. USCAR Organization Chart. RG260, USCAR, CM, Box 84, Folder 1.
18. Ibid., 8.
19. From George M. Pollard, Chief, Economic Policy-Coordinating Section. Memorandum to Mr. West, Deputy Assistant Secretary for the Far East, Subject: Organization of Civil Administration in the Ryukyu Islands. RG319, DCSOP, PA, Entry 100, Box 6.

20 Memorandum for the Record, Subject: Meeting on Proposed New Directive for Military Government in the Ryukyu Islands, 1430 hours, (14 September 1949), 2. RG319, DCSOP, PA, Entry 100, Box 6.
21 Ibid., 3.
22 Eldridge, (2003), 166–173; Miyazato, (1981), 211–246; the State Department called the USCAR Directives "civil affairs directives."
23 Memorandum for the Record, Subject: Meeting on Proposed New Directive for Military Government in the Ryukyu Islands, 1430 hours, (15 September 1949). RG319, DCSOP, PA, Entry 100, Box 6.
24 Magruder to Rusk, (1950/4/25). RG319, DCSOP, PA, Entry 100, Box 6.
25 WAR 97286, (3 December 49), 4. RG319, DCSOP, PA, Entry 100, Box 6.
26 Memorandum for Mr. R. W. E. Reid, Subject: Draft Directive for Civil Administration of the Ryukyu Islands. (1950/1/20). 2. RG319 DCSOP, PA, Entry 100, Box 6.
27 Ibid., 1.
28 WAR 83375 (CM OUT 83375), From SAOUS to CINCAFE, 1950/5/24. 7. RG319, DCSOP, PA, Entry 100, Box 6.
29 Memorandum for the Chief of Staff, (1950/8/26), FRUS, 2.
30 CX 65173, Enclosure "B" (From: CINCFE TOKYO JAPAN, To: DEPTAR FOR JCS WASH DC) of JCS 1231/16, Establishment of A Ryukyuan Constabulary and Coast Guard, (1950/11/8). RG 218, Geographic File 1951–1953, Box 49, File: CCS 383.21 POA Sec. 4.
31 General Orders Number 6, (1951/1/8). RG260, USCAR, AO, Box 264.
32 CINCPAC 7500.1C, 1961/9/18. RG260, USCAR, AO, Box 58.
33 Manpower Survey 1963. RG319, Entry A1-1964, Records of Deputy Chiefs for Military Operations; Directorate of Civil Affairs; Economic Affairs Division, Manpower Survey and Statistical Data Files Relating to the Ryukyu Islands. Box 1. 603-06 File: Personnel and Manpower Correspondences.

## Chapter 5

1 AG 091.1 (12 Oct 1951) RCA, Subject: Proposed Modification to JCS 1231/14, (4 October 1950), From: General Headquarters, Far East Command, To: Secretary of the Army. RG319, DCSOP (Deputy Chief of Staff for Operations), PA (Public Affairs), Entry 100, Box 7.
2 Staff Study re Use of GARIOA Counterpart Funds to Purchase Land in the Ryukyu Islands, op.cit.
3 Annual Command Report 1952. RG 260, USCAR, AO, Box 6.
4 Directive for U.S. Civil Administration of the Ryukyu Islands, Draft CAMG, 17 Feb 53. RG319 DCSOP, PA, Entry UD 100, Box 6.
5 Kono, op.cit., 94.
6 Tab B Draft of JCS Directive prepared by CAMG (1953/2/17). RG319, DCSOP, PA, Entry 100, Box 6.
7 Tab C Draft of JCS Directive prepared by USCAR, (1953/2/17). RG319, DCSOP, PA, Entry 100, Box 6.
8 From Ogden to Harrison, (1953/2/18). RG319, DCSOP, PA, Entry 100, Box 6.

9 Miyazato, *Nichibei Kankei to Okinawa 1945–1972*, 114–115.
10 From Robert J. M. McClurkin to Charles A. Sullivan, (1953/9/16). RG319, DCSOP, PA, Box 6.
11 From Sullivan to McClurkin, (1953/10/12). RG319, DCSOP, PA, Box 6.
12 NSC Action Number 824. The Japanese Treaty Islands (Memo for NSC from Executive Secretary, same subject, dated June 15, 1953; NSC 125/5, para. 4). RG 273, Records of NSC Actions, Box 1.
13 NSC Planning Board Report attached to Memorandum for the National Security Council, Subject: The Japanese Treaty Islands, (1953/6/15), 5. WHO, OSANSA, 1952–1961, NSC, PPS, Box 3, EL (Dwight D. Eisenhower Presidential Library).
14 Ibid., NSC Planning Board Report, 9–11.
15 Directive for U.S. Civil Administration of the Ryukyu Islands, (1953/10/6). RG319, DCSOP, PA, Box 6.
16 Proposed Directive for United States Civil Administration of the Ryukyu Islands, (1953/11/17). WHO, OSANSA, 1952–1961, NSC, OOS, Box 3, EL.
17 From Dulles to Wilson, (1954/1/11). RG319, DCSOP, PA, Box 7.
18 794C.0221/1-853. Memorandum by the Assistant Secretary of State for Far Eastern Affairs (Robertson) to Secretary of State. 1584. FRUS 1952–1954 Vol. 14, Part II.
19 CX 67023, From CINCFE TOKYO HULL to DEPTAR WASH DC FOR CAMG. (1954/2/5).
20 Memorandum for the Honorable John A. Hannah, Assistant Secretary of Defense, Subject: Proposal by Secretary of State for Revision of Directive for U.S. Civil Administration of the Ryukyu Islands, (1954/1/30). RG319, DCSOP, PA, Box 6.
21 Proposed Revised Directive for United States Civil Administration of the Ryukyu Islands (JCS1231/26, 2 February 1954), Memorandum by the Chief of Staff, U.S. Army. RG319, DCSOP, Entry UD 100, Box 7.
22 Subject: Directive for U.S. Civil Administration of the Ryukyu Islands, Mr. Hauge/CAMG for Mr. Wilson, (1954/4/30). RG319, DCSOP, Entry 110, Box 7.
23 Miyazato, 200, 94–103.
24 Supplemental Instructions to the Governor, Ryukyu Islands, (1954/4/27), RG319, DCSOP, PA, Box 7.
25 Supplemental Appropriations Bill 1955, Hearings before Subcommittees of the Committee on Appropriations House of Representatives, 83rd Congress, 2nd Session, Part 2, (1954/4/27). Printed for the use of the Committee on Appropriations (Washington, D.C.; Government Printing Office, 1954).
26 Directives for U.S. Civil Administration of the Ryukyu Islands (1954/8/2). Chronology—Ryukyu Islands and the United States. RG319, Entry UD 110, DCSOP, Box 7. Folder: USCAR Directive 3.
27 From Rowland Hughes to Secretary of Defense, (1954/8/10). RG319, DCSOP, PA, Box 6.
28 Office Memorandum, Subject: Executive Order re Administration of the Ryukyu Islands, From Public Affairs Division to General Gailey, (1955/11/29). RG319, DCSOP, Entry 110, Box 9.
29 Excerpt from Command Report (January 1955), Implementation of the New Directive for USCAR (Secret).

30 Yasuo Kurima, *Okinawa no Beigun Kichi to Gunyochiryo* (Okinawa Military Base and Land Leases), (Ginowan: Yoju Shorin, 2012), 26–29.
31 Congressional Records –House, 84th Congress, 510.
32 Congressional Records –Senate, 84th Congress, 1139.
33 AGJ 014.1 EJ-D. Subject: Draft Terms of Reference for Commission on Application of U.S. Laws to Ryukyu Islands (1955/7/8) attached to H.R. 2684, 84th Congress, 1st Sess., A Bill to provide for the administration of the Ryukyu Islands, and for other purposes, (1955/1/20). RG260, USCAR, AO, Box 180, Folder 2.
34 DA975369, From OASofA DA WASH, DC to CINCFE, TOKYO JAPAN, (1955/2), 2. RG319, DCSOP, Entry 110, Box 7.
35 Memorandum for the Chief of Staff, Subject: Implementation of President's Directive for U.S. Civil Administration of the Ryukyu Islands, (1955/1/14). RG319, DCSOP, Entry 110, Box 7.
36 Memorandum for the Record, Subject: Operational Plan for Civil Administration of the Ryukyu Islands, (1955/2/28). RG319, DCSOP, Entry 110, Box 7.
37 Memorandum, Subject: Mission Report on Implementation Procedures Pursuant to Presidential Directive for Administration of the Ryukyu Islands, (1955/3/15). RG319, DCSOP, Entry 110, Box 7.
38 Memorandum for the Record, Subject: Okinawan Problems—Matters to be handled by CAMG, (1955/3/22). RG319, DCSOP, Entry 110, Box 7.
39 Follow-up Action Check List, DA Mission to Far East Command, (1955/3/24). RG319, DCSOP, Entry 110, Box 7.
40 Request to Secretary of Defense that General Ogden be Appointed as Member Legislation Review Commission to be Created Pursuant to Enactment of Ryukyu Legislation, (1955/4/13).
41 Office Memorandum, Subject: Executive Order Providing for Administration of the Ryukyu Islands, From Public Affairs Division to General Marquart, (1955/4/19). RG319, DCSOP, Entry 110, Box 9.
42 Subject: Revision of Presidential Directive for U.S. Civil Administration, Ryukyu Islands, (1955/4/22). RG319, DCSOP, Entry 110, Box 7.
43 Progress Report on U.S. Policy toward Japan (NSC5516/1), 18. OPA 059-01586-00022-001-116.
44 Memorandum of Understanding Between the Department of Defense and Department of State with Reference to Foreign Relations Responsibilities for The Ryukyu Islands, (1955/5/31). RG319, DCSOP, Entry 110, Box 7.
45 Okinawa Lands. Hearing before a Subcommittee of the Committee on Armed Services, House of Representatives, 84th Congress, 1st Session, held at Naha, Okinawa, Ryukyu Islands, October 24 and 25, 1955. (Washington D.C.: U.S. Government Printing Office, 1957).
46 Okinawa Lands, Hearing, op.cit., 43.
47 No. 86, Report of a Special Subcommittee of the Armed Services Committee, House of Representatives, Following an Inspection Tour, October 14 to November 23, 1955 (Washington D.C.; United States Government Printing Office).
48 Ibid., 7663–7665.

49 From Katherine Fite to Phlager. Subject: U.S. Bases in the Ryukyus (1956/6/20) attached to a copy of the letter from John Foster Dulles to Charles E. Wilson (1956/6/22). RG 59, Entry A1-3069, Subject Files 1941–1962, Records of Office of Assistant Legal Adviser for Far Eastern Affairs, Box 4.
50 Office Memorandum, Subject: Provision Requiring the reporting GRI laws to Congress, From Harold Seidman to Col. Norman King, CAMG, Chief of Public Affairs, (1956/2/16). RG319, DCSOP, Entry 110, Box 9.
51 OCB Course of Action 42, Excerpt from Japan Outline Plan of Operation, approved by the Operations Coordination Board, (1957/2/27). RG319, DCSOP, Entry 110, Box 9.
52 National Security Council Progress Report on United States Objectives and Courses of Action with Respect to Japan by the Operation Coordinating Board, 5. WHO, OSANSA, 1952–1961, NSC, PPS, Box 3, EL.
53 op. cit., NSC Planning Board Report (1953/6/15), 3.
54 No. 2351, From USAMBASSADOR TOKYO JAPAN to Secretary of State, (1957/4/18). RG319, DCSOP, Entry 110, Box 9.
55 FE 804813, From CINCFE TOKYO JAPAN to SECDEF WASH DC, (1957/4/26). RG319, DCSOP, Entry 110, Box 9.
56 Summary Telegraph from AmEmb Tokyo to State re Kishi reaction to issuance of Executive Order, (1957/5/22), FE 805216, From CINCFE to SECDEF 1957/5/29. RG319, DCSOP, Entry 110, Box 9.
57 Executive Order 10713, Providing for Administration of the Ryukyu Islands, 1957/6/5(22 FR 4007, June 7, 1957).
58 From Eisenhower to Secretary of Defense, (1957/6/5). RG319, DCSOP, Entry 110, Box 9.
59 Memorandum for Lt. General Eddleman, Subject: Executive Order Providing for Administration of the Ryukyu Islands, (1957/6/6). RG319, DCSOP, Entry 110, Box 9.
60 DEPTEL 2712, From Tokyo to Secretary of State, (1957/6/6). RG319, DCSOP, Entry 110, Box 9.
61 From Crone, Signal Officer, RYCOM/IX Corps, Okinawa RI, to Sampson, Chief, Army Comm Svc Div., Department of Army, (1957/6/7). RG319, DCSOP, Entry 110, Box 9.
62 Press Release, Lt. Gen. James Moore will be designated as High Commissioner of the Ryukyu Islands, (1957/6/8). RG319, DCSOP, Entry 110, Box 9.
63 Executive Order 10713 as amended by Executive Order 11010, (10 March 1962), Providing for Administration of the Ryukyu Islands. RG 260, USCAR, LA (Legal Affairs), Box 126, Folder 1, NA.
64 Executive Order 10713 (CFR 68–71, 1958, Chapter II, Executive Orders).
65 74 Stat. 461, Public Law 86-629, An Act to provide for promotion of economic and social development in the Ryukyu Islands, H.R. 1157, (1960/7/12).
66 Draft, Problems and Issues Affecting the U.S. Civil Administration of the Ryukyu Islands, (1958/2/16), attached to Memorandum for the Operation Coordinating Board, Subject: Problems and Issues Affecting the U.S. Civil Administration of the Ryukyu Islands, (1958/2/27). OPA 059-01586-00022-001-023.

67 Executive Orders can be classified. Kevin R. Kosar, Classified Information Policy and Executive Order 13526, Congressional Research Service, (2010/12/10).
68 Oral History Interview, Alexander Liosnoff. See Chapter 8.

## Chapter 6

1 Winkler, Allan M., *The Politics of Propaganda: The Office of War Information 1942–1945* (New Haven, CT; Yale University Press, 1978), 8–37.
2 Takeya Mizuno, *Tekikokugo Janarizumu* (Enemy language press in wartime: The Pacific War and Japanese language press in the United States), (Yokohama: Shumpu Publishing, 2011), 306–350.
3 Winkler, 86.
4 Winkler, 124–125.
5 Reiko Tsuchiya, *Taigai Senden Bira ga kataru Taiheiyo Senso* (Propaganda Leaflets against Japan during the Pacific War), (Tokyo: Yoshikawa Kobunkan, 2011), 12.
6 Winkler, 137–139.
7 Winkler, 149; Congressional Quarterly Service, *Congress and the Nation 1945–1960: A Review of Government and Politics in the Postwar Years*, 210.
8 Introduction, Psychological and Political Warfare, *FRUS-EIE (Foreign Relations of the United States 1945–1950, Emergence of Intelligence Establishment)*, 615.
9 Paul Linebarger, M. A., *Psychological Warfare* (Landisville, PA; Coachwhip, 2010=1948), 249.
10 Yuka Tsuchiya, 2009, 128.
11 Kiyul Uhm, "The Cold War Communication Crisis: The Right to Know Movement." *Journalism and Mass Communication Quarterly*, 82: 1 (Spring 2005), 134.
12 *Congress and the Nation*, 211.
13 Brian Angus McKenzie, *Remaking France: Americanization, Public Diplomacy, and the Marshall Plan* (New York; Berghahn Books, 2005), 24–25.
14 Yuka Tsuchiya, 2009, 138.
15 *Congress and the Nation*, 208.
16 *FRUS-EIE*, 615.
17 *FRUS-EIE*, 364–369.
18 ORE 24-48, The Ryukyu Islands and Their Significance, 1948/8/6, Central Intelligence Agency. RG 319, Records of Army Staff, Assistant Chief of Staff (G-2), Intelligence Administration Division, Entry NM3 82A, Box 23.
19 The Ryukyu Islands and Their Significance (ORE 24-48). 1948/8/6. Central Intelligence Agency. RG 319, Records of Assistant Chief of Staff (G-2), Intelligence Administration Division. Entry NM3, 82A. Box 23.
20 NSC 13 (1948/6/2), Report to the National Security Council by the Department of State on recommendations with respect to U.S. policy toward Japan. RG 273, Records of the National Security Council, Policy Papers, Entry 1, Box 2.

21 NSC 13/1 (1948/9/24), 13/2 (1948/10/7), 13/3 (1949/5/6). Report to the National Security Council by the Executive Secretary on the recommendations with respect to U.S. policy toward Japan. RG 273, NSC Policy Papers, Entry 1, Box 2.
22 Robert A Fearey, *The Occupation of Japan, Second Phase: 1948–1950*. Published under the auspices of the International Secretariat, Institute of Pacific Relations (New York; MacMillan, 1950), 5–6.
23 Annex 8, National Security Council Intelligence Directive No. 2, Coordination of Collection Activities Abroad (1948/1/13), National Security Archives, George Washington University.
24 Document 249, Report by an Ad Hoc Subcommittee of the State-Army-Navy-Air Force Coordinating Committee, 1947/11/7, *FRUS-EIE*.
25 Document 256, Department of State Briefing Memorandum, Coordination of Foreign Information Measure (NSC 4) Psychological Operation (NSC 4-A), 1947/12/17, *FRUS-EIE*.
26 Document 256, *FRUS-EIE*.
27 Sara-Jane Corke, *US Covert Operation and Cold War Strategy: Truman, Secret Warfare and the CIA, 1945–1953* (New York: Routledge, 2008), 49.
28 Document 263, Office of Special Operation Directive No. 18/3, 1947/3/29, *FRUS-EIE*.
29 Naoki Ono, *Reisenka CIA no Interijensu* (CIA Intelligence during the Cold War: Truman Administration Strategic Policy Making Process), (Kyoto: Minerva, 2012), 218.
30 Document 268, Memorandum by the Chief of the Special Procedure Group, Central Intelligence Agency (Cassidy), Policy Liaison for SPG Activities, undated, *FRUS-EIE*.
31 Corke, 60.
32 Brad M. Ward, *Strategic Influence Operations; Information Connection*. USAWC Strategy Research Project (Carlisle Barracks, PA; U.S. Army War College, 2003), 5
33 Corke, 102–105.
34 Corke, 120.
35 General Order No. 37, Section IV, Department of Army, 1952/4/14.
36 Ron Rubin, *The Making of the Cold War Enemy: Culture and Politics in the Military-Intellectual Complex* (Princeton, NJ; Princeton University Press, 2001), 146–157.
37 Emily T Metzgar, "Public Diplomacy, Smith-Mundt and the American Public." *Communication Law and Policy*, 17:1 (2012), 67–101.
38 2013 Amendment to Smith-Mundt Act and Zorinsky Amendment, Section 1078 of the National Defense Authorization Act (NDAA), P.L. 112–239.
39 Nancy Snow, "The Smith-Mundt Act of 1948," *Peace Review: A Journal of Social Justice*, 10:4 (1998), 619–624.
40 Allen W. Palmer, and Edward L. Carter, "The Smith-Mundt Act's Ban on Domestic Propaganda: An Analysis of the Cold War Statute Limiting Access to Public Diplomacy," *Communication Law and Policy*, (Winter 2006).
41 Uhm, 131–147.
42 An Act to promote the better understanding of the United States among the peoples of the world and to strengthen cooperative international relations (H.R.

3342), P.L. 402, 62 STAT. 6., 80th Congress, 2nd Sess., (1948/1/27) (United States Information and Education Exchange Act of 1948).
43 Agreement for Facilitating the International Circulation of Visual and Auditory Materials of an Educational, Scientific and Cultural Characters, UNESCO; Records of the General Conference of the United Nations Educational, Scientific and Cultural Organization, Third Session, Beirut 1948, Volume II, Resolution, UNESCO, Paris, (February 1949); Roxanne E. Christ, "The Beirut Agreement: A License to Censor." *Loyola of Los Angeles International and Comparative Law Review,* (1984): 255–278.
44 Kenji Tanigawa, *Amerika Eiga to Senryo Seisaku* (US Occupation Policy and American Films), (Kyoto: Kyoto University Press, 2002), 427.
45 RCA Communication, Inc. (Manila) to Bernard Sloan, Communication Department, USCAR. (1951/10/11). RG 260, USCAR, LA, Box 21, Folder 4.
46 Digest, Economic Cooperation Administration, Overseas Information Program. PSB File, Box 2, File: 040 ECA Liaison, TL.
47 Report on Study of Overseas Information Program of State Department and the Economic Cooperation Administration, (1951/10/1). PSB File, Box 2, File: 040. TL.
48 NSC125 Policy Toward Japan, WHO, OSANSA, NSC, PPS, Box 3, Folder: NSC 125 Policy Toward Japan, EL; CIA-RDP80R01731R003300190002-8, Memorandum for the Honorable Allen W. Dulles, Director of Central Intelligence Agency, Subject: Implementation of PSB D-27, A Psychological Strategy Plan for Japan, (1953/2/25).
49 National Security Council Progress Report on United States Objectives and Courses of Action with Respect to Japan by the Operation Coordinating Board. 5. WHO, OSANSA, NSC, PPS, Box 3, Folder: NSC 125 Policy Toward Japan, EL.; 511.94/10-2254, Office Memorandum, A Letter to Ambassador Allison on Psychological Strategy Plan for Japan, From: NA Mr. Hemmendinger to: FE Mr. Robertson. RG 59, NA.
50 511/94/4-2852, Memorandum for Mr. John Allison, Subject: Terms of References, (1952/4/28). RG 59, NA.
51 Draft, International Operations Plan Concerning United States Personnel in Japan. WHO, OSANSA, NSC, PPS, Box 3, EL.
52 NSC Planning Board Report for 1953/6/18 NSC Meeting, 3. WHO, OSANSA, NSC, PPS, Box 3, EL.

## Chapter 7

1 CAA 1-1 (Civil Affairs Activities in the Ryukyu Islands. For the Period Ending 31 December 1952. Vol.1, No.1), 198. RG260, USCAR, CM, Box 113.
2 Miyagi, 1994, 1–2.
3 Choko Takamine, *Shimbun Gojunen* (Newspaper 50 Years), (Naha: Okinawa Times, (1973): 299–314.
4 10th Army Action Report, Chapter 11: Staff Section Report—Naval Gunfire. RG 407, Entry 427, File 110.03.

5 Jun Eto, *Tozasareta Gengo Kukan* (Suppressed speech sphere), (Tokyo: Bunshun Bunko, 1994): 99–102.
6 Eto, 30.
7 JCS 1231, Para 15, 1945/1/12, Directives for Military Government in the Japanese Outlying Islands. RG218, Records of Joint Chiefs of Staff, Entry UD2, Geographic File 1942–45, Box 170, Folder: CCS 383.21 POA Sec. 1.
8 Report of Psychological Warfare Activities, Okinawa Operation, Appendix H, Joint Intelligence Center, Pacific Ocean Areas, (1945/9/15, 35. RG 407, Entry 427, File 110.39.
9 Report of Psychological Warfare Activities, 24–26.
10 The Buckaneer, 8. RG 407, Entry 427, File 110.00.
11 No. 104, Study of Pacific Bases, A Report by the Subcommittee on Pacific Bases of the Committee on Naval Affairs, House of Representatives, 79th Congress, 1st Sess., Pursuant to H. Res. 154, (1945/8/6): 1133.
12 Fisch, Arnold G., *Military Government in the Ryukyu Islands, 1945–1950* (Honolulu, Hawaii; University Press of the Pacific, 1988), 20–21.
13 Proclamation No. 2, (1945/9/25). RG 260, USCAR, LA (Legal Affairs Department), Box 39, Folder 4.
14 Proclamation No. 8, (1945/undated). RG 260, USCAR, LA, Box 39, Folder 4.
15 Proclamation No. 10, (1945/undated). RG 260, USCAR, LA, Box 39, Folder 4.
16 Proclamation No. 2, No. 8, No. 10, op.cit.
17 Proclamation No. 1, United States Navy Government. RG 260, USCAR, LA, Box 39, Folder 4.
18 Kabira, 2011, 92–99.
19 MG Directive Number 11, From Deputy Governor for Military Government to Chiji of Okinawa Gunto. Subject: "Uruma Shimpo," publication of, (1946/5/22). RG260, USCAR, LA, Box 128, Folder 1.
20 United States Army and Navy Manual of Military Government and Civil Affairs (FM27-5/NAV 50E-3), (1943/12/22), 17.
21 James N. Tull, *The Ryukyu Islands, Japan's Oldest Colony—America's Newest; An Analysis of Policy and Propaganda* (MA thesis, University of Chicago, December 1953), 54.
22 Yamamoto, Taketoshi, *GHQ no Kenetsu Choho Senden* Kosaku (GHQ censorship, intelligence and propaganda), (Tokyo: Iwanami Shoten, 2013), Chap. 3–4.
23 Nicholas John Bruno, *Major Daniel C. Imboden and Press Reform in Occupied Japan 1945–1952* (Ph.D. Disser., University of Maryland, 1988), 181.
24 Bruno, 179.
25 CAA 1-1, 24–25.
26 CAA 1-1, 198.
27 Miyagi, 1994, 37–42.
28 Tull, ii.
29 Tull, 64, Appendix B: Portion of Report on Pre-Election Information Campaign.
30 Tull, 53.
31 Tull called CIE movies propaganda films.
32 Tanigawa, 341; USCAR CI&E Film Catalogue. RG 260, USCAR, AO, Box 178.
33 Fisch, 76.
34 Tull, 54. Civil Affairs Activities in the Ryukyu Islands.

35 Tull, 54.
36 CAA 1-1, 202.
37 Kenneth Osgood, *Total Cold War: Eisenhower's Secret Propaganda Battle at Home and Abroad* (Lawrence, KS; University Press of Kansas, 2006), 298.
38 Kayo Yasuharu, *Okinawa Minseifu* (Okinawa civilian government: A memoir), (Tokyo: Kume Shobo, 1996), 142–143.
39 Tull, 64, Appendix B.
40 Mizuno, 350.
41 Masahide Ota, and Akira Tsujimura, *Okinawa no Genron* (Okinawa Press), (Tokyo: Nanpo Doho Engokai, 1966), 13–50.
42 Gekkan Okinawa Sha (ed.), *Amerika no Okinawa Tochi Kanren Hoki Soran* (Martial law collection of the U.S. administration of Okinawa), (Naha: Ikemiya Shoten, Vol. 4, 518.
43 Mizuno, 318.
44 MG Ordinance Number 3. RG260, USCAR, AO, Box 262.
45 Tull, 54–58.
46 Tull, 66.
47 Kenneth Osgood, *Total Cold War: Eisenhower's Secret Propaganda Battle at Home and Abroad* (Kansas: University Press of Kansas, 2006), 298.
48 CAA, 1-1. 26.
49 Tull, 205.
50 Tatsuo Taira, *Sengo Seikai Uramenshi* (Secret postwar politics history), (Naha: Nampo-sha, 1963), 157.
51 General Orders Number 11, (1952/2/25). RG260, USCAR, AO, Box 264.
52 Civil Affairs Activities, 1-1. 24–27.
53 Civil Affairs Activities, 1-1. 193.
54 Hidekazu Sensui, "1952 SIRI *Kaigi* (1952 SIRI Conference)," *Kokusai Keiei Forum*, Vol. 20, (2009), 43–44.
55 CAA 1-1, 204
56 Tull, 67.
57 Tanigawa, 430–435.
58 Yamamoto, 13.
59 CAA 1-1, 26.

## Chapter 8

1 Roger Hilsman, *To Move A Nation: The Politics of Foreign Policy in the Administration of John F. Kennedy* (New York; Doubleday, 1964), 23.
2 Ibid., 77.
3 United States Civil Administration of the Ryukyu Islands (7244), APO 331, Department of the Army, 1 May 1956. RG260, USCAR, AO (Administration Office), Box 180 Folder 2.
4 USCAR Organization and Functions (USCAR Reg 10-1). RG 260, USCAR, AO (Administration Office), Box 249.
5 AICA-CIE 110.01, CIE Yen Budget for FY 1954, (1953/6/10). RG 260, USCAR, CM (Comptroller Department), Box 209.

6 Office of Public Information, USCAR Organization Chart. RG260, USCAR, CM, Box 84, Folder 1.
7 LO 9-17, Subject: Federal Service Overseas Fund Campaign of 1958, To: Captain Sam L. Amato, 01176238, Arty, Office of Public Information, USCAR, (1957/9/12), RG 260, USCAR, AO, Box 12, Folder 9; General Order Number 26 (1958/9/10), General Order Number 27 (1958/9/11). RG 260, USCAR, AO, Box 263, Folder 2.
8 USCAR Reg 10-1, 51.
9 Mass Media Preference Survey, (September 1958), Vol. III: "Konnichi-no-Ryukyu" Survey; Cultural Center Survey; Demographic Characteristics; Samples and Interviews; Questionnaires, RG 260, USCAR, PA, Box 65.
10 Position Paper, USCAR Monthly Magazine, *Konnnichi-no-Ryukyu*, (1969/8/27). RG 260, USCAR, PA (Public Affairs Department), Box 5, Folder 10.
11 Almanac 1969. RG 260, USCAR, PA, Box 94.
12 USCAR's Radio and TV Programs, 1967. RG 260, USCAR, PA, Box 5, Folder 1.
13 HCRI-PAD, Public Opinion Survey (U), (1969/11/19). RG 260, USCAR, PA, Box 5.
14 HCRI-PAD, October 1968, Revision of the Facts Book, (1968/9/10). RG260, USCAR, PA, Box 12.
15 Frank Tanabe, Japan Occupation Essays Project, National Japanese American Veteran Council.
16 Ibid.
17 Etsujiro Miyagi, *Okinawa no Beijin Kisha kara mita Nihon Fukki, Okinawa no Shinbun ga Tsubureruhi* (Okinawa Newspaper Death), Ed. Okinawa Freelance Journalist Association, (Naha: Gekkan Okinawa Sha, 1994), 292.
18 Johannes A. Binnendijk, "The Dynamics of Okinawa Reversion 1945–69," In ed. Gregory Henderson, *Public Diplomacy and Political Change* (New York; Praeger, 1973).
19 Report to Ambassador Dulles, Third draft 4-6-51, Subject: United States – Japanese Cultural Relations, From: John D. Rockefeller, 3rd, p11. RG 59, Decimal Files 1950-1954, Box 2534, 4-651.
20 Recommendation, attached to Okinawa News Highlights on (1966/5/4). RG 260, USCAR, PA, Box 93, Folder 8.
21 Alexander Liosnoff, Records of Operations. 2. June 1957 to date, with U.S. Civil Administration of the Ryukyu Islands, 1961/3/25. 2. Liosnoff Collection (Alexander Liosnoff Papers Collection), Box 24, Folder 4-9: PAD USCAR Operations Policies, Hoover Institution, Stanford University.
22 JA5501. RG 306, United States Information Agency, Office of Research, Country Project Files, 1951–1964, Japan, Entry 1015, Box 58.
23 Miyagi, 1994, 131–133.
24 Miyagi, 133; The Okinawa Times Okinawa Bureau (Ed.), *Kichi de Hataraku* (Working in U.S. Base), (Naha: The Okinawa Times, 2013), 266–273.
25 Communist Propaganda Highlights, Analysis and Trend, No. 70–69. Headquarter, 7th Psychological Operations Group, Department of Army. RG 260, USCAR, AO, Box 64, Folder 15.
26 Kobayashi, Somei, *Reisenki Asia no Denpa Senso Kenkyu Josetsu, Ouyou Shakaigaku Kenkyu (*Applied Social Science Review*)*, Vol. 52, 2010, 65–77; Document 122, Paper Prepared in the U.S. Information Agency, undated. *FRUS*

Notes

1961–1963, Vol. XXV, Organization of Foreign Policy, Information policy, United Nations, Scientific Matters; Document 102, Telegram From the Embassy in Korea to the Department of State, 1966/11/29. *FRUS* 1964–1968, Vol. XXIX, Part 1, Korea.
27 HCRI, Subject: Support of Civil Information Program (U) Commanding Officer, 7th Psychological Operations Group, APO 96248, (1970/2/27). RG 260, USCAR, PA, Box 57, Folder 4.
28 USCAR's Radio and TV Programs, 1967, op. cit.
29 HCRI, Subject: Support of Civil Information Program (U), (1971/2/22). RG 260, USCAR, PA, Box 57, Folder 4.
30 Okinawa Times (1971/11/7), Ryukyu Shimpo (1971/11/7) English Translation. Liosnoff Collection, Box 24, Folder 4–9: PAD USCAR Operations Policies.
31 Osgood, 314–321.
32 Miyagi, 134–136.
33 HCRI, Subject: Support of Civil Information Program (U), (1971/2/22), op.cit., 3–4.
34 USCAR's Radio & TV Programs, 1967, op. cit.
35 Reception of VOA Broadcasts Beamed to Far East, Southeast Asia and Oceania Summer 1970. RG260, USCAR, PA, Box 57.
36 Hearings before the Subcommittee of the Committee on Appropriations, House of Representatives, 85th Congress, 2nd Session, (1958/2/24). Department of State and Justice, the Judiciary and related agencies appropriations for 1959. United States Information Agency. 388, 400.
37 Ibid., 136, 145.
38 Somei Kobayashi, "VOA Shisetsu Iten wo meguru Kanbei Kosho 1972–73," *Journal of Mass Communication Studies*, No. 75, (2009), 129–147.
39 Alexander Liosnoff, Records of Operations, op. cit., 2.
40 FBIS Daily Report, Asia & Pacific, No. 179, Vol. II, Tuesday, 16 September 1969.
41 The Okinawa Times Okinawa Branch, 279–285.
42 FBIS Daily Report, Far East, No. 162-1965, Monday, 23 August 1965.
43 "Lansdale Memo for Taylor on Unconventional Warfare," (1971/7/1), New York Times.
44 Alfred T. Cox, "Civil Air Transport (CAT); A Proprietary Airline 1946–1955," Clandestine Services History, CS History Paper, No. 87, Vol. 1, (April 1969), 6–16. (http://www.cia.foia.gov).
45 Ibid., 14.
46 Joe F. Leeker, "CAT and Air America in Japan," (2013/3/4), 79. Special Collection, University of Texas-Dallas (http://www.utdallas.edu/library/specialcollections/).
47 The Okinawa Times Okinawa Branch, 286–399.
48 Document 10. Memorandum of Conversation, (1958/9/15). FRUS 1958–1960, Vol. X, Part 2, Eastern Europe; Finland; Greece; Turkey.
49 Oral History Interview, Alexander Liosnoff. Liosnoff Collection, Box 1. Hoover Institution, Stanford University.
50 Behind the Iron Curtain. Liosnoff Collection, Box 15, Folder 3.
51 Tape Recording Tally Sheet, Koje Islands and Compound 11, Pusan, 1952/7/6. 4th Mobile Radio Broadcasting Co./1st Radio Broadcasting & Leaflet Gp. Liosnoff Collection, Box 15, Folder 4.

52 Propaganda Analyses 1954–1955. Liosnoff Collection, Box 15, Folder 9.
53 Operation Memo #1. Liosnoff Collection, Box 15, Folder 1.
54 Oral History Interview, op. cit., 30.
55 From c/o K.S. Hsia, PAMIS, 7th Psy Op Gp. to Liosnoff. Liosnoff Collection, Box 29, Folder: Personal. T.T. Ssutu, K.S. Hsia, W. Kuai.
56 Program and Events, undated. Liosnoff Collection, Box 19, Folder II-6: Okinawa Reversion Historical.

## Chapter 9

1 Kono, 1994; Kei Wakaizumi, *Tasaku Nakarishi wo Shinzemu to Hossu* (Tokyo: Bungei Shunju, 1994); Shinobu, Takashi, *Wakaizumi Kei to Nicibei Mitsuyaku* (Tokyo: Nihon Hyoron Sha, 2012).
2 Nakajima, 34–40.
3 The original text of Sato's speech is in Japanese. This translation is exerpted from the USCAR official translation for the press releases at the time. Prime Minister Sato's Statement at Naha International Airport (Embargoed until delivery of the speech). RG260, USCAR, PAD Box 73, Folder 1 (Official Statements and Speech Primin Sato's Visit 19-21 August 1965.
4 Yoshiharu Fukui, Okinawa Henkan Kosho: Nihon Seifu ni okeru Ketteikatei, *Kokusai Seiji* (International Politics), (Tokyo: Yuhikaku, 1974), 107.
5 Nicolas Evan Sarantakes, "Keystone: The American Occupation of Okinawa and U.S.-Japanese Relations." (Texas A&M University Press, 2000), 194.
6 Operation Friendship. RG260, USCAR, PA (Public Affairs Department), Box 72.
7 Nakajima, 38: USCAR'S official English translation of Sato's statement is excerpted from "Prime Minister Sato's Statement at Naha International Airport." op. cit.
8 Operation Friendship. op.cit.
9 Daniel Dayan and Elihu Katz, "Media Events: The Live Broadcasting of History." (Harvard University Press, 1992) 26.
10 Kurt Lang and Gladys Engel Lang, "The Unique Perspective of Television and Its Effects: A Pilot Study." *American Sociological Review* 18 (1) (Feb. 1953), 6.
11 Hicom and Cincpacrep Ryukyus Opord, RG260, USCAR, PA, Box 70.
12 Miyagi, 193–211.
13 Official Statements and Speech Primin Sato's Visit Aug.19–21. RG260, USCAR, PA, Box 72.
14 Green Briefing Paper, RG260, USCAR, LO (Liaison Department), Box 263)
15 The Future of Japan, 65, RG260, USCAR, LO, Box 263.
16 Miyazato, 2000, 250–252.
17 Appointment of Lt. General Albert Watson, (June 3, 1964). RG59, Office of East Asian Affairs, Central File. Box 8.
18 Nakajima, 32.
19 Embassy Note No. 895. (April, 2, 1965). RG59, Central Foreign Policy File 1964–1966, Box 2826.

20 JCS1231/50, (1962/2/24), 307. No. 00147, National Security Archives, George Washington University.
21 News Release 65-116, (April 2, 1965). RG260, USCAR, PA, Box 3.
22 U.S. Policy Okinawa, (July 16, 1965), 8. No. 00498, National Security Archives, George Washington University.
23 From SECSTATE to AMEMBASSY Tokyo 3467, Info: HICOMRY, (June 22, 1965). RG260, USCAR, PA, Box 2.
24 From HICOMRY OKINAWA RY to DA, (July 3, 1965.) RG260, USCAR, PA, Box 2.
25 From SECSTATE to AMEMBASSY TOKYO, Info: HICOMRY, (July 8, 1965). RG260, USCAR, PA, Box 2.
26 HI-LO 518405, RG260, USCAR, PA, Box 2.
27 HI-LO 518602, RG260, USCAR, PA, Box 2.
28 Subcommittee of Public Affairs, Operation Friendship. RG260, USCAR, PA, Box 72.
29 HI-LO 518602. RG260, USCAR, PA, Box 2.
30 HI-LO 518601. RG260, USCAR, PA, Box 2.
31 Official Statements and Speech Primin Sato's Visit Aug 19–21. RG260, USCAR, PA, Box 72.
32 JCS 6582, (23 July 1965). RG260, USCAR, PA, Box 2.
33 Memorandum for: Civil Administrator and Information Coordinator, Subject: News Media Developments Concerning the Sato Visit, (21 July 1965). RG260, USCAR, PA, Box 2.
34 Memorandum for Records, (1965/7/21). RG260, USCAR, PA, Box 2.
35 Operation Friendship. RG260 PA Box 72.
36 HC–JU 5199306, (1965/7/12). RG260, USCAR, PA, Box 2.
37 Reiko Tsuchiya, 120.
38 From Amembassy to Rusk. RG260, USCAR, PA, Box 2.
39 Green Briefing Paper. RG260, USCAR, LO, Box 293.
40 Memorandum for: Chairman, Operation Friendship, Subject: Visit of Amemb and GOJ Public Relations Officials, (1965/7/31). RG260, USCAR, PA, Box 2.
41 From SecState to Amembassy, (August 17, 1965). RG260, USCAR, PA, Box 2.
42 From Amembassy Tokyo to SecState, Immediate 559, (August 18, 1965). RG260, USCAR, PA, Box 2.
43 Prime Minister Sato's Statement at Naha International Airport (Embargoed until actual delivery of the speech). RG260, USCAR, PAD, Box 73, Folder 1.
44 Operation Friendship Summary Sheet. RG260, USCAR, PA, Box 73.
45 After-Action Report, Operation Friendship. RG260, USCAR, PA, Box 2.
46 SATO, OKINAWA, LOOKS TO REUNION: Visit by a Japanese Chief Since Loss of Islands, By Emerson Chapin, Special to The New York Times. The New York Times, August 19, 1965 (ProQuest Historical Newspapers: The New York Times 1851-2009)
47 "Sato Protected by US as Okinawa Riot Flares," *Los Angeles Times*, (August 20, 1965).
48 Memorandum for: Chairman, Operation Friendship. Subject: Comments on After-Action Report from Chairman, 28 August 1965. RG260, USCAR, PA, Box 2.

49 Douglas Kellner, "Media Events and Media Spectacles: Some critical reflections." *Media Events in a Global Age*. (Ed.) Nick Couldry, Andreas Hepp and Friedrich Krotz. (Routledge, 2010). 76–91.
50 From Amembassy Tokyo to State, (1965/10/9) RG59, Central Foreign Policy File, Box 2626.
51 Weekly Intelligence Summary, Ryukyu Islands. RG260, USCAR, AO, Box 63.
52 Dayan and Katz, 189.
53 "Our Ryukyu Base." RG260, USCAR, LO, Box 263.
54 HCRI, Subject: Support of Civil Information Program (U). (1970/2/26). RG 260 PA Box 57 Folder 4.
55 Jackson Report, Presidential Committee on International Information Activities, Report to the President, (1953/6/30), 61; Sprague Report, Conclusions and Recommendations of the President's Committee on Information Activities Abroad, (December 1960), 17. Richard Helms Collection, FOIA, CIA.
56 HCRI, Subject: Support of Civil Information Program (U). (1970/2/26). RG 260 PA Box 57 Folder 4.
57 RIPO-C. Subject: Revision of PSYOPE Requirement LOI (U). (1971/2/12). RG 260 PA Box 57 Folder 4.
58 Program and Events, undated. Liosnoff Collection. Box 19 Folder II-6. Okinawa Reversion Historical. Hoover Institution, Stanford University.
59 Okinawa Reversion Planning: Transfer of Civil Administration to Japan, (1970/2/26). RG 319, HMS P1196, ARC 5716769, Background Files to the Study "History of the United States Civil Administration of the Ryukyu Islands."

## Conclusion

1 Harold D. Lasswell, *Propaganda Techniques in the World War* (New York: Alfred A. Knopf, 1927).
2 Nye, op.cit., 99.
3 Odd Arne Westad, *The Global Cold War: Third World Intervention and the Making of Our Times* (Cambridge: Cambridge University Press, 2007), p. 400.
4 Office Memorandum, From: Richard H. Lamb, To: FE/NA - Mr. James V. Martin, Jr., Subject: Comments on Draft NSC Paper on the Ryukyus, 1957/12/17, p.1. RG 59, General Files Relating to the Ryukyu Islands 1952–1958, Box 14. (This document became available at the author's request based on the Freedom of Information Act on September 12, 2014)
5 Ibid., Office Memorandum, Lamb, p.1.

# Bibliography

## U.S. National Archives and Personal Collections

RG 59 Records of State Department, National Archives College Park (NA)
RG 208 Records of Office of War Information, NA
RG 218 Records of Joint Chiefs of Staff, NA
RG 260 Records of United States Civil Administration of the Ryukyu Islands, NA
RG 273 Records of National Security Council, NA
RG 306 Records of United States Information Agency, NA
RG 319 Records of Army Staff, NA
RG 407 Records of Adjutant General's Office, NA
Records of Psychological Strategy Board, Harry S. Truman Library (TL)
Records of National Security Council, Dwight D. Eisenhower Library (EL)
Central Intelligence Agency, FOIA Website (CIA FOIA)
National Security Archives, George Washington University
Alexander Liosnoff Collection, Hoover Institution, Stanford University
Okinawa Prefectural Archives (OPA)

## Government Publications and Published Documents

*Budget of the United States Government,* Federal Archives Reserve.
*Civil Affairs Operations, Department of the Army Field Manual* (FM41-10, 1962)
*Code of Federal Regulations*
*Congress and the Nation, 1945–1964* (Washington D.C.: Congressional Quarterly Service, 1965).
*Congressional Records,* Proquest Database.
CRS Report for Congress, U.S. Occupation Assistance: Iraq, Germany, Japan Compared (March 23, 2006), Congressional Research Service.
*Foreign Relations of United States,* State Department.
*Gekkan Okinawa Sha,* ed. *Amerika no Okinawa tochi kanren hoki soran*, Ikemiya Shokai, 1983.

## English Sources

Appleman, Roy E., James M. Burns, Russell A. Gugeler and John Stevens. *Okinawa: The Last Battle*. New York: Skyhorne Publishing, 1947.

Binnendijk, Johannes A. *The Dynamics of Okinawa Reversion 1945–69, Public Diplomacy and Political Change*. Edited by Gregory Henderson. New York: Praeger, 1973.

Bruno, Nicholas John. "Major Daniel C. Inboden and Press Reform in Occupied Japan 1945–1952." Ph.D. Dissertation. University of Maryland, 1988.

Cole, Harry L., and Albert K. Weinberg. *Civil Affairs: Soldiers Becomes Governors*. Washington, D.C.: Department of the Army, 1964.

Corke, Sara Jones. *U.S. Covert Operation and Cold War Strategy: Truman Secret Warfare and the C.I.A. 1945–1953*. New York: Routledge, 2008.

Couldry, Nick, Andreas Hepp and Friedrich Krotz. *Media Events in a Global Age*. New York: Routledge, 2010.

Christ, Roxanne E. "The Beirut Agreement: A License to Censor." *Loyola of Los Angeles International and Comparative Law Review* (1984): 255–278.

Cull, Nicholas J. *The Cold War and the United States Information Agency: American Propaganda and Public Diplomacy*. New York: Cambridge University Press, 2008.

Davis, Robert T. *U.S. Foreign Policy and National Security: Chronology and Index for the 20th Century*. Santa Barbara, CA: Praeger, 2010.

Dayan, Daniel and Elihu Katz. *Media Events: The Live Broadcasting of History*. Boston: Harvard University Press, 1992.

Dougherty, William E. and Morris Janowitz. *A Psychological Warfare Casebook*. Operations Research Office: Johns Hopkins University Press, 1958.

Edelstein, Alex. *Total Propaganda: From mass culture to popular culture*. Mahwah, NJ: Lawrence Erlbaum, 1997.

Eldridge, Robert D. and Paul Midford. *Japanese Public Opinion and the War on Terrorism*. New York: Palgrave Macmillan, 2008.

Entman, Robert. "Theorizing Mediated Public Diplomacy: The U.S. Case." *The International Journal of Press/Politics* 13:2 (2008).

Ellul, Jacques. *Propaganda: The Formation of Men's Attitudes*. New York: Alfred A. Knopf, 1965.

Fearey, Robert A. *The Occupation of Japan, Second Phase: 1948–1950*. New York: MacMillan, Institute of Pacific Relations, 1950.

Fisch, Arnold G. *Military Government in the Ryukyu Islands 1945–1950*. Honolulu: University Press of the Pacific, 1988.

Gilboa, Ethan. "Global Communication and Foreign Policy," *Journal of Communication* (December, 2002).

Haydon, Craig. *The Rhetoric of Soft Power: Public Diplomacy in Global Contexts*. Lanham, MD: Lexington Books, 2012.

Haye, Grace Person. *The History of Joint Chiefs of Staff in World War II: The War against Japan*. Annapolis: Naval Institute Press, 1982.

Hillsman, Elizabeth Lutes. *Defending America: Military culture and the cold war court-martial*. Princeton: Princeton University Press, 2005.

Hilsman, Roger. *To Move a Nation: The politics of foreign policy in the administration of John F. Kennedy.* New York: Doubleday and Co., 1967.
Huntington, Samuel P. *The Soldier and the State: The Theory on Politics of Civil-Military Relations.* Cambridge: Harvard University Press, 1957.
Jacobson, Mark R. "Minds Then Hearts: U.S. Political and Psychological Warfare during the Korean War." Ph.D. Dissertation, Ohio State University, 2005.
Kellner, Douglas. "Media Events and Media Spectacles: Some critical reflections." In *Media Events in a Global Age.* Edited by Nick Couldry, Andreas Hepp and Friedrich Krotz, 76–91. New York: Routledge, 2010.
Lang, Kurt and Gladys Engel Lang. "The Unique Perspective of Television and Its Effects: A Pilot Study." *American Sociological Review* 18:1 (1953).
Lasswell, Harold D. *Propaganda Techniques in the World War.* New York: Alfred A. Knopf, 1927.
Laville, Helen and Hugh Wilford. *The US Government, Citizen Groups and the Cold War: The state-private network.* New York: Routledge, 2006.
Lee, Guy A. *The Establishment of the Office of the U.S. High Commissioner for Germany.* Historical Division, Office of the Executive Secretary, Office of the U.S. High Commissioner for Germany, (1951).
Leeker, Joe F. "CAT and Air America in Japan." 2013/3/4, Special Collection, University of Texas-Dallas http://www.utdallas.edu/library/specialcollections/.
Linebarger, Paul M. A. *Psychological Warfare.* Landisville, PA: Coachwhip, 2010.
Lowenthal, Mark M. *Intelligence: From secret to policy.* Washington D.C.: CQ Press, 2009.
Manheim, Jarol B. *Strategic Public Diplomacy and American Foreign Policy: The evolution of influence.* New York: Oxford University Press, 1994.
McCormick, James M. *The Domestic Sources of American Foreign Policy: Insights and Evidence.* New York: Rowman & Littlefield, 2012.
McKenzie, Brian Angus. *Remaking France: Americanization, Public Diplomacy, and the Marshall Plan.* New York: Berghahn Books, 2005.
Metzgar, Emily T. "Public Diplomacy, Smith-Mundt and the American Public." *Communication Law and Policy,* 17:1 (2012): 67–101.
Nye, Joseph S. Jr. *Soft Power: The Means to Success in World Politics.* New York: Public Affairs, 2004.
Osgood, Kenneth. *Total Cold War: Eisenhower's Secret Propaganda Battle at Home and Abroad.* Lawrence, KS: University Press of Kansas, 2006.
Palmer, Allen W. and Edward L. Carter. 'The Smith-Mundt Act's Ban on Domestic Propaganda: An Analysis of the Cold War Statute Limiting Access to Public Diplomacy," *Communication Law and Policy* (Winter 2006).
Price, Harry Bayard. *The Marshall Plan and Its Meaning: An independent and unbiased appraisal of the entire record.* Ithaca, N.Y.: Cornell University Press, 1955.
Putnam, Robert D. "Diplomacy and Domestic Politics: The Logics of Two-Level Games," *International Organization,* Vol. 42, No.3 (Summer, 1988), pp. 427–460.
Reischauer, Edwin O. *My Life Between Japan and America.* New York: Harper and Row, 1986.

Rubin, Ron. *The Making of the Cold War Enemy: Culture and politics of the military-intellectual complex.* Princeton: Princeton University Press, 2001.

Saeki, Chizuru. *U.S. Cultural Propaganda in Cold War Japan: Promoting democracy 1948–1960.* Edwin Mellen Press, 2007.

Sandler, Stanley. *The Korean War: An encyclopedia.* New York: Garland, 1995.

Sarantakes, Nicholas Evan. *Keystone: The American occupation of Okinawa and U.S.-Japanese relations.* College Station, TX: Texas A & M University Press, 2000.

Sebald, William J. *With MacArthur in Japan: A personal history of occupation.* New York: W.W. Norton & Co., 1965.

Shulman, Holly Cowan, *Voice of America: Propaganda and Democracy, 1941–1945.* University of Wisconsin Press, 1990.

Snow, Nancy. "The Smith-Mundt Act of 1948." *Peace Review: A Journal of Social Justice*, 10:4 (1998), 619–624.

Stone, Gerald C., Mary K. O'Donnell, and Stephen Banning. "Public Perception of Newspaper's Watchdog Role." *Newspaper Research Journal*, 18:1–2 (1997).

Tuch, Hans N. *Communicating with the World: U.S. public diplomacy overseas.* New York: St. Martin's Press, 1990.

Tull, James N. "The Ryukyu Islands, Japan's Oldest Colony – America's Newest: An analysis of policy and propaganda." Master's thesis, University of Chicago, 1953.

Uhm, Kiyul. "The Cold War Communication Crisis: The right to know movement." *Journalism and Mass Communication Quarterly*, 82:1, (Spring 2005): 131–147.

Ward, Brad M. "Strategic Influence Operations; Information connection." *USAWC Strategy Research Project.* Carlisle Barracks, PA: U.S. Army War College, 2003.

Warner, Tim. *Legacy of Ashes: The history of the CIA.* New York: Anchor Books, 2007.

Westad, Odd Arne. *The Global Cold War: Third World Interventions and the Making of Our Times.* Cambridge: Cambridge University Press, 2007.

White, David Manning. "Gate Keeper: A case study in the selection of news." *Journalism Quarterly*, 27 (1950), 383–396.

Winkler, Allan M. *The Politics of Propaganda: The Office of War Information 1942–1945.* New Haven: Yale University Press, 1978.

Zacharias, Ellis M. *Secret Mission: The story of an intelligence officer.* Annapolis, Maryland; Naval University Press, 1946.

## Selected Japanese Resources

Calder, Kent E. *Beigun Kichi Saihen no Seijigaku* (Embattled Garrisons: Comparative base politics and American globalism). Translated by Yoichi Takei. Tokyo: Nihon Keizai Shinbun Shuppan Sha, 2008.

Eto, Jun. *Tozasareta Genron Kukan.* Tokyo: Bunshun Bunko, 1994.

Eldridge, Robert D. *Okinawa Mondai no Kigen.* Nagoya: Nagoya University Press, 2003.

Gabe, Masaaki. *Nichibei Kankei no naka no Okinawa*. Tokyo: San-ichi Shobo, 1996.
Kabira, Naruo. *Okinawa Kuhaku no Ichinen 1945–1946*. Tokyo: Yoshikawa Kobunkan, 2011.
Kayo, Yasuharu. *Okinawa Minseifu*, Tokyo: Kume Shobo, 1986.
Kobayashi, Somei. VOA "Shisetsu Henkan wo meguru Kanbei Kosho," *Journal of Mass Communication Studies*, 75, (2009).
Kobayashi, Somei Reisenki. *Asia no Denpa Senso Kenkyu Josetsu, Ouyou Syakaigaku Kenkyu*. No.52, (2010).
Kono, Yasuko. *Okinawa Henkan wo meguru Seiji to Gaiko: Nichibei Kankeishi no Bunmyaku*. Tokyo: Tokyo University Press, 1994.
Kurima, Yasuo. *Okinawa no Beigun Kichi to Gunyochiry*. Ginowan: Yoju Shorin, 2012.
Miyagi, Etsujiro. *Okinawa Sengo Hoso Shi*. Naha: Hirugi Sha, 1996.
Miyazato, Seigen. *Nichibei Kankei to Okinawa 1945–1972*. Tokyo: Iwanami Shoten, 2000.
Miyazato, Seigen. *Amerika no Taigai Seisaku Kettei Katei*. Tokyo: San-ichi Shobo, 1981.
Miyazato, Seigen, ed. *Sengo Okinawa no Seiji to Ho*. Tokyo: Tokyo University Press, 1975.
Miyazato, Seigen. *Amerika no Okinawa Tochi*. Tokyo: Iwanami Shoten, 1966.
Mizuno, Takeya. *Tekikokugo Janarizumu*. Yokohama: Shumpu Publishing, 2011.
Monna, Naoki. *Okinawa Genron Tosei Shi*. Tokyo: Yuzankaku, 1996.
Nakajima, Takuma. *Okinawa Henkan to Anpo Taisei*. Tokyo: Yuhikaku, 2012.
Nye, Joseph S. *Soft Power*. Translated by Yoichi Yamaoka. Tokyo: Nihon Keizai Shimbun Shuppan Sha, 2004.
Okinawa Furi Janarisuto Kaigi. ed. *Okinawa no Shimbun ga Tsubureru Hi*. Gekkan Okinawa Sha, 1994.
Okinawa Kyokai. ed. *Nanpo Doho Engokai 17 nen no Ayumi*. Okinawa Kyokai, 1973.
Okinawa Times. ed. *Kichi de Hataraku*. Naha: Okinawa Times, 2014.
Ono, Naoki. *Reisenka CIA no Interijensu*. Kyoto: Minerva, 2012.
Ota, Masahide. *Okinawa Senka no Nichibei Shinri Sakusen*. Tokyo: Iwanami Shoten, 2004.
Ryukyu Ginko Chosa Bu. ed. *Sengo Okinawa Keizai Shi*. Naha: Ryukyu Ginko, 1994.
Sensui, Hidekazu. 1952 SIRI *Kaigi. Kokusai Keiei Forum*, 20, (2009).
Shinobu, Takashi. *Wakaizumi Kei to Nichibei Mitsuyaku*. Tokyo: Nihon Hyoron Sha, 2012.
Taira, Tatsuo. *Sengo no Seikai Uramen Shi*. Naha: Nanpo Sha, 1963.
Takamine, Choko. *Shinbun 50 nen*. Naha: Okinawa Times, 1973.
Tanigawa, Kenji. *Amerika Eiga to Senryo Seisaku*. Kyoto: Kyoto University Press, 2002.
Tsuchiya, Reiko. *Tainichi Senden Bira ga kataru Taiheiyou Senso*. Tokyo: Yoshikawa Kobunkan, 2011.
Tsuchiya, Yuka. *Shinbei Nihon no Kouchiku*. Tokyo: Akashi Shoten, 2009.
Tsuchiya, Yuka and Shunya Yoshimi. eds. *Senryo suru Me / Senryo suru Koe*. Tokyo: Tokyo University Press, 2012.
Tsujimura, Akira and Masahide Ota. *Okinawa no Genron*. Tokyo: Nanpo Doho Engo Kai, 1966.

Yamamoto, Taketoshi, *GHQ no Kenetsu Choho Senden Kosaku.* Tokyo: Iwanami Shoten, 2013.
Wakaizumi, Kei. *Tasaku Nakarishi wo Shinzemu to Hossu.* Tokyo: Bungei Shunju, 1994.
Watanabe, Yasushi, *Amerikan Senta.* Tokyo: Iwanami Shoten, 2008.

# Name Index

Allen, George V. 89, 93 126
Allison, Dean 66
Allison, John M. 95
Amato, Sam L. 117

Baron, Stuart 67
Beightler, Robert S. 41
Benton, William 84
Broger, John C. 125
Buckner, Simon B. 34

Caraway, Paul 122, 133
Carroll, Wallace 82
Cassidy, Thomas G. 90
Chennault, Claire L. 127
Coolidge, Harold J. 110
Crist, William E. 34, 41

Davis, Elmer 82
Diffenderfer, H. Earl 61
Donovan, William 81
Downs, Darley 72
Dulles, John Foster 10, 65

Eichelberger, Robert 26, 53
Eisenhower, Dwight D. 31, 59, 64, 72, 73, 75, 82
Emerson, John K. 138
Evans, Joseph S. 123

Fearey, Robert A. 88, 129, 134, 144
Fisch, Arnold G. 30
Freimath, Edward O. 136

Galloway, Donald H. 89
Goebbels, Joseph 81
Goeku, Chosho 59
Gray, Gordon 91

Harrison, W. K. 61
Hemmendinger, Noel 52
Higa, Shuhei 69, 72
Hillenkoetter, Roscoe H. 89
Hilsman, Roger 8
Hinds, John H. 50
Hirohito (Emperor) 35, 145
Hoover, Herbert 51
Hughes, Rowland 68
Hull, John E. 65, 66

Ikemiyagi, Shui 138

Johnson, Lyndon B. 134, 139, 143

Kabira, Kiyoshi 138
Kays, Robert 124
Kaysen, Carl 115
Kennan, George 6

Kennedy, John F. 114
Kerr, George H. 110
King, Earnest J. 33, 41
King, Norman D. 72
Kishi, Nobusuke 73
Kitamura, Sam 122, 125

Lamb, Richard H. 155
Lampert, James B. 129, 144
Lasswell, Harold D. 1, 35, 152
Linebarger, Paul M. A. 84
Liosnoff, Alexander 125, 128, 136, 142, 144
Lovett, Robert 91

MacArthur, Douglas 41, 103
MacArthur II, Douglas 50, 74, 84
MacLeish, Archibald 82
Magruder, Carter B. 55, 86
Marquart, William 69
Marshall, George C. 33, 46, 89
Martin, James V. 155
Matsuoka, Seiho 109, 134
McClure, Robert A. 82
McClurkin, Robert J. G. 62
McCune, Shannon 134
McNamara, Robert 133
Miyagi, Etsujiro 121
Miyazato, Seigen 8
Moore, James 74, 114
Mundt, Karl E. 85
Murdock, George P. 36, 41, 110
Mutsu, Ian 111

Nimitz, Chester W. 34, 40, 41, 100
Nixon, Richard M. 143
Nye, Joseph S. 6, 153

O'Flaherty, Edward 59
Ogden, David A. 61, 69
Oliver, Douglas L. 52, 54
Osborne, Monta L. 123
Ota, Ronald 122
Ota, Seisaku 134

Patterson, Robert 21
Pollard, George M. 51
Price, Byron 98
Price, Melvin 71, 76

Radford, Arthur W. 125, 155
Reischauer, Edwin O. 35, 114, 133
Robertson, Walter 65, 66
Roosevelt, Franklin D. 81
Rusk, Dean 55, 133, 135

Sakakida, Richard 122
Sato, Eisaku 131, 138, 143, 145
Seidman, Harold 69
Senaga, Kamejiro 102, 109
Sheetz, Joseph R. 54, 105
Sherwood, Robert 82
Shima, Kiyoshi 101
Schrum, Wilbur 91
Smith, Alan 110
Smith, Alexander 85
Smith, Walter Bedell 91
Souers, Sydney W. 86
Steadman, John N. 135
Stevens, Leslie 91
Stevens, Russell 136
Stillwell, Joseph 121, 138
Sullivan, Charles 62

Taira, Tatsuo 109

*Name Index*

Takamine, Choko  97
Tanabe, Frank S.  121
Tatekawa, Clarence K.  122
Truman, Harry S.  10, 59
Tull, James N.  103

Uechi, Kazufumi  119, 121

Vandenberg, Hoyt S.  86
Vinson, Carl  69

Warden, C. C. B.  59
Warner, Gerald  135, 137

Watson, Albert  134, 138
Webb, James  91
Weckerling, John  53, 105
West, Robert R.  26, 53
Westad, Odd Arne  154
Wilson, Charles E.  66, 69
Wisner, Frank  90, 127

Yara, Chobyo  145

Zacharias, Ellis M.  83
Zanier, Jean  111

# Policy Index

Beirut Agreement 93

China Aid Acts 25

Economic Cooperation Act 25
Executive Order 10713 58, 74, 75, 113

FEC Directive 50
Foreign Aid Appropriation Act 25

Intelligence Directive No. 2 88

Japan Peace Treaty 3, 10, 58, 60, 62
JCS 1231 3, 40, 42, 98 *see also* Subject Index "Joint Chiefs of Staff"
JCS 1231/14 48, 49
JCS 819/5 41
JCS 873/3 98

Military Establishment Act 19, 20

National Defense Authorization Act (NDAA) 92
National Security Act 80, 86

Nimitz Proclamation 34, 42, 100
NSC 4 89 *see also* Subject Index "National Security Council"
NSC 10/2 90, 127
NSC 13/3 50, 87
NSC 59 90
NSC 125 63
NSC 125/2 60
NSC5516/1 71
NSC Action 1047 66
NSC Action 824-b 63

ORE 24-48 87

Price Act 27, 76, 116
PBS D-27 73, 95

Ryukyu Organic Act 69, 114, 149

Smith-Mundt Act 11, 85, 92
Supplemental Appropriation Act 26
SWNACC 304/11 88 *see also* Subject Index "State-War-Navy-Air Coordinating Committee"

USCAR Directive 49
USCAR REG 10-1 115

# Subject Index

1947 system 157
526th CIC Detachment 38
7th Psychological Operation Group 124, 144

Administration Ryukyu Islands (ARIA) 13, 28
Air America 128
Allied Translators and Interpreters Service (ATIS) 121
American Society of Newspaper Editors (ASNE) 22, 84
area administration unit 14
Armed Forces Radio Network 22
Army, US 4, 7, 11, 13, 23, 58, 62
———— Corps of Engineers 58
———— Judge Advocate 39
———— Staff 36
  Civil Affairs and Military Government (CAMG) 59, 64, 72
  Psychological Warfare Center 91
Army-Congressional relations 59
Associated Press 85, 141
Atoms for Peace 123

B yen 43, 47
B-29 aircraft 139
Battle of Okinawa 2, 99, 150

Beirut Agreement see Policy Index
black propaganda 86, 89 *see also* "white propaganda"
blue sky position 60
Bureau of Budget 57, 60, 68

Caltex 148
CAMG see "Army, US"
Camp Chinen 128
carrot and stick policy 149
censorship 2, 32, 98, 102, 106
Central Intelligence Agency (CIA) 19, 86, 89, 95, 126, 144
  Office of Policy Coordination 90, 127
  Office of Research and Evaluation (ORE) 86
Central Intelligence Group (CIG) 86
Chief Executive see "Government of the Ryukyus"
civil administration 32, 75
civil affairs 3, 11, 30, 32, 102, 110, 137
———— teams 50
Civil Affairs Guides 83
Civil Affairs Handbook 36
Civil Air Transport (CAT) 127

*195*

Civil Information and Education (CIE) 84, 90, 93, 103, *see also* "USCAR"
civil intelligence 37
civil liberties 55
civilian camp 34, 44
Cold War 97, 148, 153, 154
Combined Chiefs of Staff (CCS) 41, 43
communication blockade 98
communism 9
Composite Service Group (CSG) 127
Congress, US 8, 12, 19, 58
 Library of Congress 35, 82
Congressional oversight 77, 149
Counter Intelligence Corps (CIC) 34, 99
counterpart funds 24, 25, 27, 46, 67
cultural exchange 2, 15, 27, 118
cultural violence 154

defense budgets 23
Defense Department 10, 11
democratic ideals 5, 9
dilemma of modern states 1
disease and unrest formula 24
Domei News Service 97
double standard 68

ECA in the Far East 25, 105 see "Economic Cooperation Administration"
economic aid 13, 105
Economic Cooperation Administration (ECA) 7, 52, 91, 94

Economic Rehabilitation for Occupied Areas (EROA) 25, 105, 107
education program (for military veterans) 22
Emperor 44 *see also* Name Index "Hirohito"
Executive Office of the President (EOP) 3
Executive Order 10713 78 *see also* Policy Index

Far East Broadcasting Corporation (FEBC) 125
Far East Command (FFC) 65
FEC directive see Policy Index
Far Eastern Broadcasting Service 124
film industry, US 93
Foreign Broadcasting Information Service (FBIS) 110, 126
foreign information policy, US 80
Federal Foreign Fund Campaign 117
field manual 32
forced land acquisition 49, 68, 72
forced land requisition *see* "land requisition"
foreign audience 9
Fort Ord 34
Free Philippines 83
freedom of speech 55, 84, 92, 100

gatekeeper 7, 9 see "public affairs officers (PAOs)"

*Subject Index*

General Accounting Office (GAO) 57
General Headquarters of the Supreme Commander for the Allied Powers (GHQ/SCAP) 84, 111
Geneva Convention 44
German Propaganda Institute 81
Germany 24, 52
Government Aid and Relief in Occupied Areas (GARIOA) 13, 19, 20, 23, 28, 36, 47, 52, 59, 70, 107
Government of the Ryukyus 4, 65, 109
   Chief Executive of ——— 12, 32, 62, 69
Governor 5 *see also* "High Commissioner"

Hague Convention of 1907 31
Hawaii 34, 41
High Commissioner 5, 20, 75, 114, 119, 137, 151
——— to Germany 45, 52
———'s General Fund 26
Voice of the ——— 119
Hoover Commission 51

information and education program 13, 105
information center 106, 108
Inter-Agency Committee 73
international broadcasting 85

Japan Peace Treaty *see* Policy Index

Japan's aid 115, 134
Japan's Communist Party 139
Japan's Socialist Party 140
Japanese-Americans 34, 35, 99, 121, 122
Japanese flag 137
Japanese Government Liaison Office (JGLO) 139
Japanese militarism 45
Japanese Outlying Islands 44
Japanese surrender 102
Joint Chiefs of Staff (JCS) 3, 11, 40, 41, 50, 151

Kaysen Task Force 134
Korea 21, 36, 52
Korean War 49, 51, 56, 128
Korean-American assistant 129

land requisition / forced land requisitions 68, 69, 72
Library of Congress 35, 82 *see also* "Congress"

Manhattan Project 22
Marshall Plan 20, 21, 25, 46, 94
media blackout 98
media events 118, 132, 142
media policy 84
media spectacles 142
Militant Liberty 125
militarism 153
military bases 136
military colony 45, 48, 148, 154
military government 3, 42, 97
Military Government, Ryukyus 6, 32, 41, 105

Military Intelligence Service 83
military necessity 1, 20
military police 33, 56

Naha Consulate 71, 114
Nampo Doho Engokai
    (Southern Islands
    Friends'Association) 28
NATCO projectors 105, 108
National Defense University 31
National Intelligence Estimate
    (NIE) 86
National Psychological Strategy
    Board (NPSB) 90, 95
National Security Council
    (NSC) 3, 10, 14, 60, 77,
    88 *see also* Policy Index
National Security Resource
    Board (NSRB) 91
nation-building 6
New York Times 141
News morgues 120
Newspaper Week 109
NHK 84, 97, 110
North Africa 4, 31
nuclear power plant 72
nuclear weapons 143

occupation diplomacy 3, 14
Office for Occupied Areas 36
Office of Censorship 98 *see*
    "censorship"
Office of Comptroller 57
Office of Policy Coordination *see*
    "CIA"
Office of Public Information
    (OPI) *see* "USCAR"

Office of Research and Evaluation
    (ORE) *see* "CIA"
Office of Strategic Services
    (OSS) 35, 82
Office of War Information
    (OWI) 35, 81, 82
Okinawa / Ryukyu 5
Okinawa problems 70
Okinawa Herald 107
Okinawa Mainichi 107
Okinawa Shimpo 97
Okinawa Times 38, 74, 107, 119,
    120, 121, 137
Operation Friendship 15, 131
Operation Iceberg 33, 98
Operations Coordinating Board
    (OCB) 73, 76, 114
Operations Research Office
    (ORO) 91
Overseas Affairs
    Administration 52

peace-building operations 31
political adviser 4
popular vote 55, 62, 68, 69
Presidio of San Francisco 35
press conference / press release 9,
    118
Price Delegation 71, 72
Price Report 72
propaganda leaflets 34
Provisional Central
    Government 59
psychological operations 5, 89,
    152
Psychological Operations
    Committee (POC) 95

Psychological Strategy Board
   (PSB)  73, 91, 95
Psychological Strategy Program
   for Japan (PSB D-27)  73, 95
   *see also* Policy Index
psychological warfare  57, 91, 124
Psychological Warfare Branch
   (PWB)  82
Psychological Warfare Center *see*
   "Army"
Psychological Warfare Team  34
public affairs  1, 38
 Public Affairs Department *see*
   "USCAR"
 ——— officers (PAOs)  9, 11
public corporations  27, 40, 46, 59
public diplomacy  2, 11, 15, 86,
   92, 114, 153
puppet  5, 65

Radio Corporation of America
   (RCA)  94
re-education program  84, 93
residual sovereignty  10
reversion
   ——— of Okinawa  59, 128, 131,
   143
   ——— of Amami Islands  65
Ryukyu / Okinawa  5
Ryukyu Broadcasting  144
Ryukyu Broadcasting
   Corporation (RBC)  137, 138
Ryukyu Koho  110
Ryukyu Legislature  59
Ryukyu Nippo  107
Ryukyu Shimpo  38, 102, 120,
   137

Ryukyu Shuho  99
Ryukyuan Communication
   Administration (RCA)  107
Ryukyuan passport  10
Ryukyuan-American Cultural
   Centers  110

SCAP *see* "General
   Headquarters of the Supreme
   Commander for the Allied
   Powers"
Scofield Barracks  41
showcase of democracy  38, 149,
   152
Shurei no Hikari  119
soft power  6, 92, 147, 153
speech control  37
SPG policy liaison  90
State Department  2, 15, 41, 62,
   76, 93
State-War-Navy-Air Coordinating
   Committee (SWNACC)  88
State-War-Navy-Coordinating
   Committee (SWNCC)  45
Statistical Bulletin  51
Status of Force Agreement
   (SOFA)  145
Summations  51
Supreme Headquarters of the
   Allied Expeditionary Force
   (SHAEF)  82

Tass News Agency  139
thought police  38, 56
threat  155
Today's Ryukyus  117, 119
Tokyo Olympics  133

Treasury Department 43, 47
Trieste 37
TV Okinawa 144

U.S. administration of Okinawa 10, 14
U.S. Territories and Possessions 68
U.S.-Japan alliance 136
U.S.-Japan Consultative Committee 134
unconditional surrender 83
United Nations 21, 93, 111
 United Nations Trusteeship 53, 57, 64
 United Nations Relief and Rehabilitation Administration (UNRRA) 24, 127
 Voice of ——— Commands (VUNC) 124, 129
UNESCO 93
United Press 82, 85
United States Civil Administration of the Ryukyu Islands (USCAR) 3, 4, 28, 37, 50, 66, 75, 109, 111, 129, 144
 Civil Information and Education Department 61, 150
 Comptroller Department 28
 Office of Public Information (OPI) 117

Public Affairs Department 113, 117, 144
Tokyo Office 29
United States Information Agency (USIA) 7, 81, 111, 123
United States Information Service (USIS) 27, 95, 111, 120, 123, 139
USIS Okinawa 80
University of Ryukyus 106, 107
Uruma Shimpo 101

veto 5, 66
Vietnam 139
Vietnam War 124
Voice of America (VOA) 22, 85, 90, 92, 126
Voice of the Army (VOA) 22
Voice of the High Commissioner see "High Commissioner"
Voice of the Ryukyus 103, 107
Voice of United Nations Commands (VUNC) see "United Nations"

War Department 86
Weekly Intelligence Summary 38
white propaganda 86 *see also* "black propaganda"